Jeffrey Rob  resident
in London. *he Risk
Takers* and aphy of
the Saudi ex

By the same author

Non-fiction
The Risk Takers
Yamani–The Inside Story

Fiction
Pietrov and Other Games
The Ginger Jar

JEFFREY ROBINSON

Minus Millionaires

Or, How to Blow a Fortune

GRAFTON BOOKS

A Division of the Collins Publishing Group

LONDON GLASGOW
TORONTO SYDNEY AUCKLAND

Grafton Books
A Division of the Collins Publishing Group
8 Grafton Street, London W1X 3LA

This revised edition published by
Grafton Books 1988

First published in Great Britain by
Unwin Hyman Ltd 1987

Copyright © Jeffrey Robinson 1987, 1988

ISBN 0-586-20289-7

Printed and bound in Great Britain by
Collins, Glasgow

Set in Century Schoolbook

For Yasmine, Philippe, Corice and Arman
with Love

Contents

Acknowledgements

During one of *The Risk Taker* interviews with Jacob Rothschild, he happened to mention that Jim Slater once called himself a 'minus millionaire'. I said, 'What a terrific title for a book.' And the very next morning this project was under way.

With thanks then to Jacob Rothschild for the germ of an idea and Jim Slater for the title.

I am naturally indebted to my agent Leslie Gardner and my editor Nick Brealey for all their help, suggestions, encouragement, caring and understanding.

And, of course, to La Benayoun.

Also on the thank you list are Liz Paton for her copyediting, plus the BBC Data Service, the Press Association, bookseller Paul Holcombe and the Houston, Texas, Public Library, who were among the numerous sources of research assistance.

Also included are the *New York Times*, the *Los Angeles Times*, the *Boston Globe*, the *Wall Street Journal, The Times* and *Sunday Times*, the *Observer*, the *Financial Times*, the *Telegraph* and *Sunday Telegraph, The Economist, Forbes, Fortune, Businessweek*, and *Euromoney*.

I particularly wish to acknowledge the many people mentioned, referred to and quoted in the book, especially those portrayed who gave me their time, answered my questions and hopefully didn't get too terribly annoyed with my persistence. To be perfectly honest, a select few people who appear, however briefly, in this book were not as willing to talk as almost all of the others. Understandably, it can't be much fun to tell the world how you've blown a fortune. Those who would not cooperate necessitated that I track down their friends, acquaintances and former business associates. So to the friends, acquaintances and former business associates of the reluctant ones, I also add my thanks.

One man, who must remain nameless, was an invaluable help with one of the stories portraited here. I have reason to believe he assisted me at some risk to himself. And I am most appreciative.

Then there are my special thanks to Sir Kenneth Cork, a thoroughly charming man, a former Lord Mayor of the City of London and the all-time superstar liquidator in the sometimes murky world of bankruptcy. Over lunch and again in his office he totally enthralled me with stories. I can only say that if he ever decides to write a book I'll be first in line to buy a copy.

Introduction

My grandmother was a philosopher.

Sure, everybody's grandmother was a philosopher. But mine really did found the school of thought known as 'Any Damn Fool Can . . .'

It was a kitchen table philosophy . . . nurtured in the ghettos of Europe, sailed steerage to a new world, refined by the raising of four daughters, then custom tailored for her grandchildren. More often than not it poured forth over bowls of soup. Break the speed limit and she'd remind you, 'Any damn fool can drive too fast.' Get an 'F' in history class and she'd tsk, 'Any damn fool can fail at school.' Come home too late and she'd shake her head, 'Any damn fool can stay out all night.'

Had she lived to see this book she would have certainly commented, 'Any damn fool can lose his money.'

But this is where her folk wisdom breaks down. Sorry Grandma. It's not any damn fool who can blow a fortune, because it's not any damn fool who can make a fortune to begin with.

New York, 1955
You were a big deal with a $10,000 yearly salary and a $25,000 house. Those were the days of 20-cent lunches and 5-cent bus fares. Just four years before, Joe DiMaggio made front-page headlines by signing his magical $100,000 one-year contract with the New York Yankees. In 1955 it was still a staggering sum

even if such matters were relegated now to page two or three.

$100,000!

It was almost unimaginable.

And, frankly, anything beyond that, especially ten times beyond that, was utterly unthinkable.

Sure, there were millionaires in America. But there weren't a lot of them. Not like today when there are supposed to be over a million American millionaires.

For the rest of us, a million dollars was such an abstract concept that one afternoon in 1955 – somewhere between the American Revolution and the weekly spelling test – Mrs Hausherr asked everyone in her class to make up a list of what we'd do if we had a million dollars. You know, if you had it, how would you spend it?

The list that at least one of us came up with looked something like this:

House – $25,000
Private DC-3 – $25,000
Yacht – $25,000
Gold bars – $25,000
Race horses – $25,000
Several Cadillacs – $25,000
A Park Avenue penthouse – $25,000
A season box seat at Ebbetts Field to see the Brooklyn Dodgers – $150

Grand total – $175,150

It was a long way from a million. Not a single kid in the class came close. Even if you bought two of everything you still weren't halfway there. But then, that was the point of the exercise. Besides being an unimaginable sum, it was also an unspendable sum.

It is not unspendable today. But it certainly seemed

to be in 1955. So unspendable, in fact, that the idea
thoroughly intrigued me. I was captivated. I may not
remember the date of the Boston Tea Party and there
are times when I still have to think to myself, 'I before
E except after C . . .' Yet ever since that day when a
white-haired fifth-grade teacher proved beyond any
doubt that a millionaire couldn't spend it all even if he
wanted to . . . ever since then I have loved watching
what some people do with money and what money does
to some people.

In its most basic form, money is really just a convenient device to simplify the barter process. Money is
for buying cars and television sets, clothes and schooling for your kids, food, and holidays at the seaside.
You know, 'God invented money to spend,' and 'You
can't take it with you.' Money is to have fun with.
Sometimes, watching someone else spend money is
almost as much fun as spending it yourself. If nothing
else, it's cheaper. Money is what you carry in your
pocket to pay for things. Money is one of the reasons
you go to work. Money is what you hold on to for a
rainy day. Money is what your Aunt gives you for your
birthday when she can't think of anything else and
knows you don't need gloves. Money is a way of saying
thank you. Money is what you want when you get first
prize. Money is something to cry about when you lose
it and to cry about when you win it. Whether you're
talking dollars or pounds, yen, francs, shekels or
drachmas . . . money is what saves you from the
trouble of constantly trying to negotiate a value for
shells, coconuts, beads, wives, camels, whatever.
Money is 'a commodity that has been legally established to be an exchangeable equivalent of all other
commodities and used as a measure of their compara-
tive market value'.

But those definitions – even the quote from the dictionary – don't really go far enough because money is not just for earning, spending and saving. It's about a lot of other things as well, including benevolence, independence and freedom.

I've always liked the story of the people who were asked, 'How much would you like to have if someone gave you as much as you want and what would you do with it if you had it?' The all-too-usual response is, 'I'd take a million and never work again.' But there was a farmer who was once asked that question and he thought about it for a long time before he answered, 'I'd want twenty grand because that's about what it costs me to live a year. And if I had that I'd sell my Jerseys and buy me some Guernseys.'

Put another way, by a friend who became a millionaire by combining enormous talent with very hard work, 'The trick is to have enough money, not so that you never have to go to work, but so that you can always afford to do whatever it is you want to do.'

So, more abstractly, money is a means to an end. Money is about attaining access, wielding power, pampering one's ego, motivating other people, doing some good, creating a sense of security and eliminating some of the pressures that can, at times, get in the way of enjoying life.

But this is dangerous territory.

All too often it's right here where money crosses the border into the land of political philosophies.

Some years ago I was in Sri Lanka and interviewed Dr N. M. Perrera, then the leader of the country's Trotskyite party. He held two advanced degrees from the London School of Economics and was the man who must be credited with the remark, 'All of the great economic ills the world has known this century can be directly traced back to the LSE.'

During that interview he raised a point about the use of money as an incentive. He wondered why money had to be the dangling carrot when, in a hot climate like Sri Lanka's, air conditioners might be used to reward faithful workers. I naïvely asked what happens when a worker is so good that he gets several air conditioners, and then trades his second or third one to someone for food or a car or clothes or a new cricket bat. Didn't that then turn air conditioners into money. He said no but never managed to convince me why not. Maybe he and my grandmother would have got along. Though I doubt it.

May I therefore explain that this book is not about capital, or about states, or about social convictions. I'm not talking about Milton Friedman any more than I'm talking about Karl Marx.

What I'm saying is that because money is so many things, including, obviously, a means to an end – rightly or wrongly – there will always be people who make a conscious effort to acquire a great deal of it. For some people, the acquisition of money and therefore material wealth is a real and extremely serious pastime. You don't have to like it. You don't have to be a player. You don't even have to be ready at the drop of a hat to voice an opinion one way or the other. I'm simply asking you to accept the idea that money as a goal is very much part of the world we currently live in.

How people acquire money is, in some minor ways, what *The Risk Takers* was all about. How they spend it – or, more accurately, how some people happened to let millions slip through their fingers – is what this is all about. Blame it on Mrs Hausherr and her fifth-grade lesson. My fascination for this really does stem from that. Hand in hand goes my interest in a good story. Yes, the world loves a winner. But in a funny way many people also share a somewhat morbid curiosity about losers. Perhaps it has something to do with the 'it can't happen to me' syndrome. Yes, I realize this is a time of great unemployment. And, yes, I know very well there is starvation and poverty in the world. And yes, I am all too aware that there are people who deeply believe that hoarding wealth or even the mere pursuit of wealth for the sake of wealth is immoral. But again, that's not what this book is about. I make no moral judgements. I simply recount these tales for what I hope they really are . . . interesting stories of the foibles and the follies, the good luck and the bad luck, the challenges and the defeats and the eccentricities that some people have known and – perhaps even thankfully – the rest of us can merely read about.

Any damn fool can write a book about people blowing money.

I do hope however that this damn fool, while trying to be a good story teller, has also somehow inadvertently stumbled on whatever lessons might be learned.

JR
London 1988

1

How to Blow a Fortune

There is no set formula for getting rich.

Although some ways are more obvious than others.

Twenty-five telephone calls to bankers, stockbrokers and analysts around the City of London and along Wall Street brought this odd assortment of first answers to the question, 'How can someone get rich?'

Nine said, 'Rob a bank.'

Six came up with, 'Marry money.'

Four suggested, 'Choose your parents well.'

Four others lit on these variations of the same theme: 'Win at Las Vegas' . . . 'Win the pools' . . . 'Win the lottery' . . . and, 'Bet big on the long shot the day the long shot wins the Derby.'

Interestingly enough, only two answered with anything even resembling 'Work very hard in a very deliberate quest for material success, know everything about what you're doing and at the same time be very lucky while you're doing it.'

Well, bank heists, weddings, the ponies and birth with a silver spoon in your mouth notwithstanding . . . there are probably as many ways of getting to the pot of gold as there are people willing to look at rainbows. And each road is almost guaranteed to be littered with hurdles. Of course, maps are readily available. There's big money to be made in writing 'How to's'. Unfortunately, in most cases, by the time you've thumbed through 'How to Obtain Financial Independence with Powdered Snake Oil', just about everybody else who's looking for a get-rich-quick gimmick has long since got into powdered snake oil, and long since got out of powdered snake oil, and, anyway, the fellow who wrote the book probably only did so because he wanted to make back the money he unexpectedly lost in his own 'sure thing' powdered snake oil scheme.

There is, after all, never a tip without a tap.

Tip: 'Psst,' the guy says. 'The hottest thing in the market right now is a company making peanut butter flavoured toothpaste. The shares should hit 100 by tomorrow morning.'

Tap: 'Oh by the way, I just happen to own a few shares if you want to buy.'

Any damn fool can read a book. But spotting opportunities usually takes a modicum of imagination.

Point One: it helps if you can recognize what face opportunity will wear.

For example: In 1932, one of the bleakest years of the Great Depression, an unemployed Philadelphia heating engineer named Charles Darrow thought he saw a great opportunity for making money by giving other unemployed people a few hours of fantasy to fill their generally empty days. So he set out to invent a game where anybody could, with minor skills and a few lucky rolls of the dice, become a game-board multimillionaire. It took time and imagination, but when he had it perfected he took it to the Parker Brothers Company who quickly came up with the terrifically far-sighted response, 'No'. They even listed 52 fundamental errors in Darrow's game. His opportunity – and theirs – might have slipped away forever, except for Darrow's persistence. He knew he was on to a winner, even if no one else did. He refused to go away. It took him two years of nagging before Parker Brothers finally agreed to give him a chance. And, today, Monopoly is the world's best-selling copyrighted game ever.

Point Two: opportunity may knock but that doesn't mean you're going to be at home to answer the door.

For example: Dr Seuss's first children's book was rejected by no less than 23 publishers. The 24th publisher managed to sell 6 million copies of it.

Point Three: not all opportunities that come along are open to every one of us. Some are less legal than others. Some may rely on skill alone when all you've got is a pocketful of luck. Some may rely merely on luck when you're top-heavy in skill. Some may simply have to do with being in the right place at the right time. Some may have nothing more to do with anything than who you know.

For example: In its first year in the soft drink business, the Coca-Cola company managed to sell only 400 Cokes. And . . . in its first year of the safety razor business, Gillette sold only 51 razors and 168 blades. And . . . in his first attempt at drilling for oil, Howard Hughes Sr hit hard rock, decided to invent a drill bit that could get through the rock, and made his original fortune on drill bits, not oil. And . . . when Raymond A. Kroc went to Florida as a young man, just after the First World War, he was trying to make his fortune in real estate. But the speculators wiped him out. Before his thirtieth birthday, he was stone broke. Over the next 20 years he bounced around from job to job, until he landed one in California, selling milkshake machines. It wasn't much, but at least he was working. Two of his customers were brothers who owned a drive-in restaurant in San Bernadino at the very start of the drive-in restaurant craze. He got to know them, clearly realized the potential of their business and struck up a deal where he would sell their franchises. Some 300 franchises later he bought them out for $2.7 million in cash. Today the 7,500 McDonald's Restaurants worldwide are worth $4–5 billion.

Point Four: losers think any defeat is where the road ends. Winners know that's not true.

For example: Sam Moore Walton trained as a clerk in a J. C. Penney store before the Second World War, learned the retailing business and came back after the war to open his own Ben Franklin Store in Newport, Arkansas. He was 27 years old. His theory was that quality goods, sold at a discount, had to be a winner. But in 1950 his landlord raised the rent. It cut too close to the bone. And Walton was forced out of business. Yet he was so sure of his formula that he refused to quit. He had to try again. Today his Wal-Mart Stores are spread across America. In a *Forbes* poll for 1985, he was listed as the wealthiest man in the United States, owning 39 per cent of a business that is worth $5.4 billion. And ... when a certain life insurance salesman lost a huge policy because his fountain pen leaked all over the contract, he knew it was time to rethink his life. Mr Waterman then gave up insurance to start manufacturing leak-proof fountain pens. And ... a young man named Francis Kane started buying sugar futures while working as an inventory clerk in a New York City supermarket. So very good with numbers, he was a paper millionaire by the age of 21. That's when Franklin Roosevelt froze sugar prices and Francis Kane got completely wiped out. He lost everything. When he decided to see if he was as good with stories as he was with numbers, he tried his hand at writing novels and before long changed his name to Harold Robbins.

Point Five: opportunity and luck are sometimes the same thing. Of course, it's not uncommon to hear ultra-successful people say things like, 'There is no such thing as a lucky break. I made all my own breaks. I made all my own luck.' But life for most people is hardly that black and white. If it was, everybody in the world who knew how to combine imagination with ambition would be on easy street.

For example: Carruthers, chairman and chief executive officer of Frongue Industries, sits in a huge office, with six secretaries at his beck and call, with Picassos on the walls, a dozen telephones on his antique desk and 5000 employees worldwide. A young man asks, 'Would you please tell me the secret of how you got so successful?' And after drawing on his Havana Havana, tugging at his gold cufflinks, then glancing out at his pale blue Rolls, he begins, 'I was born in a one-room, cold water flat, above a barber shop, where my father worked at the third chair, cutting hair six days a week. It wasn't enough to get by so my mother took in other people's washing. At the age of 16 I met a man who gave me a candle. I immediately saw the potential of the gift and sold the candle. With that money I bought two more candles. When I sold those, I had enough to buy four candles, which I then sold so that I could buy eight candles. Before my eighteenth birthday I had parlayed my candles into a used van, which I promptly scrapped. I sold off the pieces of the van for enough money to buy two more vans. Before my twenty-first birthday I turned the two vans into four. Before my twenty-second birthday I turned the four vans into eight. Then, on my twenty-third birthday I married Frongue's only daughter.'

Once big money has been acquired, the next trick is to hang on to it. Invariably, the moment wealth arrives so does a long queue of people who want to take it away from you. Tax inspectors. Friends. Close relatives. Distant relatives. Former business associates. Current business associates. Hopeful future business associates. Occasional strangers. Complete strangers. That's why, if you've been clever enough and lucky enough and ambitious enough and whatever-else enough to pluck the prize, you've then got to be clever enough, lucky enough, ambitious enough and whatever-else enough to keep it.

In 1923 a handful of the world's most important financiers met in Chicago. Among them were the president of America's largest independent steel company, the president of the country's largest gas company, the president of the New York Stock Exchange, the world's greatest wheat speculator, a US Presidential cabinet member, the greatest single speculator Wall Street has ever known, the president of a major international bank and the man who owned the world's greatest monopoly.

Within 15 years the steel magnate Charles Schwab died penniless, the gas company boss Howard Hopson went insane, the NYSE president Richard Whitney wound up in jail, the greatest wheat speculator Arthur Gutten died broke, the Presidential cabinet member Albert Fall went to jail, the Wall Street super-star speculator Jesse Livermore committed suicide, and the president of the Bank of International Settlement also died a suicide.

So did the man with the world's greatest monopoly, Ivar Kreuger.

Known as the 'Match King', at one point during the 1920s he owned or controlled the supply of nearly three-quarters of the world's matches.

Trained as an engineer, he bounced around the world before returning to his native Sweden in 1907 to start his own construction firm. He was so successful at it, building throughout Europe, that he soon branched out to banking and film financing ... and paid for Greta Garbo's first role.

In 1915, he set his sights on the match business because he found he was able to get supplies of phosphorus and potash when established local match manufacturers couldn't. He profited handsomely, took over his competitors and by 1917 was in full control of the Swedish match industry. He used that as his base to conquer the world.

In those days it was possible to secure a national monopoly in countries with questionable finances simply by paying off the government of the day. He moved into France, Yugoslavia, Turkey, Eastern Europe, Central and South America, parlaying one match monopoly into another.

As a serious businessman he was skilful and successful. But somewhere inside him ran an odd streak. Maybe it was ego. Maybe it was paranoia. Maybe it was just sheer genius playing at the wrong speed. Whatever it was, he compulsively layered his empire with mysterious companies, off-shore holdings carrying bearer shares and other conduits where he could launder funds.

Throughout the 1920s, through the stock market crash in 1929 and into the opening years of the 1930s, he continued announcing fabulous deals, and offering investors 2 and 3 and 4 points higher interest than they could achieve anywhere else. When there was a rumour that he might be insolvent, Kreuger purposely overpaid his taxes by $150,000 as a ploy to assure the world he was still in the chips.

Ever the showman, he'd impress visitors by pretending to take telephone calls from the world's leaders . . . people actually believed Stalin was on the other end . . . yet he legitimately was a frequent visitor to the White House during the Hoover years. He roamed the world putting together deals that filled the financial pages of the daily papers. Those deals brought new investors into his match monopoly. But it was all too good. His companies were making money, yet none of them was making enough to pay such whopping dividends. To keep up appearances he began forging notes. No petty thief, he forged one from the Italian government for $143 million. By 1930–31 the stress he was under while trying to juggle so many growing frauds must have been incredible. It started to affect his health. And he suffered a stroke. 'I cannot think anymore,' he admitted. 'I am going crazy.'

On 12 March 1932, in his flat in Paris, Ivar Kreuger ended his life with a pistol.

In his own mind he was a ruined man.

His businesses, without him, toppled like the house of cards they had so oddly become.

During the years 1917–1932, Kreuger had received some $650 million. But hundreds of millions had been squandered. A hundred million more had simply been lost. 'I have built my enterprise on the firmest ground that can be found,' he said, 'the foolishness of people.' A bizarre thing for him to say because, at the time of his death, he was still worth $200 million.

But then the bigger they are, the harder they really do fall.

In 1974, Kleinwort Benson Ltd, a London-based merchant bank, thought they were on to a winner when they purchased $3.2 million in shares of Nihon Netsugaku Kogyo, the high-flying Japanese air conditioning firm. Ten days later, Netsugaku was bankrupt. Out of the blue, it collapsed under the weight of $222 million worth of debt. It was then the biggest bankruptcy in Japanese history. After the fact, of course, the pundits agreed that the company was too highly leveraged and the victim of soaring interest rates. But Masao Ushida, the company's president, felt his inability to lie was the major factor in Netsugaku's defeat. 'I was honest. Being too honest in the business world is a defect.'

True or not, being outright dishonest is no sure way of making money either.

Italy's Banco Ambrosiano was undoubtedly a virtual palace of illegality, culminating in the greatest banking scandal Italy has ever known, or likely ever will. 'Although we lack great mystery writers,' commented one Roman newspaper while the affair broiled on, 'our real-life production of thrillers is unbeatable.' Well documented over the years in periodicals and books, the cast of characters in the Ambrosiano mystery includes the Mafia, the Vatican, crooks, fraudsters, murderers and plenty of victims, some still alive, some very dead.

Banker Roberto Calvi might have known what was going on, but he was found in London, in 1982, hanging under Blackfriars Bridge. Sicilian financier Michele Sindona might have known what was going on, but he was found in Milan, in 1986, lying on the floor of his jail cell having swallowed a lethal dose of cyanide, by

choice or otherwise. Anyway, he not only lost millions
with the Banco Ambrosiano crash, he also blew a
fortune when his own Franklin National became
America's largest bank collapse. Sindona's *gumba*
Licio Gelli might have known what was going on, but
he disappeared out of a Swiss jail, taking the secrets of
his Masonic Lodge P2 with him. Italian lawyer Giorgio
Ambrosoli might know where the money is, but he was
shot to death in 1979, while acting as liquidator after
the Franklin National escapade brought Sindona to
his knees. Sicilian cop Boris Giuliano might have
known something, but he was murdered in a bar in
Palermo, in 1979, while investigating Sindona. Calvi's
secretary Graziella Corrocher might have been able to
shed some light on her boss's interests, except she 'fell'
to her death, in Rome, just one day before Calvi died
in London. Of course lots of people at the Vatican
might know something – they had major money tied
up with the Banco Ambrosiano – but don't hold your
breath until you hear anything from them.

Suffice it to say that hundreds of millions changed
hands before and during the affair. And for every
winner, whoever they were, there were plenty of losers,
some of whom might even still be alive.

But then where banks are concerned, money is no
object.

In October 1983, IBH, a West German construction
company – and the world's fourth largest – went bust.
Within four weeks the Schroder Munchmayer Hengst
bank travelled the same road.

SMH was a 1969 grouping of three smaller banks,
the brain child of Ferdinand Graf von Galen, the
highly respected president of the Frankfurt stock exchange and deputy chairman of the local Chamber of
Commerce. But rather stupidly, under Galen's direc-

tion, SMH had loaned IBH nearly £280 million, which amounted to a staggering ten times its assets. So when IBH went, there was no way to save SMH.

Claiming to be the largest single victim of the crash, von Galen was forced to liquidate his own personal position, selling castles and country homes worth around £30 million.

It left him destitute.

Well, almost.

He happens to be married to a woman with $15 million worth of assets in the United States, so von Galen stayed off the dole queue.

Actually, he probably would have been better off on the bread lines because in December 1984 he was arrested and tossed into Preungesheim, said to be 'Germany's grimmest prison', to await trial. The charges against him amounted to fraud. A blue-collar crime in most cases, but at Preungesheim von Galen was oddly treated more like a terrorist. His attorneys insisted that he could not be guilty of fraud because he was the main victim of the bankruptcy. 'A man cannot be a collaborator and a victim to the same crime,' went the argument.

Whatever the truth behind SMH might be – and whether or not it is ever known – von Galen is living proof that, when you have big money, holding on to it is not always as easy as it looks.

So is Jimmy Ling.

During those high-flying, risk-taking days of the 60s, he was chairman of Ling–Temco–Vought, America's undisputed fastest-growing conglomerate. Beginning in 1948 with a $3000 investment in a Dallas electrical business, Ling was 20 years later an indus-

trial giant dealing in planes, rocketry and communications equipment.

His style was decidedly financial-macho. When he
saw something he wanted, he went after it. In early
1968 he liked the Transamerica Corporation so he
bought it for $500 million in securities. They owned
Braniff Airways, National Car Rental, the First Western Bank, a number of insurance companies and some
real estate. In the next breath he sold the insurance
companies, the bank and National. He followed that
with a cash tender offer of $425 million for the Jones
& Laughlin Steel Corporation of Pittsburgh.

It was all part of a Ling game called 'project rede-
ployment'. Based on the theory that investors will rate
a company by its assets, he divided L-T-V into three
entities, like stockings hanging from a mantle on
Christmas Eve, and filled each with goodies. Then he
went public with shares in those offshoots. The conglomerate logically created a market for its own holdings, increasing the values of those assets over book
when they were just a part of L-T-V. So his subsidiaries
could now raise additional money in support of the
parent company's purchasing of new assets for those
subsidiaries.

He ran into trouble, however, when suddenly, out of
left field, the US government slapped L-T-V with an
anti-trust suit of dubious origins. It appears that
Richard Nixon's Justice Department might simply
have felt Ling had got too big for his britches.

The suit nevertheless punctured Ling's balloon. L-T-
V's share prices started tumbling. One of L-T-V's
directors became concerned because he owned a pair of
insurance companies that had loaned L-T-V $30 mil-
lion. Joining him was a Texas millionaire who was
holding L-T-V debentures and was not pleased at

seeing them go down in value daily. Then along came a banker who owned $5 million worth of Ling's IOUs, and with him the fellow who had guaranteed those IOUs. When the smoke cleared after a series of fancy boardroom manoeuvres, the L-T-V director had feathered the board with the other three and together they unceremoniously showed Ling to the door.

A few years later, having sold everything, including his own house, to stay alive, Ling tried to recreate L-T-V with a company called Omega-Alpha. But in its first two years it managed to lose $47.8 million while amassing debts of $178 million. And the market wouldn't back him. With his shares nearly worthless, he went after the Transcontinental Investing Corp, a New York real estate holding company from the 60s that had branched out into consumer finance and owned eight independent record distributors. Ling thought he was buying a company with $17 million losses. It turned out to be twice as much. And that mistake was enough to sink Ling a second time.

In 1980 he was trying yet again. But times had changed and so have conglomerates, and when you ask a bank to stake you in a crap shoot it's tough to convince them that there is sound economic sense in the theory, third time lucky.

Jose Maria Ruiz Mateos was also flying high when the government shot his plane out from under him.

In 1961, Ruiz Mateos was running his family's business. They were wine traders from Jerez. He was 29 years old, filled with ambition and hope for the future. Using the wine business as his base, and with 300,000 pesetas as capital (then about $4,000 or just under £1500) he went out into the world to see what he could do.

The company he formed came to be known as Rumasa . . . it was an acronym from the first letters of Ruiz and Mateos and the abbreviation of the Spanish equivalent of Inc. or Ltd, 'S.A.'.

By 1983 Ruiz Mateos was wine and retailing, import and export, checking accounts and car loans. In the UK he owned several companies, including the Augustus Barnett chain of cut-price off-licences, a company to control the British distribution rights to Dry Sack sherry, and a catch-all investment operation called Multinvest (UK). For a while he was Spain's single most important employer, with more than 60,000 people on the payroll. At the same time, he was undoubtedly also Spain's richest man. But the house that Ruiz Mateos built turned out to be a pyramid. And in February 1983 it came tumbling down.

Or, more accurately, it got shoved.

The socialist regime that had just come to power in Spain looked into the workings of Rumasa and decided that the company was almost broke, that at least 18 banks controlled by the Ruiz Mateos group were endangering the entire Spanish banking system by being overvalued five fold, that discrepancies in the company's assets amounted to more than $500 million, and that Rumasa owed 38 billion pesetas in withheld taxes and social security. Their solution was to seize the company.

When the people of Spain demanded to know why the socialists were nationalizing the nation's largest private holding company . . . especially after those very same socialists promised in the elections three months previously that there would be no nationalizations . . . the government replied, 'No habla nacionalizacion. Esta est expropriacion.' But a rose by any other name is just as complicated and the difference between nationalization and expropriation must have been lost somewhere in the translation.

Described as a success fanatic, Ruiz Mateos had always been pretty much an outsider. The kind of fellow who never played the game. Or when he did, he wanted to be the one to make up the rules. Despite being linked with Opus Dei – Spain's sometime influential Roman Catholic political organization – he had a reputation among friends and enemies alike for political independence. That was, and still is, a rare quality among Spanish industrialists. He had apparently remained indifferent to the courting rights demanded by the inner circle of Spanish businessmen. Homage wasn't always forthcoming. That obviously didn't sit well with the inner circle. For instance, Ruiz Mateos figured that as long as he was Rumasa's chairman and largest shareholder there was no reason why his board of directors shouldn't consist of his five brothers and one sister.

A man of enormous charm, a man who accomplished something that no one else in Spain had ever done and something that now looks as if no one else in Spain will ever do again, Ruiz Mateos built his empire the hard way.

Backwards.

In Spain, where banks are the centre of the business world, the unwritten rule is that banks will own the industries. Therefore, the same unwritten rule dictates, industries will not own banks. But Ruiz Mateos either hadn't read the rules or simply didn't like them, because in 1962, after forming Rumasa, he bought a small ailing bank and nurtured it into the robust and healthy Banco de Jerez. Using that as his pass key into the world of Spanish high finance, he bought more companies. And those companies in turn bought more banks.

His financial skills were considerable. But coupled with those skills were two factors that worked strongly in his favour. First was Spain's financial climate in the mid-1960s. Second was a few choice connections.

During the 1960s, for the first time ever, the old guard Spanish banks began losing their grip on the nation's banking business. Much like the High Street 'monopoly' enjoyed by the four major British clearing banks, the 'Big Seven' Spanish banks thought they had the nation sewn up tight. But somewhere in the mid-1960s newer, smaller local banks started popping up all over the country. Spain was prosperous and an entrepreneurial spirit was rippling through the economy.

At the same time, with Franco's hand strongly on the tiller, a number of bankers came perilously close to being formally accused of knowingly violating the government's exchange controls. However, one man in particular, Ramon de Rato, did not get off with mere warnings. He paid a heavier price. As the owner of two banks found to be in flagrant abuse of the law, he went to jail. The government put a clamp on his holdings. And it seemed as if de Rato would be forced into a fire sale situation. But when two Spanish banking groups and one Mexican company tried to buy, the Bank of Spain rejected their offers. Then, about four months later, at a secret 6 A.M. meeting held in de Rato's jail cell, control of the Banco de Siero and the Banco Murciano was signed over to Ruiz Mateos.

Rumasa prospered, even through the oil crisis that ripped through Spain and ruined any number of businesses. Dozens of small banks fell by the wayside, only to be absorbed by the larger banks . . . and now also by

Ruiz Mateos. Within ten years he owned at least 20 banks, which represented more than 1200 branch offices.

While nothing succeeds like success, a frequent by-product is jealousy and suspicion.

Ruiz Mateos started raising eyebrows in the mid-1970s. After all, here was Spain in the midst of a deep recession, yet the hard times appeared to have no serious effect on Rumasa. Questions were raised, the Governor of the Bank of Spain queried Ruiz Mateos for information, he couldn't be bothered to supply it, and the Suarez government never asked again. Such was the way of transition from the Franco regime to democracy.

Pressure on Ruiz Mateos to disclose details of the Rumasa empire built up again under the Calvo Sotelo government. They requested a voluntary audit and, in 1981, Arthur Anderson and Company was called in for a limited review. Anderson hoped to look at 100 Rumasa entities – by this time there were about 700 in all – focusing primarily on the banking operations and especially on the question of whether the Rumasa banks were violating lending limits. But the accountants eventually pulled out, using as their excuse that Rumasa would not cooperate. Then, in the autumn of 1982, Rumasa's banking chief quit. He claimed ill health. But his rapid recovery to good health fuelled rumours that he had seen what was about to happen and wanted to get out while the getting was good.

When Felipe Gonzalez and the socialists came to power, one of the very first things they did was to demand an official audit of the Rumasa books. Ruiz Mateos balked. And the socialists came down on him with both fists. One evening that February there was a cabinet meeting and the expropriation was decided. Within an hour – in the middle of the night – the Spanish police raided the Rumasa headquarters and laid claim to everything.

Ruiz Mateos fled first to London where he lived for a year. When his visa expired, he moved to Germany where he spent three months in jail awaiting extradition and 16 months on bail fighting extradition. In the end he lost and was returned to Madrid to stand accused and face trial.

While always denying that it was a nationalization, the government felt they were more than justified to look into three specific areas of the business. One concerned withholding taxes that Rumasa should have passed along to the government. Another concerned social security taxes Rumasa owed. But the third was the most important. The Gonzalez regime insisted on finding out for certain whether or not Rumasa was solvent.

According to Juan Robredo, a Spanish journalist with *El Europeo* – the Iberian equivalent of *Business Week* or *The Economist* – the real problem lay in the fact that the Rumasa structure was too closed. No one could get any accurate information. The government couldn't get the facts. No one knew what was happening. Rumours ran wild. By 1981, the Spanish Banking Association was cautioning its members to be careful when dealing with the Rumasa banks. And the association suspected that Rumasa's assets were wildly exaggerated.

'Inflating asset values', says Robredo, 'is as much a sport in Spanish business as avoiding taxes is a part of French business. But no one knew at the time how large Rumasa was. There were the companies that everyone knew about and then there was a whole list of secret companies, and no one knew about them. And then there was yet a third group made up of foreign companies, like those in England, which Ruiz Mateos tried to keep from the government.'

The man who actually pulled the plug on Ruiz Mateos was Spanish finance minister Miguel Boyer. 'The Rumasa Group always tried to create an image of great prosperity which is not a true picture. Their shares were over-quoted in the stock market and they weren't paying dividends.'

Boyer claimed right from the start that a very early audit of 100 Rumasa companies brought to light the fact that assets amounted to a mere 5 billion pesetas and not the 119 billion pesetas the company was claiming. In addition, the government listed only 500–600 companies in the group, not 700 as often stated by Ruiz Mateos. Then they managed to whittle that figure down to somewhere between 200 and 300 actually functioning companies. The rest were empty shells. And, while Boyer agreed that expropriation was a serious step, he felt the government had little choice. 'We could have left Rumasa alone, except Ruiz Mateos was doing business without money and the situation would have got worse. They would have continued over-expanding. For a new government not to have faced these problems at the beginning would eventually have meant the risk of being criticized later on for leaving the problems alone. We were faced with a 20-bank problem and it was so severe that we believed it threatened the entire Spanish banking system. It was an exceptional problem, which is why we took exceptional measures.'

The final game score, according to the government referees, tallied this way: of 776 companies in the Rumasa group, 338 were wound up as empty shells. There were 152 companies in which Rumasa held a minority stake, and they were returned to the majority shareholders. Of the remaining companies, another 224 were sold . . . including all of the banks . . . and 30 more have been liquidated. The rest have been put on the market and are awaiting buyers. To date, the government says, they've spent 500 billion pesetas to untangle Rumasa (that's $3 billion or £2 billion).

Throughout his ordeal, Ruiz Mateos has steadfastly maintained that Rumasa was a sacrificial lamb on the socialists' altar. He has always totally disagreed that there were wrong-doings on his part . . . 'Rumasa never did anything that was not general practice in the behaviour and customs of Spanish businessmen' – although that remark can cover a multitude of sins.

Ruiz Mateos had it and lost it.

So did Jacques Borel.

In 1958, the short, swaggering Frenchman visited the ruins at Pompeii. And it might have been just another holiday had he not discovered the slaves' dining room. He remembers standing there in awe, fascinated by the basic concept behind the organization of the room. He remembers standing there thinking to himself, hmmm, a self-service restaurant. And hmmm, he thought again, I'll bet this would work in France.

Having spent ten years working for IBM – his sales included the first computer in Europe – no one had to remind him that efficiency means money. The slaves' dining room seemed so ultra-efficient that, back in Paris, Borel thrust himself into the restaurant business, even though he admittedly couldn't boil an egg.

'I didn't create the need for self-service restaurants in France. I didn't create the market for fast foods. That was always there. All I did was what I've always done. I simply saw what the public wanted and gave it to them.'

But . . . fast food for the French?

Borel called his first restaurant L'Auberge Express.

And he supervised everything. He designed it himself, exactly as he had seen it at Pompeii. He oversaw the construction, developed the menus, handled the buying, wrote instruction manuals to train his staff, took the cash and worked behind the counter. He learned the trade from the inside out and it wasn't long before he realized that his formula could lead to future successes. It wasn't long before he understood, 'Food must become an industry.'

The naturally sceptical French were suddenly faced with the fact that Jacques Borel had started a revolution. That Jacques Borel had begun his single-handed campaign to 'borelise' the world.

Boreliser: -er ending verb of the first group. Je borelise, tu borelises, il borelise, nous borelisons, vous borelisez, ils borelisent. It means, 'to Howard Johnson', 'to Little Chef', 'to Berni Inn', etc. The word was coined, not surprisingly, by Monsieur Borel.

His next venture was to take the self-service concept into what had then been called canteens and what he now called company restaurants. He sold the first one to an insurance firm, saying in effect, 'I'll pay you for the right to feed your employees.' Fifteen years later Borel ran 800 of these company restaurants, including the dining room at the German Bundestag.

All of this, out of one visit to Pompeii.

And 'all of this' was not all.

When he came across a company too small to have its own dining room, he sold them luncheon vouchers . . . scrip that could be exchanged for meals in neighbourhood restaurants. Employees ate cheaply, enjoying a valuable fringe benefit at minimal cost to the employer. In return Borel had an enormous two – three – four-month cash build-up to float other ideas.

Like hamburgers.

Ever fearless, he risked the wrath of the French by importing the Wimpy franchise from England. Most people thought it would be suicide. A hamburger joint in France? Le Cheeseburger? Borel, his critics said, had to be out of his mind even to entertain the notion that the French would eat hamburgers.

But he wasn't.

And they did.

'Je boreliserai (future tense) le monde,' he continued to think. And by 1969 he was well on his way.

'There never was a miracle called Borel. Above everything else there was a lot of hard work. Very hard work. I worked 100 hours a week. That was the basis of it all. At the beginning of 1977 I had 17,000 employees, but they weren't concentrated where I could see them work, where I could come to know them all. So I travelled all over the world. 300,000 miles a year. Maybe more. I visited, on the average, three restaurants or hotels a day.'

At one point he even predicted, 'By 1985 I will employ 100,000 people around the world.'

As the 1960s came to an end, Borel couldn't help but notice that the automobile had finally become a necessity in European life. So before too long there were 80 Jacques Borel restaurants decorating motorways in France, Italy and Spain.

'I studied the problem and personally designed my Restoroutes to provide fast food at a reasonable price and to bring in a sound profit.'

He went into that phase of the business the same way he went into everything . . . calculatedly. He could tell you that a hamburger cost him 2.65 francs for 56 grams of meat with a tolerance of 2 grams. He could tell you that every time someone flushed a toilet in one of his Restoroutes, it cost him 11 centimes.

'Power goes to the man who manages, not to money. Now, some people say I'm a nasty type, but how do you expect me to react to that? The problem isn't to be loved, it's to be respected and to be followed. Perhaps I've got a reputation for being nasty because I've always been ruthless with my competition. But I consider myself a combat leader.'

The way he liked to see it, his role was to stand up to three attacking forces. 'First there are the clients who want more for less money. Then there are the personnel who want better working conditions for higher salaries. Then there are the stockholders who want guaranteed profits. The man with the power must deal with these three and neutralize them. He must know how to say no because he's paid to be courageous.'

With some sort of John Wayne complex branded onto his ego, Borel's blitz-like expansion style created the constant need for more capital. He shopped around for French bankers, but refused to kiss the ring, genuflect or lick boots. Bankers of course like that sort of thing. Borel knew it, but he wouldn't play their game. As a matter of fact, much of the time it seemed as if he was being purposely abrasive when it came to dealing with bankers. 'All I want from you is your loot,' he would remind them, often talking down to them as if they were children, using enormous amounts of slang, not sparing his 'tu' for the more polite 'vous', going as far as to tell some potential investors, 'Bugger off'.

Not surprisingly, many Parisian bankers found him vulgar. His excuse was that he modelled himself after the ways of American business. Well . . . maybe he was smart, and yes he was pushy, and yes again, he had a definite Gallic cockiness. But he also upset a lot of people in the otherwise dull world of French business.

At the same time, he excited W. R. Grace and Company.

Borel went to America looking for fast cash and convinced Grace, 'I'll never make a major financial error.' They picked up 60 per cent of his stock. For the next five years he reigned under the watchful eyes of Grace, showing 40 per cent profits on $160 million worth of annual business. He served 15 million customers a month. And the deals he was able to make with Grace's money earned him the title of Emperor Borel I.

'I love to be on top, to command, to decide, to lead my men into battle. I learned many lessons by watching business in the United States. The systematic approach, the efficiency, the way to fight, the way business is treated like a battle where you're forced to plan everything.'

Borel fought his battles well enough to turn the initial Grace $7 million investment into a reported $35.6 million, after taxes. That's when the Grace folk decided to go back to chemicals and consumer products. They said, 'Merci Jacques', packed up and went home fat. Their shares were divested among small French banks. And those small French bankers seemed helpless in the face of Borel's new-found freedom. He plunged into a whirlwind of deals, deciding that he had to become Europe's largest hotelier. He estimated that Europe's food and lodging market would be worth $125.5 billion by 1980.

And he wanted a very large slice of that pie.

He dressed for battle by purchasing the financially troubled Sofitel chain. They were 17 four-star hotels that he guessed would lose him a few francs over the next few years, at least until he could turn the business around.

This time he guessed too low.

Borel's stock started fluctuating. He walked onto the floor of the Paris 'bourse' in a grandstand effort to rally his troops. He travelled at a faster pace than ever before. He went to the Middle East and came back with an Egyptian hotel contract worth $60 million. He leaked word to the press that when he gathered his executives at one of his hotels for a weekend meeting everyone had to make their own beds. 'It's the only way to get the hotel business under your skin.'

At the height of his power Jacques Borel controlled some 900 restaurants and 37 hotels throughout Europe. His sales were reported at nearly $400 million a year.

But at the end of 1976 the axe started falling.

Suddenly everything went wrong. The system short-circuited. His bottom line tumbled into the red by 76.7 million francs (about $15.3 million).

The bankers panicked.

As far as they could see, the choice was 'him or us'. They phoned him at home on the morning of 2 May 1977. The coup d'état was swift and effective, just the way Borel himself might have organized it. Two days later, with his palace under heavy siege, he conceded defeat. 'I'm stepping down.' And just like that the former emperor went into exile.

The bankers selected a man with a good solid multinational background to run the company. Ironically he had been a classmate of Borel's at the Hautes Etudes Commerciales, the French equivalent of the Harvard Business School or the LSE. The very first thing the new management did was to de-borelise everything.

Projects were abandoned. Divisions were sold. Consolidations were made.

What had happened, the new man believed, was that Borel had made some very basic tactical errors. He had fatally underestimated the breakeven point when he went into Sofitel. And the name Jacques Borel on everything created serious confusion in the market place . . . Jacques Borel's Restoroutes were known for fast food while Jacques Borel's Sofitel was trying to present a four-star image. The customers couldn't get it straight in their own minds.

Borel, of course, saw it differently. 'If I made a mistake it was only in the short term. I ran up against the elements. I was at the mercy of a 400 per cent increase in the cost of oil, price ceilings, a cheap dollar versus an expensive franc, and the escalated prices of coffee and potatoes. I ran up against nine months of unfavourable elements.'

He also ran up against Sofitel's lack of clients, although he refused to consider that a mistake. 'In 1975 they lost 26 million francs. In 1976 their losses were cut to 1 million. Jacques Borel was on his way to solving that problem. Perhaps I put too many soldiers and too much money into the combat, but I won the battle.'

On a personal level, Borel was a strange breed of cat. He was the sort of guy who, when you rang the bell at his house in a small village a dozen miles outside Paris, would answer 'Yes' instead of 'Oui'. Even on a Sunday afternoon he'd wear gaberdines and worsteds, with a supply of business cards in his pockets. His office, in the then brand new and ultra-chic Tour Montparnasse, had been enormous. The view of Paris from his corner suite was breathtaking. There was always a suitcase next to his desk, ready to go. A television set was built into the wall, and there was a microphone near his chair, reminiscent of the gadgetry in a Buck Rogers master control room, where Borel could shout, 'Buy that hotel . . . sell that restaurant . . . tell that banker I said go to hell.'

But it was all a little too foreign for the French.

When he was deposed, he vowed – like they always do – to continue in business, to start all over again and build another empire. He moved to considerably less impressive surroundings, a small suite of rooms in Neuilly sur Seine, and now there were no more microphones. Even his car telephone was disconnected.

He said at the time, 'I don't have a yacht. I don't have a second home. My wife doesn't wear designer clothes. I started my business in 1958 and I'm the same man with the same wife and the same house. Money never changed me. I left that business without a cent. I left with my head high, with the satisfaction that I created something, but I want you to know that I left broke.'

He insisted at the time, 'I'm not bitter. Bitterness does nothing. It's a sterile emotion. I don't look at this as a check. It's an experience. What's the difference? An experience is a setback that we don't let happen twice. So if you've come to see a beaten Borel, a guy who's finished, forget it. I left with my head high, and I left with no money.'

He promised at the time, 'Watch me. I'll bounce back. Will I ever.'

Except he didn't.

Ruiz Mateos had it and lost it.

Borel had it and lost it.

And so did John Bloom.

In those heady days of the swinging 60s, Bloom

owned a Rolls-Royce and a Bentley, a yacht, a plane, a speedboat, and a big flat in Mayfair. When he got married, he ordered a pair of wedding cakes that reportedly weighed over a ton and took a whole army of chefs more than 15 hours to make.

Between 1958 and 1961 Bloom had cornered a large share of the British washing machine market. At the height of his success he was selling 6000 machines a week, surpassing even the market leader, Hoover.

Entrepreneurship came to him early. Raised in London just after the war, he found he could stand in a queue for a couple of hours to buy fireworks at a penny a piece and then resell them to other kids at sixpence a shot. While doing his National Service with the RAF, he organized JB Productions to put on shows for the troops, and JB Coaches to ferry his fellow airmen home for leave. While in the after-hours transport business, it seems that he broke some laws and wound up in a magistrates' court. Looking up at the bench, Bloom tried to make the judge understand, 'There's no sin in making a profit.' The judge reportedly answered, 'I wish you had been in my unit.'

Getting out of the military, he opened his own firm called Ace Transport. But the company failed. Next he tried his hand at selling drapery. And that's when he met a man named Mick Cosgrave who told him about the immigrant demand for paraffin.

According to Cosgrave, the West Indians who were coming in droves to Britain reacted more harshly to the cold weather than natives. There was money to be made, Cosgrave believed, in selling paraffin to the West Indians to help them keep warm. He claimed that they could make a handsome 1s 6d profit per gallon. So they went into a partnership. Unfortunately, their profit estimates were off, their clients often complained of short measures and even when they offered a free fountain pen to anyone buying 11 gallons they still couldn't generate enough trade.

Undeterred, Cosgrave now suggested they might try to make their fortune in washing machines. He promised it was the coming thing. They found a man importing machines from Holland. He sold them to Cosgrave and Bloom for £29 and they sold them for £44. Starting with a table near the phone in a pub, they quickly moved on to more serious office space and found they could quite easily sell three machines a week. Then they put salesmen on the road to flog the machines door to door. One lovely side story is that early on in the game, after selling a machine to one housewife, they actually managed to convince her to let them borrow the machine no less than five times so that they could have one to show to potential customers.

It was then a curious slip of the tongue from their wholesaler that turned their business around. Bloom must have said something about a trip to Holland when the wholesaler warned him not to bother going. Bloom wondered why. The wholesaler explained that it wouldn't be worthwhile because he had every Dutch washing machine manufacturer already sewn up. But Bloom didn't believe him. The wholesaler's premises just didn't look as if he was doing that kind of business. So he went to Holland and swung a deal there for a machine that he could price at 49 guineas . . . giving him nearly £7.50 more profit per machine than through the wholesaler. And even at 49 guineas his machines were still cheap because most British machines were then selling for £70–90.

His next step was to take out a £424 back-page ad in the *Daily Mirror*, hoping at best to move perhaps 200 more machines. But the response was beyond anyone's wildest imagination. The ad brought in nearly 7000 orders. The problem was, at best, they could only fill 100 a week. For the next few weeks Bloom and Cosgrave, with the help of Bloom's sister, ran around Europe trying to find manufacturers who could fill their orders. It was two weeks of total chaos, during which time many prospective clients cancelled their orders and took their business elsewhere. That's when Cosgrave said he wanted out, that it was just too crazy. He sold his share of the business to Bloom.

By the end of 1959 Bloom had increased his turnover to the point where he was selling 500 machines a week. That's when he got a call from someone in the City testing the take-over waters. Bloom turned him down. Instead he set his sights on Rolls Razor, once a fashionable company, which had fallen on hard times with the advent of electric shavers. Merging his own operation into Rolls Razor, he put them in the washing machine business and flooded newspapers with a massive advertising campaign. The main feature of his ads was a mail-back coupon, which helped guarantee a good reception for the salesmen who would call.

As the business grew, he opened retail branches in the provinces, relished the personal publicity that surrounded his success and drove head first into diversification . . . central heating, dishwashers, cosmetics, holidays in Bulgaria and cameras. For a time there was simply no stopping him. A millionaire by the age of 28, he must have thought he could do no wrong. He moved into television rentals, home movie kits, a £10 million bid for a chain of radio and television shops, and as 1964 came around he was even getting on to the trading stamps bandwagon, with his own likeness on the stamps.

That's when they – figuratively speaking – stopped his clock.

It was July. Bloom was cruising on his yacht somewhere off the coast of Bulgaria . . . he always claimed it wasn't a holiday but rather a business trip . . . when the directors passed a resolution to wind up the company. That might have been a surprise to his fan club. But it had been clearly on the cards.

When he first took over, Rolls Razor shares went from 1s to 7s, at which point dealings were suspended by the Stock Exchange. In 1961 he produced a trading profit of £369,000. The next year the shares came back on to the Exchange at 23s. Washing machine sales doubled in 1962 and rose another 50 per cent in 1963. As profits soared, the share prices hit a high of 48s.

On the surface, Bloom's was a great British success story.

To round out his stature as a City gentleman, Bloom peppered his Rolls Razor board with men such as Richard Reader Harris, MP, and Sir Charles Colston, the former managing director of Hoover. Bloom even went after control of the Queen's Park Rangers football club, although he lost when the directors managed to rally enough support to keep their own jobs. Anyway, only a couple of years before he was proudly bragging that he was an Arsenal supporter, so not being able to install himself as chairman of QPR couldn't have been too serious a blow to his ego.

But just beyond the glitz and glitter, there were troubled waters.

To begin with, money had been lost on ventures into cosmetics, dishwashers, and central heating. Then, there was Bloom's 13 per cent interest rate for time payments. In those days that was considered exorbitant. Finally his selling methods fell under fire. It seems his sales team had perfected the gimmick known as the 'switch'. A genuine Arthur Daley type routine. While he was advertising his 39 guinea machines – and getting housewives to fill in coupons inviting a salesman to visit to discuss that machine – his articulate salesmen were really on a high-pressure sell for the more expensive 59 guinea model. It got to the point where the Rolls Razor selling techniques were even questioned in the House of Commons ... defended there, of course, by Harris.

Then Bloom had negotiated a deal with a company called Pressed Steel, which involved a substantial share exchange between the two firms. Rolls Razor agreed to sell Pressed Steel's refrigerators while Pressed Steel re-geared one of its factories to produce washing machines. But that deal went nowhere, mainly because the product was designed for their own convenience instead of the customer's. The washing machines had to be light enough to transport, yet they also had to have a very powerful spin dryer so that demonstrations could be done quickly and efficiently. It was a good idea. But it was much too expensive to be competitive. As *The Economist* eulogized the affair, 'Mr Bloom failed because he had not learnt his own lessons: never manufacture when you can import more cheaply; think first of the consumer and only then of your own convenience.'

Nor did Bloom's futile take-over of a company called Bylock Electric do much for his year-end reports. They turned in an £85 million loss and had to be liquidated.

Throughout all of this, Bloom liked to tell people that he was Sir Isaac Wolfson's protégé.

One of the great 'risk takers' of the 1950s–1960s, Wolfson controlled the General Guarantee Corporation. While the rightful owner of the 'Wolfson Junior' honours has always been Isaac's son Leonard (now Lord Wolfson) who, for many years, has happily and successfully run Great Universal Stores, Bloom seemed to have latched on to the title at least long enough to convince some people in the City that it was true. Looking back, the Wolfson protégé claim was definitely one of the factors that contributed to the meteoric success of both Rolls Razor and Bloom's holding company, English and Overseas Investments. The only problem was that, in reality, Bloom and Wolfson weren't as close as Bloom led people to believe. In spite of frequent references in conversation to 'Uncle Isaac' and comments such as, 'Isaac's is the only advice I listen to', Bloom's business with Wolfson was limited to one £10 million deal where Wolfson bought Rolls Razor's hire-purchase paper.

When he was riding high, Bloom could boast of a 30 per cent share of the washing machine market, as opposed to Hoover's 25 per cent. But, as competition hotted up, Bloom's costs rose. He spent nearly £1.8 million on advertising alone in 1963. Then he added 'give-aways' to his sales techniques. He started by offering every housewife who bought a washing machine a free £14 fan heater. When sales slowed, the give-aways got better ... free crockery, saucepans, food mixers, cook books, fur coats, encyclopaedias, holidays abroad. Yet as the give-aways got better, not only did the housewives get suspicious – if the machines were so good, why all the free gifts – but his costs got higher. It eventually got totally out of hand. Sales slipped from a high of 6000 a week to a mere few hundred a week.

The slide was quick and irreversible.

Shares plummeted back down to the 1s level where

they had once been. Paper losses eventually went as high as £13.5 million. Creditors claimed £3.5 million.

Bloom and Rolls Razor were very soundly bust.

The way *The Economist* saw it, 'He was unable to come to terms with two forces with which his success brought him into contact, that of mass publicity and that of the City. To the popular press he was no more than a phenomenon. The thoroughness of exposure of any new "personality" gave him an image more tycoon-ish and businesslike than the reality, at the same time insulating him in many ways from some harsh commercial realities.'

They claimed that Bloom never realized the full extent of the credit crisis in which he was suddenly thrown. But then, they always seemed to have cast a jaundiced eye towards Bloom anyway. 'This is the crash of a salesman, not of a tycoon, except as built up, perhaps fatally for his own picture of himself, by the press and television in which he was so frequent a performer.'

Sir Kenneth Cork, now retired from the City accountants Cork-Gully, looks at it in a different way.

Bloom, he says, invented a new kind of fraud.

'No one had ever done it before. That was putting money into a business instead of taking it out. He had a successful business in white goods and in those days if you were running a profitable company you could get yourself a multiple of say 20 times. Bloom's greatest cost in selling these fridges was advertising. He had to advertise every day. So for three months before reversing his own company into Rolls Razor, he charged all of his advertising costs to his little £2 company. There were purchase taxes in those days and he had all of those charged to his £2 company as well. Of course he couldn't possibly afford to pay them. But

by taking out the advertising costs and taking out the
purchase taxes, he could show a great profit on the
books of the company selling the fridges. It was almost
a net profit. With that he got the multiple under his
agreement to reverse his company into Rolls Razor. He
got all these millions of shares. He sold about 2 per
cent of them and with that he paid his advertising and
his VAT. It was very difficult to persuade a jury that a
man who decided to help his company by paying his
advertising costs and his purchase taxes that way
wasn't a criminal. The prosecutor couldn't get a jury to
believe him. Now, concealing costs to get a multiple is
illegal. At the time it was genius.'

Immediately following the crash, Prime Minister
Edward Heath ordered a Board of Trade inquiry into
Bloom and his affairs. The Fraud Squad was called in.
But after six years of investigations, no fraud charges
were ever proved. Bloom was however fined £30,000
. . . two-thirds of that for making a false statement in
the 1963 balance sheet, the remainder for making a
misleading statement in a circular concerning the
Bylock merger. At the end of the trial all he cared to
say was, 'I shall miss my Rolls-Royce and yacht, but
now I have peace of mind.'

Years later Bloom claimed he had wanted to fight
the court case against him but it would have cost him
too much. 'Despite all the stories, when Rolls Razor
collapsed, there were no millions hidden under my
bed.'

Although his reported £5 million fortune went down
the drain with Rolls Razor, English and Overseas
Investments didn't fail and he managed to get out with
a few bob. However he told the *News of the World* in
1974, 'After the company went bust I was left with just

£30,000. And when you've been used to millions, that's what you call being down.'

He tried to make a comeback in London with topless nightclubs, but the mob supposedly moved in on him. He found life healthier in California, where he opened a chain of restaurants. When those failed, he jumped on to the video bandwagon. But this bandwagon turned out to be more like a runaway stagecoach. The posse caught up and discovered a distribution ring for pirated films. Bloom was sentenced to 300 hours' community service plus two years' probation. As community service was obviously not to his liking, he skipped to Spain, to Palma de Mallorca, where he was last seen, an apparent fugitive from justice with a £200,000 personal bankruptcy hanging over his head.

Ruiz Mateos.
  Borel.
  Bloom.
  They pale when compared to a minus millionaire of super-star status like Adnan Khashoggi.

Once acclaimed as the richest man on earth – which he almost certainly wasn't, although he might have been in the running for numbers two or three or four – he supposedly spent in excess of $330,000 a day to support his lavish and very public lifestyle. He had a dozen homes around the world, ranging in character from a 180,000-acre ranch in Kenya to a $30 million conversion of 16 apartments which he turned into a 30,000-square-foot duplex on New York's Fifth Avenue. He had more than 100 cars including a dozen stretched Mercedes limousines, three private planes including a $40 million DC-8, a 282-foot $70 million yacht named *The Nabila* after his daughter, and a wife called Soraya who once presented him with a much-publicized $2.5 billion divorce suit.

Born without money in Saudi Arabia in 1935, he was the eldest son of a doctor who became a royal court physician. As such he had access to the young royal princes whom he befriended and to privileges like schooling abroad. After boarding school in Egypt, where classes were taught in English, he went on to study in the United States. He enrolled in the Colorado School of Mines but soon transferred to California State University at Chico, north of San Francisco. He lasted three semesters there before he moved on again, this time to Stanford University in Palo Alto.

He began with courses in geology and engineering but eventually turned to marketing. Yet by the time he was 20, Khashoggi had discovered that there were more profitable ways of spending time.

He had stumbled into the world of the middleman.

Whenever he heard that anybody needed anything, he did his best to fix the deal and cut himself in for a commission. In boarding school, as a 15-year-old, he learned that the father of a classmate was looking to import sheets and towels to the Lebanon. He arranged for that man to meet with the father of another classmate, an Egyptian who happened to be in the sheet and towel business. The introduction earned Khashoggi his first commission. Depending on whose version of the story you hear, that payment was anywhere from $200 to $1000.

Before he was 21, Khashoggi was already cutting himself into half-million-dollar tractor deals between an American manufacturer and a Saudi importer, with a 10 per cent commission for his trouble.

He lasted only one semester at Stanford before returning to Saudi Arabia to set up his own companies and start full-time wheeling-dealing. He went into bricks, furniture, tyre recapping and, with two royal princes as his partners, convinced the king to give him a 50-year monopoly for the production of gypsum board.

However, Adnan Khashoggi didn't become Adnan Khashoggi until he discovered that there was serious money to be made in the arms business.

It was 1956.

Israel invaded the Gaza Strip.

Saudi Arabia pledged military equipment to the Egyptian army.

Khashoggi obtained the equipment, supplying $3 million worth of trucks. His cut this time was $150,000.

Parlaying one success into the next, he became an agent for western companies wishing to do business in Saudi Arabia – Rolls-Royce, Marconi, Fiat, Chrysler, Westland Helicopters and, before long, Lockheed and Raytheon, defence systems contractors whose mega-million-dollar contracts with the Saudi military took Khashoggi's commissions into the hundreds of millions of dollars. Between 1970 and 1975, Khashoggi earned $106 million in commissions from Lockheed alone.

As long as oil was moving from $5 a barrel to $40 a barrel, as it did between 1973 and 1979, the Saudis had billions to spend. Khashoggi spent his time help-ing them spend it while always cutting out a slice for himself of anything from 2½ per cent to 15 per cent. Then oil fell out of bed. The glut caused the Saudis to cut way back. Now Khashoggi tried to diversify into banking, hi-tech industries, real estate and basic busi-nesses like farming.

He committed $600 million to a tourist resort in Egypt that went bad when local politicians convinced the government that it posed a risk to the pyramids.

He went into the oil business with President Numeiri of Sudan, but Numeiri got himself deposed and Khashoggi got stuck with an $80 million loss.

He sank $1 billion into a building project in Utah where his Triad Center office and shopping complex would have dominated downtown Salt Lake City. But his creditors started hearing rumours of cash flow problems and a few of them called in their loans. When he couldn't pay those creditors, others joined the queue.

Before long, everything was going wrong for Khashoggi.

He got himself involved as the middleman in CIA Director William Casey's 'arms for Contras' deal – now known as Irangate – and even lost money there. He supposedly borrowed $7.5 million from Tiny Rowland at Lonrho to finance his diplomatic efforts – although Rowland denies the money was lent to Khashoggi for that purpose – and he put up a pair of planes as collateral. When Khashoggi failed to meet his obligations, Rowland seized the planes.

Law suits piled up in Utah.

He borrowed $50 million from the Sultan of Brunei – who is these days reputed to be the richest man on earth and probably has been for many years – and had to put up *The Nabila* as collateral. When Khashoggi couldn't meet the payments, the Sultan put *The Nabila* up for sale. It sat in the port of Antibes, France, while buyers offered as much as $25 million and the Sultan turned them down. Eventually he got over $30 million from New York real estate magnate Donald Trump.

Khashoggi still needed cash so he mortgaged some of his homes.

But by February 1987 his Utah problems were simply too overbearing. No less than 31 law suits had been filed against him, asking for in excess of $800 million. To take the pressure off, Khashoggi's company, Triad America, filed for Chapter 11 protection.

At least in the United States, Khashoggi was broke.

Now, it goes without saying that it would require an acutely sensitive personality even to consider shedding a tear for him.

Anyway, he isn't asking for sympathy.

How the mighty can be brought back to earth.

And how easy Khashoggi made it seem.

It's a good bet that he never carried any money in his pockets anyway.

Of course, he couldn't have lost it if he didn't have it.

And no, he doesn't actually have to worry where his next meal is coming from.

And yes, he still has 100 custom-made suits hanging in his closet so he can dress for dinner. Rags and tatters are definitely not on the cards.

And he still has a bunch of homes.

And it's no secret that he's always stashed a few rials away for a rainy day. Or more accurately, in his case, the monsoon season.

However, the bigger they are the harder they fall.

So if you've got a spare $50 million sitting around, he'd probably like to have his yacht back.

2

The Fall and Rise of Jim Slater

When times were very good, when Slater Walker Securities Ltd was flying very high, when the 60s were swinging and 'conglomerate' was the 'in' word, Jim Slater and Peter Walker controlled an empire capitalized at £290 million. That may not sound like a lot of money by today's corporate standards, especially not when you see companies like Hanson Trust bidding billions to win control in take-over battles where the wars are fought with newspaper ads, teams of lawyers, poison pills and shark repellent. But in those gentler, slightly less sophisticated days £290 million was a staggering sum.

Then the bubble burst. The market crashed. And conglomerates came tumbling down like Humpty Dumpty, splashing egg over all the King's horses and all the King's men. And all the pundits sat around sneering and said, 'We told you so.' And Jim Slater's personal fortune, valued at £8 million, completely dissolved. He went into the hole to the tune of £1 million.

He was the man who invented the phrase 'minus millionaire'.

Pressjack is not a game.

It's a gamesmanship philosophy. A way of looking at the game. A way of approaching the game. An insight into the way his mind works.

'It's a name I coined with some friends for a way of playing blackjack.' Jim Slater sits in his comfortable

corner office, with a splendid view up the length of the
Thames and across to the Houses of Parliament. 'It is
also a way of playing the commodity markets. In
essence I'm referring to a stake system. For example,
at blackjack you'd bet one chip and if you won the
hand you would then add another. That would mean
you had three chips riding on the next hand. If you
lose you'd immediately go back to one chip. If you win,
you'd let the six chips ride. This then becomes 12 chips
if you win the next hand and at this point I usually
remove two, leaving myself with 10 chips riding. This
is, of course, ten times my original stake so if I then
have a winning sequence, I win a great deal. As soon
as there is a loss the stake is immediately cut back to
one chip.'

Lean and fit and well dressed, he speaks with the
assurance of a man who once had it all, who knows
better than anyone what it is to lose it all, but who has
since made a lot of it back.

'Exactly the same principle can be operated with
commodities. Take a small position first and cut losses
quickly. In this way losses are always small and based
upon a small stake. Conversely if there is an upward
movement, buy more and in that way profits are
always larger and based on higher stakes. Needless to
say, with commodities it is vital to also operate a stop
loss system even when the play appears to be winning.
There is a classic saying in share investment that one
should run profits and cut losses. In this way losses are
always small and profits can be very big. The staking
system I have referred to simply exaggerates this
tendency.'

Jim Slater is a game player. Bridge. Backgammon.
There was once a famous and much publicized game of
Monopoly with grown men in pinstripe suits sitting

around the board, buying and selling hotels on Park
Lane, rolling dice, trying to land on Free Parking. He
lost. The man who won had only learned how to play
the night before, having been given a crash course by
his chauffeur. But winning or losing may not always
matter as much as the game itself. He looks at games
in a unique way. Life too. The game is dead. Long live
the game.

An only child, raised in North London, Slater qualified
as an accountant in 1953 at the age of 24.

And almost right from the beginning he proved
himself to be extremely capable when it came to
understanding the game called corporate management. Early on he was hired by a company reporting
£40,000 losses.

As he later wrote, 'I had learned the importance of
controlling overheads, making sure that the selling
prices were properly structured, and, above all, ensur-
ing that cash flow was controlled and adequate.'

With sound management techniques and his own
special flair for gamesmanship, he turned the company
around to show a £20,000 profit in just a year.

That filled his head with the taste of success. So he
formed his own company. He went out on his own to
give the world his best shot. Three months later he
was brought back down to earth with his first failure.

Badly in debt, he took a job with Park Royal Vehicles, a bus and coach body builder, moving on three
years later to become commercial director for sales of
Park Royal's parent company, Associated Commercial
Vehicles Ltd (ACV). But after a year or so, while on a
lengthy business trip, Slater fell ill and was taken out
of action for three months.

It was during this convalescence that he developed his 'Zulu Principle'.

The title, he says, comes from having been a subscriber to the *Reader's Digest*. Simply stated, the theory is, 'If you take a relatively narrow subject and study it closely, you can become expert in it.'

The way he puts it, if you found an article on Zulus in a copy of *Reader's Digest*, and read it thoroughly, you would then know more about Zulus than, say, someone on your block who hadn't read the article. If you then went to the library and borrowed both of their books on the Zulus, you might know more about them than anyone in your town. If you then ventured to South Africa and continued your research there, you might be able to say you knew more about Zulus than anyone in England.

'The important point is that Zulus are a fairly narrow subject and you would be putting a relatively disproportionate amount of effort into it. It is the same principle as using a laser beam rather than a scatter gun.'

His idea was to apply the Zulu Principle to the stock market.

Instead of studying a company's assets, he decided to look closely at the more narrow field of earnings. By studying dozens of back issues of investment magazines, he traced the history of shares that, following a poor period, had a steadily rising earnings trend. His theory was that the City is slow to forgive and forget. When a company has performed poorly, the City downgrades its rating. Often that rating is much too low for the company's earnings trend. The next report by the company, which might show a 30 per cent increase in earnings, then jolts the City into a new rating. But that status change overcompensates and the shares increase by considerably more than 30 per cent.

On paper it made great sense. But he wasn't out simply to prove his point. He was out to make his fortune. What Slater was particularly fond of in those days were previously downgraded companies with a strong earnings trend that were liquid, that had a strong asset backing and that had a widely held share base. His thinking was that they were the most prime candidates for a take-over.

Testing his equations against the progress of various companies followed through the back issues of those magazines, he also decided that there could be only one 'best bet'. His aim, contrary to everything building society branch managers preach, was to put all his money on that rather than spread his risk. He took £2000 from his own savings and combined that with an £800 loan from the bank. Three years later he had £50,000.

That's about the time he started writing a monthly column for the *Sunday Telegraph* under the by-line 'Capitalist'. In the column he made share suggestions, adding and subtracting to the portfolio, which, over a two-year period, appreciated 68.9 per cent against a market average of 3.6 per cent.

While playing the markets in a serious amateur way, he climbed up the corporate ladder to become commercial director of Associated Equipment Company. Then when the Leyland take-over happened he moved into Leyland's offices as commercial director of the new group. For the next two years he worked his way through the post of deputy sales director until he was invited to become the group's financial director. But his health was fragile and his investment sense was keen. He turned down a highly secure corporate future with Leyland and left in the spring of 1964 to become a full-time professional investment adviser.

By then he had already met and befriended Peter Walker, who was Shadow Minister of Transport.

Beginning with a handful of small clients' accounts, his career immediately gathered tremendous momentum. Within six months Slater received a Board of Trade licence to deal in securities. Six months after that, Slater Walker Securities Ltd was a publicly floated company, with the beginning of what would become serious interests in banking, investment and industry. Seven years later, those businesses had matured and expanded into very heavyweight interests and Slater Walker was well on its way to becoming one of Europe's major financial entities.

By 1972 Slater Walker was £290 million worth of companies dealing in banking, property, insurance, industry and investment management. In all, Slater Walker had its fingers in nearly 400 different pies.

Then came 1973.

The stock market crashed.

There was the secondary banking crisis.

The property market fell apart.

And Slater Walker took a whole mess of direct hits broadside.

Within two years the ship was sunk.

The game was over in October 1975 when Jim Slater resigned from Slater Walker and found himself a minus millionaire. He also found himself facing criminal charges in Singapore.

A new game was about to begin.

The story of his meteoric rise is the story of his autobiography. It is also a story told by investigative journalist Charles Raw who decided it was time to take a long, less passionate look at Slater's rise and fall. Both books were published in 1977. Not as a two-volume set. Hardly. But rather as distinctly separate histories trying to describe the same era.

Slater's book was called *Return to Go* (Weidenfeld & Nicolson).

Raw's book was called *Slater Walker – An Investigation of a Financial Phenomenon* (André Deutsch).

Separately they read all right. But together they give a keen insight into the way the same story can be viewed from at least two different viewpoints.

For instance:

Slater: 'In my case, the early success of Slater Walker, and the satellite system in particular, created a monster that was beyond my personal control. I then went into areas like banking and insurance which, because of their fiduciary nature, are not suited to risk taking on a massive scale, and then came a bear market of incredible intensity.'

Raw: 'Just as Slater was in no sense an industrial risk taker, or entrepreneur, nor was he a genuine speculator, in the sense of a gambler, in stock market dealing. Throughout its life Slater Walker took the appearance of many different things – money manager, financial adviser, industrial renovator, conglomerate, bank. But, it was really about one thing, the manipulation of share prices.'

Slater: 'There was no doubt that I began to believe some of my own publicity. I was constantly reading in the newspapers how clever I was and on many occasions being referred to in the City pages as "the master". It was very heady stuff and without doubt it affected me.'

Raw: 'Slater Walker had erected a mammoth paper chain of companies in the UK, Australia, South Africa, Canada, Singapore and Hong Kong, each with its own stock market quotation; and this was matched by a string of investment vehicles, its dealing companies, unit trusts, investment trusts, life assurance companies. Shares were then churned around this complex, with the effect that the value of the investments once again lost contact with any growth in the underlying business, but was determined only by the malleable forces that rule share prices and the eagerness of investors to join any promotion bearing the Slater Walker imprimatur.'

Slater: 'To an extent we stirred up some of the more slumbering elements in the City, as many of our ideas were highly innovative . . . On the other hand, we tried to be rather too clever in some instances by adopting the minimum disclosure required by the law rather than a higher level to make the nature of our activities completely clear.'

Raw: 'Slater may, perhaps, be granted the benefit of what one might call the ripple effect, that Slater Walker acted as some sort of bogyman the mere voracity of which was enough to goad some firms into greater efficiency. But it is far from self-evident that, after a decade of the activities of Slater Walker and its imitators, British industry is any more efficient than it was before.'

These days, Slater looks at Raw's book as basically nothing more than argumentative. 'On everything that is arguable, Charles Raw takes the attacking stance. It's more the tone of the book than anything else. Take for example the question of Peter Walker's age. Raw argues that Peter Walker says he was a year older than he was, or a year younger, I don't remember which, and he takes about a chapter to demonstrate this without to my mind proving the point either way.

He makes an issue out of the smallest thing and was obviously out to do an assassination job.'

But in reviewing the two books for *The Times*, Andrew Goodrick-Clarke came up with some impassioned but very astute observations. 'Certainly it is easy to see, by reading both books, that when the Slater Walker bandwagon was rolling in the late 1960s, with all the Byzantine dealings which the mind of Mr Slater and his executive colleagues could think of, no one not intimately connected hour-by-hour could possibly understand what was happening.'

Further along but in the same review he added, 'Perhaps the real truth is that Mr Slater was never really accepted by the financial establishment by whom he was often regarded as a parvenu. Encouraged by his political connections and the atmosphere generated in the 1960s, he was always inclined to fly in the face of conventional wisdom – he may have defined it as taking the contrary view – without stopping to question whether such conventions were right or wrong, or indeed, whether different conventions applied in other parts of the world.'

Jim Slater has now spent more time putting the Slater Walker conglomerate years behind him than he actually spent living them.

But they were special years.

Looking back, they were years that perhaps changed forever the face of British business.

'I think it's perfectly fair to say that Slater Walker was one of the first British conglomerates that was the equivalent of a US conglomerate. At the time, L-T-V and Jimmy Ling were riding high in America. So was Gulf & Western. Whereas in England, the equivalent of the conglomerate was what we call a holding company, like Thomas Tilling or Cope Allman, a group with multifarious interests, but all held in one company.'

The difference between the conglomerate concept of Slater Walker and the holding company as Britain knew it then and as Britain certainly knows it now is that the conglomerate will buy absolutely anything. It doesn't matter. The acquisition is being made for strictly financial reasons.

'A holding company will tend to add to its existing interests in a very deliberate, planned manner. Industrial logic is the prime reason. A conglomerate is strictly a financial animal. Also, the conglomerate will issue shares very readily. It usually gets a high-flying rating, at least it did in my time, and will be very aggressive with paper on a strictly financial tack. Hanson is a conglomerate, for instance. But that is a grey area now because there are very few holding companies in Britain in the sense there were then. But Slater Walker always bought strictly for financial gain. And that just wasn't being done in those days. Even in America it wasn't being done then as aggressively as it is today.'

But then it all went wrong.

Gains turned into losses.

And these days he feels that the fall of Slater Walker was a chain reaction of events.

'Number one, there was the secondary banking crisis. In other words, an awful lot of other banks or companies of a similar nature, like First National, a £150 million company, Jessel Securities, a £100 million company, fell at that time because they were very highly geared. Slater Walker, caught in the same squeeze, was not an accepting house so they didn't have the full backing of the Bank of England. That was critical for banks to survive at that time. And so that was the first thing. We lasted out, by a long long chalk, all the other secondary banks. And probably would have survived except confidence was shattered by the Singapore incident.'

In 1972, a company in Singapore called Haw Par, in which Slater Walker had once owned shares, acquired a pair of Hong Kong companies to form a new entity called Spydar. Slater, with several other Slater Walker executives, took a financial stance in the deal as part of an incentive scheme for Haw Par executives. However at a meeting in Hong Kong a few weeks later, Slater allocated the shares he had purchased to Spydar at cost, in accordance with a prior agreement, and in exchange for restrictive covenants from the various executives concerned. The matter was left in the hands of a solicitor. And Slater says he left that meeting thinking that everything had been and would continue to be handled properly. But authorities in Singapore felt something less than kosher had taken place. First of all, they didn't like those shares being transferred at cost. Then they didn't like the idea that Haw Par's shareholders were never given a chance to approve the incentive scheme. Slater argued that no one had at any point tried to conceal the incentive scheme, that Haw Par solicitors had been consulted, that although there was no disclosure requirement under Singapore law he naturally expected that those executives who benefited from the scheme would have taken the proper advice beforehand. He says that he provided the Singapore authorities with full details of what had taken place and hoped that would be the end of it.

He was wrong.

It was merely openers.

Government officials in Singapore plus lawyers in

Singapore, Hong Kong and the UK managed to keep the matter alive for three years. It wouldn't go away. No matter how he tried, Slater couldn't put it to rest. The Singapore government seemed to want their pound of flesh.

That's when Slater stepped down from Slater Walker, handing the chairmanship over to Jimmy Goldsmith.

'The Singapore incident was the straw that broke the camel's back. Unquestionably.'

Refusing to leave it alone, the Singapore authorities continued to press for reparations. It became a major financial scandal and aroused the wrath of the Department of Trade. On 23 September 1976 they issued no less than 15 summonses against Slater claiming breaches of the Companies Act. While each summons carried a minor fine that he could have paid, they also brought along with them criminal charges.

The next day the Singapore government applied for an extradition hearing, naming Slater and four other Slater Walker directors.

One month later a warrant was issued for Slater's arrest.

'I spent a good year of my life where my major preoccupation was in defence of the Singapore incident.'

There were six charges on the extradition request. He had to fight them one by one, never losing sight of the fact that if he lost even just one, he'd be bundled off to Singapore to stand trial there. Staunchly convinced that he would never have received a fair trial in Singapore, he was severely burdened by the fight because it came at the worst possible time in his life.

'It is difficult when you've got the other problems with it as well. In other words, you're suddenly made

minus a million. From plus 8, that's a big swing.
Secondly, when you have a family to support. Then the
threat of extradition. And when you compare that with
the heights, I would say it's one of the more extreme
falls.'

Although he says he only occasionally lost sleep over
the matter ... 'Occasionally. Not often. I tend to be
fairly pragmatic. In other words, every now and then I
would lose a bit of sleep but basically I usually think
about what I can do to get things right' ... he's the
first to admit that the mental stress was considerable.

'It's a nightmare to defend yourself against a sover-
eign state because the courts don't like to say no to
them. All they have to do is to prove there is a *prima
facie* case. They only have to prove that you're sneez-
ing. And then you have to go to Singapore to see if
you've got a cold. They only have to prove there's a
sneeze. That's all. Your nose is itching. Your eyes are
running. That's all they have to say and then you've
got to prove you haven't got a cold.'

The case is well recorded in both the Slater autobiography and the Raw book. Regardless of their differing
views, the fact remains that the courts ruled in Slater's
favour. They denied the extradition.

Now he's asked, what would you have done had the
courts gone against you? And here he answers with a
slight shrug and a long pause, 'I don't know. I really
don't know.'

As the *Financial Times* once put it, 'Slater Walker has
from the beginning carved out its own traditions.
There have been success stories in the City before and
will be again, but never has there been anything quite
so big, so successful and so singular as the growth of
Slater Walker Securities.'

That means the high was very high.

Which therefore means the fall was very hard.

'The low was very low. There was a risk of being extradited. That was the biggest single part of the low, that was the most worrying. The Singapore affair. Secondly, I suppose the loss of money. But I've never actually been very hooked on money. So that didn't stop me from doing anything. My children still went to school where there were expensive fees. I still had a gardener. I still had a chauffeur. I've had the same house for 22 years. So I didn't have any period of great privation as a result because I didn't have a very high-flying lifestyle. I sold off a lot of pictures and I sold off farms, and things like that. They were investments. But it didn't affect the core of my life.'

In other words, he says, his lifestyle was never as high-flying as the Slater Walker success could have propelled it. Through it all, he tried to keep his feet on the ground. 'Well, I suppose, reasonably so. I have one wife and four children. The same wife and the same children.' There were no private jets. There were no big yachts. But here he admits, 'Not for any puritanical reasons. I just don't like big yachts. I wouldn't like to own a yacht.' As for the pictures and the farms, 'I liked some of the pictures but never sold one that was in my house. I bought many pictures just as an investment.'

On the other hand, the fall brought with it a great deal of mental strain. 'The main thing was the threat of extradition. That was the main single worry. Then loss of power and status, and all that. It was obviously very unpleasant. Then being in debt and wondering if you can get out of it. I did believe I would, but it was still a problem.'

At the same time, he says he was able to discover who his real friends were. 'That's one of the advantages. You do find out who your friends are. But there were, I must say, no major disappointments. Many years ago my wife and I audited our friends. We went to a dinner party when we were just married and on the way home we both agreed that it had been a wasted evening. Not unpleasant, just wasted. We decided there and then we wouldn't invite the people back. And we've only since then accepted invitations where we intend to invite people back. That's a very good technique because it saves you an awful lot of going through things just for the sake of it.'

These days the main core of friends are the same as they were when all the troubles started. 'Absolutely identical. Didn't lose one. On the contrary, I had some nice experiences with friends. They not only stayed with me but were very helpful.'

Just as an aside, over lunch one day with Sir Kenneth Cork, Slater's name came up. And Cork's reaction was instantaneous. 'I have a lot of time for Jim Slater. It's interesting because on his way up he always had time for everybody. You could always get to him and he'd always have the time to listen and, if he could, to help. He was nice to people on his way up which is why, I suppose, people were nice to him when he found himself on the way down.'

But friends are one thing. Business associates are another. Slater continues, 'The big thing that happened to me in that sense was in the stock market. Brokers and people like that wouldn't want to be associated. The City as a whole would sort of contract. It would be not wishing to be associated with you or back you in a period of difficulty.'

It was 1967.

One morning, while lying in bed, Jim Slater realized he was – at least on paper – a millionaire.

Eight years later he was a minus millionaire. But that revelation didn't happen quite the same way.

'You don't actually lose from plus 8 to minus 1. You go from 8 to plus 2 and from plus 2 to plus 1, and then from 1 to minus 1. It's a gradual process. Of course you have a lot of other things to worry about too. I've always been very confident in my ability to make money so I never really worried about not having money because I know I can make money. It's always been a game for me. That's why I called my book *Return to Go*. I think, as it's a game, well, someone's turned the board upside down and I've got to play a different way. I quite liked the challenge because I'd really grown out of challenges in a way with Slater Walker. I'd done that. It wasn't a welcome challenge and, as I sometimes say to people. I don't recommend the route. But I recommend the result.'

Because it was a game, his comeback began the very day he resigned from Slater Walker.

'I'd wanted to get out of it for years. I liked some of the people involved, but most of the businessmen one didn't have much to do with. For example, I don't see how I can be attached to a company making window frames. Now I'm attached to salmon fishing. Yes. I actually enjoy that business.'

The first thing he knew he had to do was to create an alternative business structure because he needed something to pay his salary and cover his overheads. 'The minus 1 million was, if you like, plus 2 million and minus 3. So I had 2 million in assets, like farms and pictures, but I owed 3 million. Now the 3 million borrowings were from a joint stock bank, an insurance company on the farmland and a merchant bank on the pictures. I'd lost a lot of money on my own shares, so I had to first of all do a deal with the creditors. I saw them individually.'

First stop was that joint stock bank.

'I went in and saw the manager and two of his colleagues. These were people I'd dealt with previously. So it was slightly embarrassing for them. I suppose it was embarrassing for me but I didn't, to be absolutely honest, feel embarrassed. I started to take my coat off and said to them, look, if you want to take the hard line you can take the coat off my back. Oh no, no, they said, that won't be necessary.'

He told them the alternative was to accept the money as lost and have an orderly liquidation of the assets so as to get the maximum return. That couldn't have pleased them too much. But he also told them he had a business plan to make the money back. 'I said you've got to look at your upside or downside, whichever route you follow. I had a Rolls-Royce parked outside, a second-hand one by the way but it was a very nice car, and I had a chauffeur, and I said if you affect my lifestyle then you affect my credibility and you affect my capacity to earn the money back for you. So I said it was a simple equation. And they agreed. They said, we'll back you, but we'll keep it under review, of course. I said I'll keep you posted every month about what's happening. And that was agreed.'

He makes it sound simple. But one should remember that his name was legendary in the City and he had a proven track record for making money. So the joint stock bank agreed. With that in his pocket, he was able to swing the same deal with the merchant bank and the insurance company.

'Then I gradually sold the pictures. You can't sell pictures in a hurry or you lose a lot of money. I sold the farmland, quite well. I made a good profit there. It was still a loss of money overall. But gradually I got it down so I was straightforwardly minus 1 million. The big thing I did was save interest because, when you're minus 3 million, the farmland doesn't earn much, the pictures don't earn anything, and you've just got a £300,000–400,000 interest bill. I was paying interest on all these things.'

Being £1 million in the hole doesn't mean that £1 million will get you out of the hole. Just to get off the 'Go' square, he had his interest bills, and his living expenses plus the overheads to employ one or two people, plus rent and all the other expenses incurred when running an office. 'With all that, I reckon, looking back on it, one would have to make at least £2.5 million over three or four years to put back the minus million, which from a minus million base is quite difficult.'

How to do it, or at least how to start doing it, is a three-step process. 'The first thing is to hold the creditors. The second thing is to preserve some sort of credibility. The third thing is you have to think in millions. In other words, if you're going to be short a million, then it's no good trying to make 10,000. So you have to think in big numbers.'

Fortunately for Slater, one of his friends was Tiny Rowland of Lonrho. 'He had rung me up on the very night I resigned and said, if ever you want any help, come and see me, we'll work out something.' So he took Rowland up on the offer, went to see him and about a week later Rowland agreed to back him in a joint real estate venture called Strongmead. Lonrho put in something like £100,000, which was to match Slater's £100,000 which he says came from the sale of 'more nebulous assets, like fixtures and fittings from the office. Not very good assets. And tax losses. Things like that.'

Lonrho then lent to their joint venture some £2.5–3 million against security. Of course there was nothing in the company at this time. But the idea was to buy blocks of flats, because the market was tremendously depressed. There were some very good deals to be had, he says, like the one they made for a mansion block near Battersea. It was 192 flats, for which they paid £308,000. The building was then insured for £2.25 million, which was the cost of rebuilding. And they then sold many of those flats for an average of £20,000 retail. The key point was that most of the flats were occupied, which meant they either had to do a deal with the people living there to share the colossal difference between the market value and the tenant value, or, alternatively, wait for them to die or move. On that deal alone, they made somewhere in the area of £700,000–800,000. Then they bought another building, Berkeley Square House, near Hay Hill in Mayfair, for £500,000. Six weeks later they sold it for £700,000.

'We made quite a bit of money very quickly. So that was my business base. It paid my overheads, my living expenses, and started to make money. It gave the banks some confidence that money was being made on the road to repaying them.'

In parallel to that, he started to write books. He wrote *Return to Go*, and then a whole series of children's books. He had never written before. He simply sat down and scribbled it all out by hand as quickly as he could. 'It took my mind off the other things. It was therapeutic. It was pleasant. I quite enjoyed writing but had a lot to learn. I had four young children and thought, there aren't many good books, especially for boys, so I started to write some. It was a hobby. But I made quite a bit of money out of it. Not an enormous amount but it needed no capital, it was a pleasant thing to do. I wrote 29 books in all. Some of them were just 1000 word books.'

Over a four-year period he wrote Puffin books and monster books for children aged 4 to about 8. Little bedtime stories, like the one about the giant snowman who melts. 'If you ever go to Switzerland and see a mountain that moves, you'll know that Big Snowy is waking up again.' Now he writes fishing stories. 'And I shall write again. I shall write more children's stories because I enjoy writing. But I've stopped it because I'm busy making money at the moment.'

Once the real estate deals were moving along, and his writing career was on its way, he decided to branch out into shares. 'But Tiny was not so keen. His administrative people rightly pointed out that if I started to buy a share and they had control of the company — they had 50.1 per cent and I had 49.9 per cent — that the shares we bought would have to be in their disclosures. They were of course aggressive in take-overs and felt I could buy something that would inadvertently embarrass them. So I did a deal with him to buy Lonrho out. Tiny got his money back with interest. He multiplied Lonrho's equity cost several times.'

That's when another friend of Slater's came in and bought 25 per cent of Strongmead. 'I went from 50 per cent to 75 per cent. I still had my debts but I was paying the banks in instalments. I also made a bit of money on shares. I was dealing in shares on my own account and had one or two good investments. Then I started two little companies in the stock market here. Very small. One was called Laganvale, a property company. And another was called Yelverton Investments. I think Yelverton when I took it over was about 3 or 4 pence a share. I eventually sold it several years later at about 38p. It had gone up much higher, at one point to 70p or 80p, but basically I did well on it, although arguably it was a big disappointment for people who came in much higher up. Laganvale also did well. I came in there at 10p, I think. Then I reversed Strongmead into that. I put Strongmead into Laganvale so I ended up with a lot of Laganvale shares. I subsequently sold out of that. I also did a deal with that friend at a certain point to buy him out of his 25 per cent. So I ended up with 100 per cent of me, rather than 50 per cent or 25 per cent, or whatever.'

And all the time the banks were being repaid. 'It takes a long time. Four or five years. Interest rates were very high. I had no compromise on any debt at all. I paid them all in full with interest. It was a long process that. And, frankly, I don't think any of them ever suggested compromising because they thought I'd repay it. There was a growing conviction I'd repay it. I never approached them because by the time I got that far anyway, it became a matter of pride. It wasn't at the beginning. I'd have willingly compromised in the beginning. But near the end it got to the point where one thought, I might as well repay everyone fully to deal with it in a nice way. To round it all off. Everyone was paid in full.'

So as debts kept getting paid, confidence kept building.

That's when he started to like the look of gold.

'I had this idea with a friend of founding a gold mine. Especially North American gold. We put about $1 million together with some people, and I had a stake in it, although he had a bigger stake as he was going to be more actively involved. The company was called Centennial Minerals. We found a man who had a lot of mining experience and we made a very good deal with a quoted American company called United States Minerals Exploration. It was quite remarkable because we did a $22 million deal and our company was only $1 million. We managed to conclude our deal and went public.'

In 1985 they sold out to a well-known Canadian mining house for about C$30 million.

'During this time I also started to sell gold short. Gold was at that time $500 an ounce and everyone thought it was going to $2000. Well, if it went to $2000 we were going to make the most unimaginable fortune because of our stake in the gold mine. But I would rather make a fortune no matter which way gold went. So I started to short gold, quite heavily, and I made a lot of money as gold went down. The price of the gold mine went down, but it was up from the base price. Let me try to explain that. We started it at about 50 cents, and I came in with an issue at $1. We subsequently went public at $5. It's been sold out at about $4. But gold came down from $500 an ounce to $320. Now the problem is, if gold comes down that much, you get a much more than pro rata fall in the price. If you produce at, let's say $250, and gold is $500, you're going to make $250. But if gold is $320 you're only going to make $70. So it has a very highly geared effect on the price of what you're doing.'

Fishing came into his life in 1973–74, just as everything around him was turning sour. 'It helped a lot. I fished two or three weeks a year then. Now I fish ten.'

Another game. A new game. And now that game has also become a business. A few years ago Slater formed a company called Salar Properties – Salar is Latin for salmon – and that company is in the business of fishing beats in Scotland.

For the sake of non-fishermen, a beat is a stretch of river, say a mile or two long, where if you own or lease the beat you can fish any part of it. Slater has, under the Salar umbrella, several beats, including two on the River Tay, one on the River Annan and one on the River Eachaig. To buy fishing rights along rivers like that would normally cost several hundred thousand pounds. Slater's thinking was that most people, obviously, haven't got half a million that they might spend or otherwise tie up in fishing rights. Secondly, most people don't want to fish all year anyway. Most people really only want to or have the time to fish for a week or two each year. However, most serious salmon fishermen might be able to afford the more manageable sum of £5000 or £10,000 or £20,000 if they were approached with the idea that it was an investment.

'This is making a business out of a hobby. The idea was to time-share prime salmon-fishing beats. It had been done before but only with inferior beats, when someone couldn't sell a beat conventionally. Whereas I bought some of the very very best ones, like Lower Redgorton on the River Tay.'

And now he coins another phrase. This is where Slater says he can make money by 'arbitraging ignorance'.

Until he came along, some of the rivers like the Eachaig and Forss were netted at the mouth, which meant that the salmon couldn't get upstream to spawn. What he did when he bought the rivers was simply to take the nets off. Along a netted river, the average catch per annum was 23 fish with nearly 3000 in the nets. 'We bought a large part of the river for £20,000 and we also bought the nets for £20,000. Which is £40,000. Well, if they'd taken the nets off, which we did, they'd have caught 142 fish in 1985. Now you can sell a salmon fishing river at £3000 a fish. Well £3000 times the extra 120 fish is £360,000, isn't it? So whoever was netting the salmon was ignorant of the fact that they should have taken the nets off.'

Since then, he says, he's also bought one of the most beautiful beats in Canada, on the Miramichi. It's 600 acres with a golf course, a skeet shoot, and lots of fish. He says they caught 144 fish there in just 18 days. 'It's phenomenal. Beautifully kept. Immaculate.' He says it cost a quarter of a million dollars and is easily worth 2 or 3 million.

While dabbling with gold and setting up Salar, he moved into oil. He invested in a company dealing in heavy oil, which is treated with steam to lower the viscosity so that you can pump it out of the ground. Most of the interests are in Texas, Missouri and New Mexico.

He followed that by forming a small company with interests in global communications and satellite link-ups.

'The only other thing over and above that I do, of any substance, is in commodities. I trade in commodities quite substantially. But nearly all my trading is in gold. I concentrate on gold.'

One of the strange little quirks one picks up when talking to him about investments is that he refers to returns as percentages, never as a total in pounds and pence. 'Yes, always percentages. Take, for example, British Telecom. If you'd invested £1000 and made £130 in a few weeks, that would be all right. But if you made £130 over a year, well, that's just 13 per cent. You could have done as well on a gilt. If, on the other hand, you had invested £10,000 to make £130 it's 1.3 per cent, which is no good at all. If you'd invested £100,000 it would be 0.13 per cent, so what's the point of it. I always look at it all like that. I wouldn't invest in anything if I *thought* I wasn't going to make 50 per cent per annum, minimum.'

How does he know when to get into an investment? He follows a newsletter that shows percentiles on bears and bulls, and immediately goes against the extreme trend. If that newsletter gave gold an 80 per cent bullish rating, he says he'd be a raving seller. If the newsletter's rating got down to something like 15 per cent bullish – or 85 per cent bearish – he'd stop being short of it. In that event, he explains, he wouldn't be short of it for anything. 'It's going to go up because everyone is saying sell, and that reflects the position they've already taken. They're saying sell because they've already sold so it's only got one way to go which is the other way. It's a question of timing. There's a stampede element in it. To turn a stampede you have to wait until they're beginning to tire. It's the same thing.'

Conversely, he generally gets out when everyone starts to agree with him. 'When everybody says this is a good investment, that's when I want to get out. For example, I liked the look of an American share named Celanese in 1984, in America, and I remember on the 8th of August the shares were $64. I remember because eight times eight are 64. I bet a friend it would do very well. I liked them at $64, their cash flow was $28 a share, which is colossal. The P/E ratio was only 5. The dividend yield was over 5 per cent. The asset value was a massive premium over book. All these things were terrific. And the earnings were going up. Now the shares are $190, a premium over book, the dividend yield is much lower, the cash flow at $28 is a lot less as a percentage of $190, and leading brokers have started recommending the company. So all the market buying power that was potentially there to come into Celanese is now in it and that is the time to sell. Although it may do well in the future, and I hasten to say I wish it well, I have also wished it goodbye.'

So Jim Slater has bounced back.

He's alive and well and doing what he does best . . . wheeling and dealing. Although these days he wheels and deals in the American markets.

'Now I have nothing in the English market. No shares. Nothing. I'm a dollar man in my thinking. I prefer the dollar to the pound and I prefer an American investment to an English investment. It's a better bet. I'd rather buy the Dow. I'd rather buy the dollar.'

It's not the way it was. But then he says he wouldn't want it that way again. This way is quiet and fun – and profitable – and it suits him just fine.

This way is a good game.

A game of skill.

At least he doesn't consider luck to have played a very big role. 'I suppose I would say that my luck has been pretty normal. Average. I don't think it's been exceptionally good. I can't remember any particularly lucky break. I certainly can't remember any series of lucky breaks. And equally I can't have many complaints. It's like at bridge or something, you sit down and some people say they always get bad cards. Well I don't think anyone always gets bad cards. It pretty well averages out.'

On the other hand, he suggests, 'If someone happens to have a lot of luck and gets somewhere then I think they can't necessarily make it again.'

But what if . . . God forbid . . . what if he should find

himself down a million again. Could he come back yet one more time?

He smiles. 'Well, I'd imagine it's progressively more difficult because I think your credibility the second time around and the third time around is very severely strained.' The smile fades. 'And secondly, your energy would be strained. You need energy and vitality.' Now there's a pause. 'It would take a lot out of you, so I imagine it would be much more difficult.' The thought of having to go through it all over again is hardly very appealing. 'I think one should arrange one's affairs more carefully so that the risk of that happening is minimized.'

And has he done that?

Finally there's a satisfied and very convincing nod. 'I argue that I have.'

3

Winners and Losers

How about, 'He who lives by the press dies by the press.'

Or, 'The bigger they are the harder they fall.'

Or, 'Fame is a fleeting thing.'

Freddie Laker was once an international front-page success story.

When he went broke – or, as some people now believe, when he was given an unfriendly shove over the side of the cliff – the newspaper headlines barking his defeat were bigger than before, bolder than before and the story ran much longer than before.

Lancelot was eaten by the dragon while trying to save the damsel in distress.

It seems that folk heroes fall harder than mere mortals.

Starting in the airline business in 1938, at the age of 15 ... Laker says he swept out the hangars ... he trained as an engineer but quickly got into the buying and selling of parts and planes, where he first made some money after the war. Then, when the Berlin Airlift came along, he got into charters and his planes were part of the constant stream that flew the corridors. He repeated the performance again in 1951 when Berlin was blockaded a second time. He flew supplies in and refugees out.

Twenty-five years of airline experience later, he decided it was as good a time as any to take aim at the lucrative trans-Atlantic market.

His Skytrain no-frills DC-10 wide-bodied daily ser-

vice from London to New York and back again began
in 1977. The major airlines pooh-poohed it at first,
figuring it would never last. But the public beat a path
to Laker's door. Then the major airlines figured they
had better compete so they lowered their fares. And
still the public voted with their wallets for Laker. His
first year in the air produced a profit of £2 million. At
its peak, Laker Airways showed revenues of £500
million and shareholders' equity was $50 million. On
31 March 1981 Laker reported that his company was
£3 million in the black.

By February 1982, with a pair of brand-new A-300
Airbuses to pay for in dollars that had to be purchased
with pounds at a time when sterling had taken a 26
per cent nosedive, and with the major trans-Atlantic
carriers having so severely lowered their prices to give
Sir Freddie a real run for his money, and with interest
rates still high, Midland Bank called in the receivers.

Emotions ran the gamut.

First came Sir Freddie's deification as a genuine folk
hero. The knight in shining armour who had brought
cheap airfares to millions of people was down but
hopefully not out. Many of his former employees cam-
paigned openly to raise money so that the company
could keep flying. Such was Laker's appeal to the
general public that cash arrived in batches, £3 million
worth, shoved into envelopes and sent through the post
from charitable fans. Laker sent it back with a note of
thanks. One woman who found her donation returned
immediately sent it back to him. He returned it a
second time and she sent it to him a third time. It was
like having a pen pal. The lady's money went back and
forth for over a year until she finally gave up.

Next came indignation.

Within a matter of days, the travelling public – the

little man on the street who was holding a paid-for Laker ticket – realized that his money had just gone down the drain. At the same time, Laker passengers flown out to the United States or already on holiday realized they were now stranded and there was a fair amount of confusion getting them home.

As the weeks went by, Laker employees understood their game was lost. Laker's creditors saw their game had just begun. Christopher Morris of Touche Ross was called in to see what he could salvage. The press made it sound as if Freddie was the cause of the creditors' problems, constantly confusing Laker Airways, the company, with Freddie Laker the fallen hero. Laker himself claimed to have been the biggest single loser, the victim if you will, forced to sell everything he owned and mortgage his house just to stay off the dole queue.

That's when Morris took aim at a consortium of trans-Atlantic carriers and advanced the theory that they had conspired to put Laker out of business.

Talk about David and Goliath!

In those early days of his full-frontal attack on the major carriers, it looked as if Morris was foolhardily firing his guns at anything that moved. Pan Am, TWA, British Airways, British Caledonian, McDonnell Douglas and the others said Morris's case carried no weight, was without any basis whatsoever and would go nowhere.

In those early days, the public probably believed the major carriers. After all, would IATA members ever lie? And, even if they did, what possible chance could Morris have against them?

A whole host of other legal actions against the major carriers in America followed Morris's. Among them was a suit on behalf of a group of travellers who

claimed that because of the Laker crash they had to
pay higher trans-Atlantic airfares. That was eventually settled by the defendants' issuing vouchers for
reduced airfares to those claimants. Then there were
suits by former Laker employees. And then there was
one filed by an American travel agent who claimed
that his business was destroyed when Laker collapsed.

But the main attraction, spotlighted in the centre
ring, was the Morris action.

It took years before the smoke finally cleared.

After some very bitter legal wrangling the airlines
agreed to end the matter 'without prejudice' – which
means they did not and would not admit to any wrong-
doing, such as a conspiracy to force Laker out of
business – on the basis that all of the creditors would
be 'satisfied' in full. Not necessarily paid in full, just
'satisfied' in full. The no prejudice settlement cost the
defendants roughly $80 million, not counting a $12.5
million fee to Bob Beckman, the creditors' attorney in
the United States, and $8 million to Laker himself.

Throughout the case Laker told anyone who asked
that he was happy for the suit to continue because he
wanted the story told. He reminded everyone that it
was not Freddie Laker versus the major airlines but
Laker Airways and the liquidator. However, at the
end of the case, Laker tried to have Morris removed as
liquidator saying that he felt the $100 million package
wasn't enough. In particular he wasn't all that pleased
with the $8 million offered to him. Although Laker did
in fact accept the no prejudice settlement at the eleventh hour, he opened himself up to a great deal of
criticism in the press. They suggested that the one-
time hero was now something less than a hero, having
walked away from the rubble of his crash as a big
winner. However Laker alleged that at the time his

business was destroyed it was worth much more than $8 million and that in those days he could have sold out to someone else for much more. He claimed that as a result of the airline's demise, his shares were valueless.

The only story to rival Laker's at the time was the demise of another folk hero, John Z. De Lorean.

He was born in Detroit in 1925. His father was a Ford employee. And so it was a natural thing – like so many kids raised in the Motor City – to think of a career in the automobile business. But after graduating from university, De Lorean's first venture was selling advertising space for the Yellow Pages . . . or, more accurately, 'a' Yellow Pages. The Michigan Bell telephone company published the famous version of the book for the Detroit area. De Lorean however was sort of a silent partner, selling ads for his own version of the tome. When the phone company found out, they tried to institute criminal proceedings against him for fraud. He only managed to sidestep that by paying back all of the money he had taken from unsuspecting small businesses.

For a while he sold life insurance and then moved on to auto parts. Finally he enrolled as an engineering trainee at the Chrysler Institute. Graduating there, he landed his first job in the automotive industry with the now defunct Packard Company. But they folded after a few years. De Lorean then followed some other Packard executives over to General Motors where he rapidly worked his way up the ladder to become the youngest ever general manager of the Pontiac Division.

From there he took charge of the even more important Chevrolet Division.

And from there found himself bounced up to the executive suite at GM's world headquarters.

While all of this was going on he became totally obsessive about his physical appearance. There was weight lifting and face lifting. His nose was sculpted and he had his chin entirely reworked, giving him a square-jawed, slightly clefted look. He also divorced his wife of 15 years, married the daughter of American football hero Tom Harmon ... she was then only 19 and De Lorean was 45 ... divorced her and later married a successful model who was nearly 28 years his junior.

While all of this was going on he was also getting deeply involved with his own investments. He had an interest in an oil field, a small percentage of the San Diego Chargers football team, and some real estate.

Then came 1973.

At the age of 48, when most men are extremely squeamish about their careers – too young to retire, too old still to be up and coming – General Motors announced that John De Lorean was quitting the company. They made it appear as if it was his choice. You know how those press releases are worded ... he is leaving to pursue other interests. The truth is that there had been talk of kickbacks to De Lorean from Chevrolet dealers, so the one-time fair-haired golden boy of GM was being gently shown the door.

Over the next couple of years De Lorean bounced around from deal to deal, most of them less than successful. There was a franchise operation in mini-race tracks. W. R. Grace & Co. spent a million dollars with De Lorean to develop a motor home, but after a year they pulled out. Then there were discussions with the Soviet Union's favourite capitalist, Armand Hammer, which was supposed to have culminated in

De Lorean becoming head of US sales for the Russians' Lada motor car. Those talks also went nowhere.

There were missed deals in CB radios at a time when they were the craze, in a bus network for Saudi Arabia and in a Japanese-designed diesel engine.

Then along came De Lorean's idea to manufacture a two-seat, gull-winged sports car that was heavy on safety features.

Not an original idea, it probably began with the collapse of Malcolm Bricklin's company in 1974.

Bricklin was from Philadelphia and made his fortune in hardware. When the fuel crisis hit the big American motor car, Bricklin went into the car business, importing Subarus from Japan. Then he decided to build cars. Especially cars where the doors open up, instead of out, giving them a winged look. He managed to find backing in the form of grants from the Canadian government. And so, working out of two plants in eastern Canada, he designed and produced a two-seat, safety-laden, gull-winged car.

In the first year, 3000 of them rolled off the assembly lines.

But Bricklin's cars were riddled with problems and his first year in business was his only year. The company went broke.

De Lorean aimed to avoid Bricklin's mistakes.

The original financing of De Lorean's car was set up in 1975 through the John De Lorean Sports Car Partnership, 35 units to be sold at $100,000 each. But investors were slow to take up the deal. The funding was only completed at the end of 1976 when certain incentives, such as dealerships, were thrown in to sweeten the pot. By then the first prototype had been completed. However more money was needed the following year, so more shares were sold – including half a million dollars' worth to TV talk show host Johnny Carson – and more dealerships were arranged, although throughout this period there were several infractions of Securities and Exchange Commission regulations.

Needing a site to manufacture with a built-in inexpensive labour force, De Lorean had negotiated a deal with the Commonwealth of Puerto Rico to set up his factory on the site of a former US Air Force base there. For a while there had been flirtations with Spain as well, but the Spanish government wouldn't give De Lorean all the control he felt he wanted, so Puerto Rico was to be the place.

Then Great Britain came along.

The Labour government under James Callaghan decided that in return for various subsidies, which would be channelled through the Northern Ireland Development Agency, De Lorean could build his cars in Belfast and bring much-needed exogenous dollars to one of Britain's more depressed areas.

The deal amounted to $97 million, almost one-third of which was an outright grant. If employment goals were achieved, another $20 million was to be made available. Some $32.5 million was then offered in NIDA equity, while just over $12 million came as a loan on the factory.

Enter here GPD.

On 18 October 1978, on John De Lorean's instructions, a cheque for $12.5 million was drawn on the De Lorean Research Limited Partnership Account at the Wall Street office of Chemical Bank, and handed to De Lorean. The cheque was made out to a company called GPD Services. Over the course of a year, another $5.15 million – making a total of $17.65 million – was sent from De Lorean Motor Corporation subsidiaries to GPD.

But no one knows much about GPD. Or, perhaps better stated, the few people who might know aren't talking. It now appears that GPD had a subcontracting deal with the Lotus Group to engage the expertise of the Lotus designer, the late Colin Chapman. But it's not clear who has or then might have had beneficial ownership or control over GPD. Registered in Panama, GPD's address is a post office box in Geneva, Switzerland. Some people think it's owned by De Lorean. Other people believe it was owned by Chapman. Possibly it's owned by someone totally different. According to a lone reference in the prospectus of a De Lorean stock offering, GPD's role was to assist with 'completion of product-design development'. Yet in November 1978, De Lorean and Chapman met in Geneva where they agreed that, in exchange for $17.65 million, GPD would handle both vehicle engineering and develop a plastic moulding system for the body panels of the car, known as VRIM (Vacuum Resin Injection Moulding). The agreement stipulated that any additional costs were to be paid by De Lorean directly to Lotus. The ten-page contract was signed by De Lorean on behalf of De Lorean Motor Cars, Ltd. Signing for GPD was a Swiss woman named Marie-Denise Juhan, who seems to be GPD's sole employee.

While the partnership existed, Lotus records show receipts directly from De Lorean Motor Cars, Ltd for $24 million. There is no mention in anyone's books of the unaccounted for $17.65 million.

Through good sound detective work, *Sunday Times* journalists in London eventually claimed to have deciphered GPD. Although De Lorean had hinted that it stood for 'General Product Development', the *Sunday*

Times Insight team came up with 'Grand Prix Drivers', a fund they suggested was linked through a maze of off-shore companies to Chapman, who filtered tax-free monies through the company to his Formula One drivers.

By 1980 De Lorean employed 1000 people and the roster was growing rapidly.

But by then the company was also in serious trouble. There were shortfalls in New York, De Lorean began insisting that the British still owed $46 million on their deal, cars were slow coming off the assembly lines, and certain company funds seemed to have been diverted into a personal land deal that De Lorean had swung in California.

New channels of finance were sought and new bank loans were negotiated because debts were piling up. There was $18 million due to the Bank of America, $22 million to his own British subsidiary and $25 million to Renault.

Desperate, De Lorean tried to hustle funds wherever he could. He asked the British Export Credit Guarantee Department for $65 million. The then Secretary of State for Northern Ireland, James Prior, was the one to tell De Lorean, no. Prior also summoned the accountants, asking for both a thorough audit of the De Lorean books and a total review of the government's relationship with De Lorean.

In Britain, Sir Kenneth Cork was appointed the receiver of De Lorean Motor Cars, Ltd.

In the States, Detroit bankruptcy lawyer Lawrence Saunders was called in to discuss a possible Chapter 11 rescue of the De Lorean Motor Car Corporation.

Generally speaking, bankruptcy laws in Europe tend to favour the creditor. In the United States, however, they favour the debtor. Chapter 11 of the federal bankruptcy code was written into the law books to give a company in difficulty a moratorium on its debts . . . a breathing space during which it can pick itself up off its knees and try to survive without the burden of creditors hanging on its back.

However, over the next few weeks there was talk of Middle Eastern money, about $100 million worth, coming along to save the company. De Lorean said that the British government had offered a $70 million write-off if he would put up $5 million. First the British government denied that, then they said, yes, it was a deal but only after De Lorean came up with his $5 million.

Some company assets were sold.

De Lorean also unloaded some of his own personal assets.

Somehow he managed to convince his creditors that he could come up with enough money to win back control of his company. De Lorean even signed an agreement with the British receivers that would have returned the Belfast factory to him upon payment of $10 million, to be paid no later than 18 October 1982.

And he almost made it.

On 19 October 1982, while having just concluded a $16 million 'business' deal – more than enough to save his company – agents of the Federal Bureau of Investigation and the Drug Enforcement Agency shut him down.

He was busted for selling a fortune's worth of cocaine and, to support their case, they had it all on video tape.

Against all the odds, he eventually managed to beat those charges. He won by convincing a jury that he had been illegally lured into the deal by the federal authorities. He walked away a free man, albeit a financially ruined man. Since then his third wife has divorced him and he's found Christ. He left in his wake an empire crumbled under $250 million debts. Not to mention the not-so-minor question of $17.65 million in Switzerland.

A more recent fall from grace – although he didn't go bankrupt – was Sir Clive Sinclair. Coming as close as he possibly could to the edge without going over, he has the dubious distinction of being the only man fully portraited as a success in *The Risk Takers* to be included here.

Born in 1940, Sinclair is a shy, smallish man with a receding hairline and a bright-red beard. He is also, without any doubt, a genius in the field of electronic innovation.

When the personal computer boom came along, he took on the giants by producing PCs that were marketed for a fraction of his competitors' prices . . . under £100. Until he came along, the home computer was an upper-middle-class folly. Sinclair single-handedly brought computers within the reach of the working classes.

In the early 1970s his company, Sinclair Radionics, was the leading manufacturer of pocket calculators in the UK. From there he went on to digital watches and the world's first pocket television set. But in 1976 he ran short of cash and needed the assistance of the National Enterprise Board. They put in a managing director who had his own ideas about the future of the company and by 1979 there was a formal parting of the ways. The founder walked out to form Sinclair Research.

By October 1984, Sir Clive Sinclair was ranked number six in a *Sunday Times* list of Britain's wealthiest men. He was said to be worth £100 million. A 10 per cent private share placing of Sinclair Research brought him £12 million, while some analysts in the City say that, at its height, Sinclair Research was valued at £136 million.

Sadly for him, it's been downhill from there.

While Sinclair continued bringing out new models and advancements to his line, the market quickly flooded with imitations of every possible home computer, spanning the range of prices. Sinclair's sales ground to a halt. Problems developed with two of his principal manufacturers, Timex and AB Electronics. Then the banks – Barclays and Citicorp – began putting pressure on him. Around the same time he unveiled his C5 Sinclairmobile and ran smack into a brick wall of total public apathy. He personally took a huge multi-million-pound loss. In the summer of 1985 there was a brief flirtation with Robert Maxwell who came up with a £12 million rescue package. But Sinclair just managed to skirt away. Instead he did a deal with the High Street chain Dixons to unload heavily discounted back stock, and for a while it seemed as if he had got his retailing act together.

In November 1985, several weeks late, Sinclair Research produced its year-end figures. They showed an $18 million deficit, against previous year's pre-tax profits of $14 million. That's a $32 million swing in 12 months.

The writing was on the wall.

With his back up against it, in April 1986 Sinclair announced that he was selling his entire computer business to Alan Sugar, whose own company, Amstrad, was an upstart in the home computer business but whose rising fortunes have been as phenomenal as Sinclair's fallen star.

Although Sir Clive lost the right to his own name in

the computer business, he retained control of Sinclair Research. That became a holding company with two entities, one in the telecommunications field, the other involved in microchip development.

But the £5 million that he got for his computer business – all of which goes to paying his company's debts – is just about as far away from £100 million as you can get.

Seven years after his first fall, Sir Clive was back to what he knows best, back to being an inventor. £95 million later, he was back to square one.

Up twice, down twice, for whatever it's worth . . . little comfort perhaps to Sir Clive . . . other inventors have known financial difficulties.

Eli Whitney, a man who changed the course of world history with his invention of the cotton-gin, which took him 14 years to perfect, was shamelessly robbed of his patents and never made a dollar over his expenses.

Much the same happened to Charles Goodyear. The man whose name is synonymous with the invention of vulcanized rubber, tyres and dirigibles that fly over major sporting events, was also robbed of his patents. He fought the pirates as best he could, ran up huge bills with his lawyers and died a broken and bitter man, in poverty, at the age of 60.

Up twice, down twice, nor is Sinclair the only businessman to know the yo-yo effect of fleeting success.

In fact, there are some people who believe that in business, as practised these days in the western world, you're really a nobody unless you've gone bankrupt three times.

It's one-upmanship of the most snobbish variety.

After all, if you go broke once and are never heard from again, that can only mean no one had enough confidence in you to stake you to a second shot. If you go broke twice and are never heard from again, it's probably because your backers are now sitting around commiserating with each other, and one of them is mumbling, 'I told you so.' But if you go to the wall three times, there's no denying that somewhere someone has been willing to give you at least two other chances when most people would have written you off long ago.

Losers, it should be pointed out, are not necessarily born to failure. Many of them work long, hard hours to attain it. It's what they then do with it, it's how they cope with it once they get there, that separates the men from the boys. Pick yourself up, dust yourself off, and fail all over again. You might even say that the most common road to failure is via failure. If success breeds success, the opposite should be just as true. It's a little tougher on the spirit, however, if you come to failure from success. You can also spot those folk by the way they explain, 'I've been rich and I've been poor and I can tell you it's a lot better to be rich.' If they're currently rich, they say that with great pride. If they're currently broke, look for the tears streaming down their face.

While some high flyers who know failure bounce back ... De Lorean probably won't because of that cocaine deal, Freddie Laker may or may not depending on his own inclination to give the airline business another shot, while Clive Sinclair is probably worth the best odds on a return to grace ... there's still another category. Call them the former losers who came to their first success via various failures.

And they're very special.

Rowland Hussey Macy is one of those who did it the hard way.

Born in Boston in 1822, he was a young man who yearned for the sea. As soon as he could, he shipped out on a whaler and spent four years roaming the oceans before returning home to think about his future. Sometime around 1844–45 he chose the world of commerce and opened a small shop to sell thread and needles.

In no time flat, he went broke.

A year or so later he tried again. He opened another thread and needles store and promptly struck out for the second time.

Then, in 1849, with a perfect batting average of failure, he offed to California. News of the Gold Rush had reached Boston, so Macy and thousands of other adventurous young men headed west. But instead of panning for his fortune, Macy, his brother and some friends reckoned they could make their fortune in catering and set up a business to supply meals to the '49ers'.

Easier said than done.

Those panners who found gold could afford better fare. The ones who didn't, couldn't afford anything.

So, three for three, Macy failed again.

Returning to Massachusetts, he went straight back into the drapery business . . . obviously he was either a man who wasn't easily discouraged, or simply couldn't take a hint. And this time he didn't just go broke, he wound up flat-arsed in bankruptcy.

All of this before the age of 35.

As long as his drapery act wasn't working in New England, he actually had the nerve to take the show on the road. He opened up in New York – on Sixth Avenue and 14th Street – and a ledger from his first day's trading in 1858 showed a total taking of $11.06. These days R. H. Macy & Co. is the world's largest department store, taking up the entire block from Broadway to Seventh Avenue and from 34th Street to 35th Street, in the heart of Manhattan.

Another retailer who knew failure first was James Cash Penney.

Born in 1876, he was raised in Missouri. His father was a full-time farmer and a part-time preacher who wanted to see his children learn the meaning of hard work. After raising pigs, horses and watermelons to earn money through his high school years, young Penney was given a job in a drapery store where for 11 months his total salary was just $25.

But his aptitude for trading was soon apparent and for his second year in the store his wages were raised to $200. The next year he was up to $300.

Then his health deteriorated.

A doctor suggested the outdoor life. Penney moved to Colorado, but instead of doing something outdoor-healthy, like lumberjacking or mountain climbing, he took jobs clerking in various stores before deciding it was time to go out on his own.

He sunk his entire life's savings in a butcher's shop in a small town about 40 miles from Denver.

The most important customer in town was the local hotel. And the hotel's chef, who did all the buying, liked to drink. One day the chef came in and explained the facts of life to the young Penney. The chef promised Penney all of the hotel's business if Penney would promise to come across with a bottle of whisky each week. Penney saw it as a bribe . . . today it's called a business promotion . . . and he steadfastly refused.

The hotel's business went down the block.

And J. C. Penney went bankrupt.

With no money, he had no choice but to find himself

a job clerking again in various drapery stores. It was a long haul, but in 1902 he managed to convince the two men who owned the store where he worked that they could use a third partner. When they realized that this could mean the expansion of their business, they allowed him to buy his way in and open a new store, which he alone managed. Unbeknownst to them, the J. C. Penney philosophy of chain store enterpreneurship had just begun.

Over the next several years Penney bought out his partners and launched his Golden Rule chain. Building slowly, he allowed his own employees – known in the company as associates – the same chance he had been given. A Golden Rule store manager with enough capital of his own would be offered the opportunity to buy a one-third interest in a new store. He'd have to train someone to manage the store, and once the new man was in place the store would be opened. That new manager and the manager of an already established store would have the right to come in with the remaining two-thirds of the necessary capital. In turn the new manager would train others who would eventually set out on their own as one-third partners.

It was a gigantic snowball.

In 1913, with 34 stores in the chain, the company changed its name from Golden Rule to J. C. Penney. Today the chain is 2000 stores ... almost nine times the size of the Marks and Spencer chain ... with additional interests in banking, credit services and electronic systems. And none of it would have happened had Penney not gone bust for the sake of a bottle of booze.

By the middle of the nineteenth century, just around the time when Penney was born, most Americans ate nothing more adventurous than meat – smoked, dried or salted – bread, potatoes, and the occasional plateful of root vegetables. Sometimes, usually in winter, there might also be cucumbers and pickles. But there was never salad, not even in summer. In those days real men never ate salad. Seriously, it was considered unmanly.

Eating habits were not very adventurous for several reasons. Commercial tinning and canning was a relatively new art form. Along with mass market preserving came chemicals, which brought with them all sorts of new and strange digestive maladies. Then too, rail and communications networks, which would eventually link every corner of the United States, were still in their infancy. Food was not easily moved about from region to region. Grapefruit was hardly known outside of Florida. Tomatoes were thought of as an exotic fruit from Mexico called 'love apples'. And oranges were a rare treat, especially in the north. Especially in the small towns of western Pennsylvania where 12-year-old Henry John Heinz first started peddling produce from the family garden in 1856.

Before long, by working his way up from a pushcart to a horse and wagon, he had 4 acres of land and was making three-weekly trips into Pittsburgh, six miles down the Allegheny River. In 1869, at the age of 25, he joined forces with his friend, L. C. Noble, and their speciality was horseradish.

In those days, horseradish was consumed in great quantities, not only because it helped to sharpen the appetite and give some flavour to frequently tasteless food, but also because it was said to possess wonderful medicinal qualities. It was supposedly useful for catarrh and the grippe. Even today experts insist that the very best horseradish should smell strong enough to drain your sinuses.

While learning everything anyone ever wanted to know about horseradish, Heinz and Noble discovered that it kept best if they actually grated it ... most horseradish was being laced with adulterants to make it look as if it had been grated ... then added vinegar and put it in clear bottles. Unfortunately, grating it made their eyes water. And, their customers were used to buying horseradish in green bottles. To sell theirs they advertised that they only packed the whitest and best-quality horseradish, with no leaves, no wood fibre and no turnip filter. Makes you wonder just what was in the other stuff.

It took some time, but Heinz and Noble Horseradish in clear bottles started selling.

When it did, Heinz realized he had stumbled on a pair of very important clues that could guarantee his future. One, a pure article of superior quality will indeed find a ready market through its intrinsic value if properly packaged and promoted. Two, housewives were willing to allow someone else to take over a share of their kitchen operations, such as the bottling and preserving of food.

Based on nothing more complicated than that, Heinz and Noble were, by 1863, one of the country's leading producers of condiments. They had 100 acres of farmland along the Allegheny – 30 acres just for horseradish – and a vinegar factory in St Louis. They turned out 3000 barrels of sauerkraut, 15,000 barrels of pickles, and 50,000 barrels of vinegar. They were also pickling 600 acres of cucumbers.

They were moving ahead at full steam.

And ran smack into the middle of the Jay Cooke banking panic.

The very day that Robert E. Lee surrendered on the steps of the court house at Appomattox to end the Civil War, the North declared itself the winner and Wall Street declared Jay Cooke a hero. They called him the 'banker-patriot'. He was, without any doubt, the greatest financier of his era, honoured and revered more than any other financier before him ... and maybe even since. He achieved wealth and fame and status through hard work and a keen sense for business. There was never the slighest hint of scandal surrounding his affairs. And 'as rich as Jay Cooke' was the expression of the day.

Raised in Philadelphia, where he learned his banking trade, he started his business by financing canals and railways. He made money on loans to the government during the Mexican War and took that experience with him into the Civil War. In 1861 the Commonwealth of Pennsylvania – that's what the state is officially called – needed to sell a large bond issue to finance its participation on the Northern side. The only banker who dared go for it was Cooke. He sold it with a rousing appeal to patriotism, which was the first time any bond issue in the United States was ever sold that way. His success was so impressive that when the Civil War broke out the federal government called for Cooke's help. He moved to Washington DC, set up offices across the street from the Treasury, and launched a nationwide campaign for war bonds, complete with newspaper ads, brass bands and flag-flying rallies. In four years he sold more than $3 billion worth of bonds.

The war over, Cooke spent $1 million of his own money to build his family a 52-room mansion where he would entertain President Grant with rare wines and fine cigars. His reputation was secure. But the thrill of the chase was addictive. He set out in search of a new challenge, and found it in 1869 in the Northern Pacific Railroad. It was to be America's second transcontinental network, linking the Great Lakes with the Pacific Northwest. Even though some people pooh-poohed the idea of a railway going 'from nowhere to nowhere', Cooke agreed to sell $100 million worth of bonds to finance the venture. With his usual flair he fired up America. But this time his call for patriotism was a bit too heavily mixed with imagination. Over-zealous copy-writers led the public to believe that the railway would wind its way through orange groves, banana trees, and tropical fauna with monkeys swinging from vines. Around Wall Street they called it 'Jay Cooke's Banana Belt', because they knew the truth. They knew that the railway was cutting straight through the Dakota 'badlands', complete with harsh winters and angry Indians. So Wall Street didn't back him this time the way they had for the Civil War. Money did come in from small town America ... taken out from under the mattress ... because Cooke was, after all, a great American hero. But that didn't raise anywhere near $100 million worth.

Now Cooke sent his salesmen to Europe. He had to sell those bonds. It wasn't just his reputation this time, his wallet was also on the line. He was overextended and everyone on Wall Street knew it. His salesmen canvassed Germany where there should have been plenty of money. Except the Franco–Prussian War got in their way and what buyers they had signed up quickly reneged.

Back in the States, pressured to get the bonds moving somehow, Cooke was forced to heavily discount them. That didn't help his hero-status among the people of small town America who had paid full price.

As his overdrafts mounted, his revenue declined. He appealed to friends in Congress to help him obtain a new charter for the railway. That would give him more time. But they were slow in reacting. Word got out that Cooke was on the ropes. John Pierpont Morgan appeared from out of the woodwork, merged his banking house with Philadelphia's Drexel & Company and took aim at Cooke. Then America's second largest financial house, Morgan, now saw a chance to become number one. He wanted in on the business of government financing . . . long a Cooke monopoly. So with Cooke weighted down by the Northern Pacific deal, Morgan raided his patch and made deep inroads. Sniping at Cooke's reputation, Morgan built up enough momentum to totally undermine Cooke's credit and steal his business.

At 12:15 P.M. on 18 September 1873, Jay Cooke went broke to become America's first well-known minus millionaire.

That afternoon, trading had to be halted on the floor of the New York Stock Exchange as no less than 37 banks and brokerage houses sank with Cooke. Over the next few days the rippling effect closed other banks across the country and completely shut down building on several railways, not just the Northern Pacific. Within three months, more than 5000 businesses had failed.

Heinz was about to join the club.

To save their own hides, banks tightened their grip on credit. Heinz and Noble got caught in the squeeze. They had enough to pay for salaries and for rent and had even budgeted for an average autumn cucumber crop. Ironically, just then, a bumper crop came in. They were committed to take it all. Their cash flow was shot to hell. Heinz personally endorsed his own life insurance policy as collateral on a loan, borrowed from friends and mortgaged his house. And still the banks squeezed him. Always happy to give you an umbrella on a sunny day, banks then – and still today – are the first to ask for it back when the rain begins.

In December 1875, there was nothing left. The vultures had picked the bones clean. Heinz and Noble filed for bankruptcy. Heinz personally lost everything. His house. His furniture. His self-esteem. He was reduced to begging three local grocers to trust him so that he could feed his family. He gave them his word that he would pay them as soon as he could get matters straightened out.

And they turned him down.

He wrote in his diary, 'Bankruptcy changes a man's nature. I feel as though every person had lost confidence in me and I am therefore reserved.'

The one thing that people who face financial ruin seem to have in common is that sooner or later they discover who their real friends are. In Heinz's case, it was a man named Jacob Covode. He was willing to stake Heinz to a $3000 loan. H. J. put the company in the name of his brother John and his cousin Frederick, and listed himself as just another employee.

F & J Heinz went into business . . . and within a year H. J. was nearly broke again. In fact, life for Heinz was such an uphill struggle it wasn't until 1879 that the new company finally started to see a small profit. By then Heinz had added ketchup to the line, along with chilli sauce, mincemeat, mustard, pickled cauliflower, pickled onions, sweet pickles . . . he was the first ever to market those . . . and baked beans with tomato sauce.

Six years later he was released from his bankruptcy having personally paid off all his old debts. The follow-

ing year he sailed to Europe. On 16 June 1886, as
recorded in his diary, he put on his best clothes, packed
seven varieties of his finest and newest goods in a
Gladstone bag, left his rooms on Great Russell Street,
marched down London's Piccadilly and straight into
Fortnum and Mason. Instead of going to the trades-
man's entrance and trying to arrange an appointment,
he stepped through the front door, surveyed the main
hall smartly, found a clerk and with home-grown
American moxie announced that he was there to see
the Head of Grocery Purchasing. When a gentleman
appeared, Heinz introduced himself as 'a food merchant from Pittsburgh, in the United States of America', gave his spiel and showed his wares. The British
gentleman tasted the horseradish, the chilli sauce and
the ketchup, then told him, 'I think, Mr Heinz, we will
take them all.'

Pub lunches would never be the same.

Two years later the company name was changed to
H. J. Heinz. But that day in London was the turning
point. That's when the former bankrupt realized, for
the first time, the world was his market.

At least in his own head, the world could be the market
for a young man named Henry Ford who, sometime
around 1899, got himself some backers and formed a
group called the Detroit Automobile Company.

He was a farmer's son who hated farms and became
an engineer because he was talented – his father once
described him as having 'wheels in his head' – but also
because by becoming an engineer he planned on forever avoiding work in his old man's fields. Oddly
enough, in later years, Ford would be a staunch advo-
cate of the 'you are what you eat' movement. Perhaps
it was some sort of latent throwback to his distaste of

a rural childhood. In any case, over the years he spent both a great deal of time and a great deal of money campaigning to rid the world of cows.

Ford and his Detroit Automobile Company, working out of a shed, spent two years and blew $86,000 to build just a dozen vehicles. When the public's response was a big yawn, the financiers decided there was nothing in the automobile business besides more debts. Ford quarrelled with his backers . . . this was the start of a life-long habit . . . and, because they staunchly refused to see things his way, he walked out.

His pockets were empty.

However a few very loyal friends walked with him. They wanted to see him set up again and felt he could succeed if he had a free hand to build another vehicle. In 1902 the Henry Ford Company opened for business. But almost as soon as the paint was dry on the front door sign Ford was once again fighting with the money men. They saw the future in passenger cars. Much to their astonishment, he produced a racing car. They couldn't see any sort of profit in such a folly, in spite of the fact that Ford actually won his first race, driving the car himself. He argued that a racing car would help promote his ideas. They told him they just weren't interested. And for the second time in as many years Ford and his angels parted company.

Because the backers of that second company still wanted to build passenger automobiles, they brought in new engineers, geared up the factory and changed their name to honour the man who had founded the City of Detroit. They called themselves Cadillac.

At the same time, twice down, Henry Ford now formed his third company. That was June 1903. He somehow managed to can his belligerence long enough to come up with a dozen new backers, and issue 1000 shares of stock at $100 a share. But only $28,000 of the total investment came in cash. And half of that was gone before the end of June. Two weeks later, the Ford Motor Company's bank balance was a mere $223.65.

That's when the Model A took America by storm.

Paul Galvin was also a Midwesterner.

Born in 1895, north of Chicago in the small town of Harvard, Illinois, he was of strong Irish peasant stock, and raised to believe in what used to be called the work ethic. Never afraid of hard work and ever enterprising, he was 13 when he noticed some other kids selling popcorn along railway sidings where trains stopped to be serviced. It struck him as a pretty good business, so he launched himself into the world of railway siding popcorn. What he didn't know at the time was that the kids who owned the turf weren't interested in any competition. To help him understand, they grabbed his popcorn and spilled it all over the street. The next day, to protect himself, he showed up for work with a big friend as a bodyguard. The day after that, the original popcorn magnates arrived with their own big friend in tow. War was declared and quickly escalated to the point where it was just the big kids doing all the fighting, while the original popcorn vendors sat on the benches and negotiated a peace. There was, in the end, more than enough business for everyone and within a few years Galvin had expanded. He brought two of his brothers into the business and added sandwiches to his stock. He built a pushcart. And when the sandwiches proved a winner, he started selling ice cream too.

As Galvin's business grew, the competition got tougher. Kids started rushing up to the trains before they even stopped, trying to be first down the aisles with their fare.

And that's when disaster struck.

One day, one of the kids missed his footing and slipped under the wheels. With a Draconian sweep of his hand, the station master put every one of those kids out of business, right there and then.

It was Galvin's first flop . . . albeit not of his making. But out of that story came the Galvin philosophy, 'Recognize the signs. If you're going to take a licking, take it, and get on to the next job.'

He graduated from high school, spent two years at the University of Illinois, quit, and offed to the Army to fight the First World War. Returning home in 1919, he decided to try his luck in the oil fields. He got himself a job with a crew in Waco, Texas. But they didn't want him to report down there for another two months, so he went to Chicago looking for temporary work. He just wanted something to tide him over.

He found it at the D&G Storage Battery Company.

Electricity was now lighting up the country's rural areas and automobiles were no longer as much a luxury item as they were fast becoming a way of life. D&G made batteries for cars and it was a tremendously fast-growing business. Galvin's eyes started to open.

Comparing notes with a home-town friend named Edward Stewart, Galvin concluded there was a great future in batteries. So dreams of Texas oil were abandoned. The Stewart-Galvin Battery Company was born in a small Wisconsin village, about a day's drive from Chicago. But batteries in those days were heavy, awkward to handle, and the acid made them especially expensive to ship. Chicago was the crossroads of the country's railway network, which meant that before they could send their batteries anywhere in America they first had to get them to Chicago.

No matter how enthusiastically they tried, they couldn't make it work.

Bills piled up.

Orders ground to a halt.

The end came swiftly in 1923. Paul Galvin left the plant for lunch one day, only to return to find the front door padlocked by Federal Agents who were seizing their assets for non-payment of excise taxes.

The Feds wouldn't even allow him inside to retrieve his only overcoat.

With nothing left – he literally had only $1.50 in his pocket – he put his wife and their baby into a borrowed car and headed back to Chicago.

For the next three years Galvin found employment with a family friend. But then in 1926 he hooked up again with Edward Stewart. And this time they went into the radio business. Stewart had spent those years still dabbling in the battery business and, even though his new company was now doing well, they both saw the possibilities of radio. In 1920 there were an estimated 3000 sets scattered around America. Two years later that figure had been multiplied by 100. By 1926 annual sales were already close to the $500 million mark. However those radios were all battery powered and it was just a matter of time before AC current radios came onto the market. The problem, as Galvin and Stewart saw it, was that the 5 million people who owned battery radios weren't going to just throw them out in favour of the new AC sets. So they came up with something called the A-Eliminator. First you plugged the A-Eliminator into an electric outlet. Then you plugged the battery radio into the A-Eliminator. The result was a battery radio that always stayed charged.

It was a terrific idea.

Except it didn't work too well.

There were too many technical problems, sales were not fast enough and by 1928 they were in financial trouble again. They managed to improve the A-Eliminator while holding off the sheriff for a while. But he eventually padlocked their doors and whatever assets they had went onto the auction block to pay their debts.

Just then fate played its hand.

The head of the radio department at Sears – the Chicago store that would literally invent shopping by post – placed an order for that new generation of A-Eliminators. Seeing this as a great break, Galvin shopped around for other potential clients. A few lined up, so he went to the auction to buy back the Stewart-Galvin assets. With borrowed money in his pocket, he paid $750 for the A-Eliminators. With an additional $565, he started the Galvin Manufacturing Corporation. The plan was to create a cash flow with those perfected A-Eliminators, then immediately move on to the product that would be the future of the industry . . . radios with AC tubes.

Galvin rented a workshop in a building on Harrison Street in Chicago. But . . . as the born entrepreneur is ever one with an eye for a good deal . . . when he saw vacant floors above him, he immediately appealed for the extra space. He told his landlord, 'You know how much money I have. Signing a lease doesn't mean anything because that is all there is. And this is a good time for me to tell you that I can't pay the first month's rent until the end of the month. I know it's customary to pay in advance but I'm working so close I just won't have the money for a few weeks.'

He got the space.

The first week's payroll was $63.

And, interestingly enough, one of the designers on that payroll was a young man named Bill Lear . . . as in Learjet.

By Christmas 1929, with all that extra space and with all those A-Eliminators and with talent like Lear working with him, Paul Galvin was still broke and just about out of business.

He figured he had one last chance.

He was going to try to put his radios into automobiles.

That wasn't being done on a very large scale in those days and Galvin couldn't be sure that there was even a decent market for such things. The popular cry was, 'Who wants a car radio? It will ruin your motor.' There were also all sorts of technical problems to overcome, like how to make the radio work without picking up massive interference from the spark plugs. And, like where to put the radio and the battery, which was the size of a fishing tackle box, when car dashboards weren't yet being designed with enough space for radios and batteries.

By Christmas 1930, Galvin Manufacturing was $3,745 in the red.

Years later, when corporate accountants talked to him about restructuring debt and expansion, Galvin would tell them, 'You fellows have never been broke and never had the problems I've had. One Saturday night in 1930 I got home and, before I had my coat and hat off, my wife Lillian, who had the rent to pay and the food to buy, asked me, "How much did you bring?" And I said, "I brought 24 bucks, and that's all they could give me." All the company could spare was 24 bucks. Now debt can smother a man and give him a false sense of security when the truth is that even the 24 bucks he brings home might not really be his.'

Today the house that Galvin built is named after the first car radio . . . Motorola.

4
Wall Street Crash

It was the best of times.

It was the worst of times.

It was the roaring twenties. It was the flapper. It was the Lindy Hop. It was black men up from New Orleans to play something new called jazz. It was white men in Chicago with Tommy guns guarding hooch they smuggled in from Canada to wet a constitutionally dry America.

Sinclair Lewis wrote *Main Street*. Fridtjof Nansen won the Nobel Peace Prize. Babe Ruth hit home runs. And Alexander Graham Bell died.

Nicola Sacco and Bartolomeo Vanzetti were executed for a murder they almost certainly did not commit. Charles Lindbergh flew to Paris. Maria Callas was born. And Paavo Nurmi ran a record mile in 4 minutes 10.4 seconds.

Pius XI ruled the Vatican. Joyce wrote *Ulysses*. And Magritte painted surreal. *Show Boat* opened on Broadway. Marilyn Monroe was born. An earthquake destroyed Corinth. The British elected their first Labour government. And Lenin died.

The *Reader's Digest* was founded. George Gershwin composed *A Rhapsody in Blue*. The BBC went on the air. And John Scopes was fined $100 plus court costs for teaching evolution in a Tennessee high school.

Al Johnson was *The Jazz Singer*. Rudolph Valentino was *The Sheik*. Jack Dempsey was the heavyweight champ. Bill Tilden was the Wimbledon champ.

And the stock market exploded.

It was the golden age of minus millionaires.

The decade began in September 1920 when a bomb went off on Wall Street and killed 30 people. It ended in October 1929 when the great American dream crashed through the floor, when the paper in the punters' pockets was so worthless that men literally threw themselves out of windows.

It was an era when a fortune was a fortune. And the times belonged to men like the one whose middle name was Fortune.

Thomas Fortune Ryan was born in Virginia, the son of penniless Scots-Irish immigrants. As a young man he worked in a drapery store in Baltimore before moving to New York to take a job as a clerk on Wall Street. By 1885, as a full-fledged broker, he began seeing opportunities in railway and tram properties. Within a year he befriended another man with public transport interests, William C. Whitney ... of the New York Whitneys, son-in-law of the major Standard Oil shareholder and a man who would serve as Secretary of the Navy during President Grover Cleveland's first term from 1885 to 1889.

In those days New York was a web of independent public transport companies. Everybody was in business for himself. Confusion reigned. The city was ripe for plucking. So Ryan and Whitney plucked it to the bone.

Beginning with horse-drawn buses, they quickly moved on to electric tramways and elevated trains, manipulating the shares and bonds of various independent companies with such skill that, long before the New York underground system was opened in 1904, they had all but monopolized the city's transport industry. They called their company the Metropolitan Street Railway. The total capitalization was $260 million –

$144 million in shares, the rest in bonded indebtedness. After some $236 million was sold to the public, Whitney described Ryan as 'the most adroit, suave and noiseless man that American finance has ever known'.

Unfortunately for the city of New York, what Ryan and Whitney were up to simply wasn't kosher. Not by any stretch of the imagination. Yet because they managed it on such a huge scale, they proved the adage that if you steal a pound you're a crook, but if you steal a hundred million pounds you're adroit, suave, noiseless and maybe even a romanticized tycoon.

However, their antics did not go unnoticed. The press had a field day. It was their prodding that finally moved the politicians to act. Investigations were commissioned which, typically, dragged on for years. Some $90 million had gone missing and a select circle of men had grown very rich ... most particularly Whitney and Ryan who had amassed two of the quickest and most important fortunes to come out of that frenzied time when quick, important fortunes were not necessarily a rarity. They had also left New York's public transport network a shambles. But by the time the commissions, the committees and the investigators finally got around to anything more useful than commissioning, committeeing and investigating, Whitney was dead and the statute of limitations had run out. A grand jury ended the matter by concluding that the transport take-over had been dishonest and probably even criminal, but that it was not necessarily actionable. Not one single person was ever prosecuted. Today, Whitney's fortune is considered 'old money' in New York, where it has long since intermarried with some of the Guggenheim wealth and these days actively finances hospitals and museums.

Ryan, who was by then said to be worth $50 million, went on to wheel and deal in tobacco, and hob-nob with the Vanderbilts. In 1906 he was summoned by Belgian King Leopold II to handle his personal financial affairs in the Congo. A few years later Ryan secured control of the Equitable Life Assurance Society ... beating New York's ever-powerful Harriman clan at the tape. A robber-baron of the least glamorous sort, Ryan was eulogized in obituaries when he died in 1928 as one of the last of the financial Titans of the 1890s. The *New York Times* actually went so far as to label his career, 'as good an example as any in American history of the possibilities that this country offers to a poor uneducated boy'.

It was into this world that Allan A. Ryan was born and raised.

Like so many first-generation Americans for whom formal learning was not always possible, Thomas F. made certain that Allan A. had the best education money could buy. He sent his son to private schools and then on to Georgetown University in Washington DC. In 1915, when Allan was 35 and had satisfactorily served a Wall Street apprenticeship at his father's knee, Thomas rewarded his son with a seat on the New York Stock Exchange. Three years later, when Thomas began thinking about retirement, he asked Charles Schwab, of US Steel and later Bethlehem Steel, to keep an eye on Allan. With the backing of his father and the patronage of his father's cronies, Allan A. Ryan and Company became an important Wall Street player.

To Allan A.'s credit, there was a critical difference between father and son. Even though young Ryan was considered a tough man to do business with and a righteous member of the Wall Street fraternity, for better or worse *fils* didn't possess *père*'s buccaneering spirit. He might have inherited some of Thomas F.'s sense of competitiveness and at least some of his old man's financial skills, but somewhere along the line he also picked up a strong sense of right and wrong, which most definitely was not one of his father's stronger suits. That sense of right and wrong manifested itself quite visibly in 1917 when Allan's mother died and the mourning widower remarried a scant two weeks later. Allan couldn't hide his disapproval. A rift developed between father and son. The two stopped speaking. And Allan was left unprotected.

As 1919 headed towards 1920, Wall Street knew one of its all-time great bull markets. Share prices shot skywards. Allan Ryan was always known for being very bullish . . . that eternal optimist who buys believing his shares will rise in value. But lurking in the shadows are the bears . . . those punters who are willing to bet that certain shares are about to fall. What bears do is sell short, unload shares now that they don't own, gambling that somewhere down the line they will be able to buy them back at a lower price. In a bear market they make money. In a bull market they lose money. But when one tries to squeeze the other, life for both of them can get nasty.

The bulls play for a corner. They want to own all the shares and therefore dictate the price. The bears are out to prevent that corner, any way they can, doing whatever is necessary to force the share prices down. In some ways it's a lot like high stakes poker. You need the same kind of nerves, the same sang-froid. But manoeuvring through the mine fields also takes the imagination of a world-class chess master. The risks are enormous. If you lose, the devastation can be a financial holocaust. If you win there are usually some

very handsome spoils. Cornelius Vanderbilt finessed
three important corners during the 1860s, including
his take-over of the New York & Harlem Railway. He
bought up all of Harlem's shares while purposely
spreading rumours around Wall Street that the company was about to go broke. He cornered the market
for about $9 a share, hyped the price, then sold the
borrowed shares back to the defeated bears for $197.
But when Jay Cooke tried to corner the Northern
Pacific Railroad market, the bears won and he flamed
out, going down in ruin.

Among the operations in which Ryan owned a controlling interest was the Stutz Motor Car Company,
makers of the legendary Stutz Bearcat. In the early
months of 1920, Stutz shares began rising at a very
steep angle. From an average price of $100 at the end
of 1919, the shares were up to $134 by February. To
many people it seemed as if the shares were priced too
high. So, willing to stake their money on those shares
being overpriced, the bears raided. They shorted Stutz.
Sell orders came flooding in.

Ryan quickly saw that in order to save Stutz, and
more importantly to save himself, he had to drive the
share price upwards until he could corner the market
and squeeze the bears out of business. His fortune was,
in those days, estimated to be worth something in the
neighbourhood of $30 million. He wasn't as rich as his
father, but he was still no slouch. He certainly had the
means to fight. So he started buying every Stutz share
that poured onto the market. It consumed an enormous
amount of cash. And the first month's campaign went
against him. The bears squeezed the price down. From
$134, Stutz ebbed at the $100 mark. Knowing that
total catastrophe was his downside, Ryan had to sink
more and more money into the war. Because he was

the one who had to put up cash – the bears were selling so they could sit tight, at least for a while – he was forced to borrow from the banks, using his entire personal fortune as collateral.

It turned out to be enough.

Into the second month of battle the Stutz share price started rising again.

It quickly passed the $134 mark.

Now greed set in among the bears. They knew that if Ryan faltered he'd be wiped out. His losses would be their gains. They convinced themselves that he couldn't support the Stutz price forever. They kept selling. Ryan kept buying. The faint-hearted were left by the wayside. Anyone smart enough to know what Ryan was doing took their profits and went home. Only the really heavyweight bears continued going short, wagering everything that the share price absolutely had to come tumbling down.

The shares hit $200. Then $250.

And still they sold short.

And still he bought.

Then they hit $300.

The Stutz frenzy actually got to the point where there weren't any shares left on the market. Allan Ryan owned them all. But there were still bears wanting to play the game. Now Ryan told them that if they wanted to stay in he'd lend them shares.

They borrowed to sell.

He loaned to keep buying.

At the end of March Stutz shares scratched the dizzying height of $391.

That same day he snapped the bear traps shut.

Ryan had finessed a beautifully classic corner. Perhaps the most beautiful ever managed. The bears had grossly underestimated his resources.

Now they had only two choices. Either they bought the shares back from him that they had promised to sell, or they faced criminal prosecution for a breach of contract. In other words, by going short they had contracted to sell him shares at a certain price. In order to get those shares, because no one else had any, they were forced to negotiate with him. He was only too pleased to sell any of the bears the shares they needed to fulfil their contracts ... but the price was now $750 per share!

To put it mildly, he had them firmly by the gonads.

The Business Conduct Committee of the New York Stock Exchange tried to fight fire with fire. They called Ryan in on charges of unethical dealing. It was a feeble ploy, but they had to do something because a number of the members of that specific committee had been caught short. Ryan stood his ground. The committee threatened to strike Stutz shares off the trading list. Ryan said that if they did that he'd raise the price from $750 to $1000 per share. The Governing Committee then suspended trading on Stutz. They said, 'Check'. And effectively they had put Ryan in a bind. strained by borrowings that everyone knew he had to repay. But he argued that a contract was a contract and he was going to collect. That's when the Law Committee of the Stock Exchange ruled all of Ryan's contracts void. They said they would not treat any failures to deliver Stutz shares to Ryan as a failure to comply with the contract. Adding insult to stupidity, the Law Committee said that, if Ryan didn't like it, he could go crying to the courts.

Ryan then informed the members that they could negotiate with him *en masse* if they wished, which would save him the bother of negotiating separately with each short seller. The not-so-subtle inference was that, should they renege on those contracts and should he win in court, the reputation of the nation's most powerful financial institution – not to mention the wallets of its most esteemed members – would be irreparably damaged.

The NYSE shrugged off the threat. Their trump card was that, should Ryan lose in court, he too was risking financial ruin.

For a while it looked like a stalemate. The NYSE hired a fancy firm of Wall Street lawyers who assured them that Ryan's contracts were unenforceable. Ryan hired a firm of Wall Street lawyers who assured him that the NYSE members had to make good on their bond.

Then, in a surprise move, Ryan resigned from the Stock Exchange.

The Governing Committee pondered that one, until it dawned on them that his resignation freed him from the NYSE's rules. But, they assured themselves, Mr Ryan will still behave like a gentleman. Except, within hours Mr Ryan broke the rules of gentlemanly Wall Street warfare. He released to the press the names of the Stock Exchange members who were trying to renege on their contracts.

Stuttering its way through various denials and revisions of the truth, the NYSE said that honouring those contracts was never in question . . . no, that's not what we meant at all . . . they changed their tune and said that it was exactly how to honour those contracts that was a matter for negotiation.

If the NYSE had been playing for Ryan's king, they had somehow missed seeing that, piece by piece, he was taking their men off the board. Knights tumbled. Then bishops. Then the queen. Now Ryan pierced the last defences in a final assault for mate. He formally called in the stock he had loaned.

Because the bears had borrowed shares from him to fulfil their short contracts, even if those contracts were ruled null and void, they still owed him for the borrowed shares. They either had to come up with them – which of course they couldn't because Ryan owned them all – or he could pay himself any price he wanted, and simply pass the bill on to the borrowers. And that was well within the rules of the game as set down by the NYSE itself.

Desperate, with their backs squarely against the wall, the NYSE set up a mediation panel. But there wasn't anything to mediate. They had no other choice but to make an offer. They suggested $550 for each of the 5500 outstanding shares.

Ryan accepted. And the game was over. He won. Yet his victory was not without its pound of flesh. His debts to the banks were several times his profit from the corner. His main asset was the Stutz shares, but, without a Stock Exchange listing, selling them could be a problem.

In Wall Street jargon, there has always been what is called 'a curb market' . . . its name stemming from the buyers and sellers who literally stood on the street in front of the NYSE, buying and selling outside of the Exchange's regulations. Today it all works by phone and computer, but the concept still exists. There is a similar activity in London where buying and selling goes on between brokers' offices before and after official trading hours, and also by over-the-counter brokers who are not directly governed by the Exchange. In order to sell his Stutz shares, Ryan's main source of buyers had to be on the curb. But even if he valued each share at anywhere from $550 to $1000, the curb price could be anything the curb market decided it would be.

While all of this was going on – taking up most of Ryan's energies and certainly all of his resources – his other investments were signed over to the banks to support the Stutz squeeze. By early summer of 1920 the great bull market was in a general decline. And the value of those other investments was evaporating very quickly. Almost too quickly. It seems that some of the discontented bears had opened secondary fronts to chip away at Ryan, dollar by dollar, to somehow get even. As those share prices fell, the banks demanded that Ryan top up the security. In order to do that, he needed cash. His Stock Exchange seat had been sold for $98,000, and that money would have come in handy, but the NYSE made a point of holding on to it for as long as they could. Why get angry when you can get even! Thinking of ways to make some fast money, Ryan filed a million-dollar defamation suit against the NYSE President and the Governing Committee. He was sure they would settle and that would help keep the banks at bay. But they didn't. He barked. They wouldn't roll over. And now the banks were snapping at his heels.

He simply couldn't meet his obligations.

In November the banks announced that they were forming a committee to take over Ryan's affairs, even though they were fast to add that they believed Ryan to be in the black so that all debts could be covered. But on Wall Street, business is almost always interwoven with confidence. And by this time there wasn't much confidence to go around where Ryan was concerned. Creditors lined up. His cash flow was shot to hell. He sold what he could, but at fire sale prices. The squeeze had turned into a stranglehold.

The money finally ran out.

On 21 July 1922 Allan A. Ryan was declared bankrupt.

And he never recovered.

Ryan's debts totalled $32.5 million . . . including $1 million to Harry Paine Whitney, his father's partner's son, $3.5 million to the Chase National Bank, $8.7 million to the Guaranty Trust Company and $300,000 to his mentor, Charles Schwab. His assets were listed as $643,000 . . . although that did not include 135,000 shares of Stutz. The market for them had simply dissolved. No one on the curb would touch them. They were eventually sold at public auction at around $20 a share, ironically enough, to Charles Schwab. In his heyday Schwab might have been the most important steel man in the world. However, when it came to the automobile business he was less than brilliant. The Stutz Bearcat had been out of production since 1920 and the company never had another 'best seller'. By 1932 they were surviving, but only just, making grocery wagons. By 1938 they were broke. That was the same year Schwab died a pauper, having lost everything on bad business deals like Stutz, being forced to spend his last years living on whatever he could borrow from friends.

Overlapping the Ryan affair was the Piggly Wiggly saga.

Clarence Saunders never hid his preference for all things ostentatious, was generous to the point of being suspect, and had early on mastered the skill of self-promotion. Born in 1881, he made his fortune in retailing before the First World War and was known around Memphis, Tennessee, as 'that fellow putting up the Pink Palace'. Built to his own specifications, he

planned it to be a home that would stand for 100 years
... lavishly done up in pink marble, with a huge white
marble atrium, and grounds enough for his own private golf course. Even though he never finished it, the
house was so extravagant that it would be more than
half a century later, when Elvis Presley lived at
Graceland, that any estate in the south would create
quite as much interest.

In the boom that followed WWI, Saunders launched
a chain of self-service grocery stores where customers
pushed a cart through aisles stacked with goods, then
paid for everything at a check-out counter near the
exit. It sounds pretty commonplace these days, but it
was a brand-new idea then. Although he probably
didn't realize it at the time, Saunders had invented the
modern supermarket.

He called the chain Piggly Wiggly ... this was a guy
with a sense of humour ... and when anyone wanted
to know why he had chosen such a name, he'd answer,
'So people would ask me what you just did.'

By 1922, there were some 1200 Piggly Wiggly stores,
mostly scattered around the Southern states and heading west, although there were also some in the North.
About 650 were owned outright by Piggly Wiggly
Stores Inc. while the rest were franchised.

In June of that year, Saunders went public. Piggly
Wiggly shares opened on the NYSE's big board at
around $50. They stayed there, doing nothing much of
anything until November when, through no fault of
Saunders, a handful of the Piggly Wiggly stores in
New York, New Jersey and Connecticut ran into
problems. They were franchised, not owned by Saunders, and their troubles should never have become his.
But when word hit the street that some Piggly Wiggly
stores were about to call in the receivers, the bears

took a closer look at the company. They guessed that, as long as those shares had gone nowhere since their listing, word of a few failures could drive them down. The bears sold short, rumours spread, and the prices tumbled to under $40.

Saunders, who had never owned a share of quoted stock until Piggly Wiggly, decided to support the share prices. He committed his own fortune, plus $10 million borrowed from Southern banks to beat the Yankees at their own game. He was going to square the account with those Northerners for the sake of Robert E. Lee and Gettysburg, the burning of Atlanta and *Gone with the Wind*. Southerners, in case you've never noticed, are a special breed of cat.

In later years the legend would have it that Saunders headed north with the $10 million-plus in small bills, bulging out of the carpet bag. He always denied that. But whether he stayed in the South or came to New York, it is true that he hired the legendary Jesse Livermore to help general his battle against the bears. That in itself was a strange choice, as Livermore was probably the most famous bear of all.

With 200,000 shares outstanding, Saunders came into the market and on his first day he bought 33,000. Within a week he owned 105,000. At the same time, he took his fight to the newspapers where he bought full-page ads, just in case anyone should doubt who were the good guys and who were the bad guys. One ad was entitled, 'Shall the Gambler Rule?' Totally in character with someone who would name his business Piggly Wiggly, it read, 'On a white horse he rides. Bluff is his coat of mail thus shielded is his yellow heart. His helmet is deceit, his spurs clink with treachery, and the hoofbeats of his horse thunder destruction.

Shall good business flee? Shall it tremble with fear? Shall it be the loot of the speculator?'

By February 1923 Saunders had forced the shares up to the $70 mark. That's when he went back to the newspapers and made a startling offer. He said he was willing to sell shares to anyone who wanted them at $55. At first glance it looked as if he was giving away $15 presents. At first glance it looked as if he had gone a little crazy.

'Opportunity! Opportunity!' The ad proclaimed. 'It knocks! It knocks! It knocks! Do you hear? Do you listen? Do you understand? Do you wait? Do you act now? Has a new Daniel appeared and the lions eat him not? Has a new Joseph come that riddles may be made plain? Has a new Moses been born to a new Promised Land? Why, then, asks the skeptical, can Clarence Saunders be so generous to the public?'

Far from having lost a few of his marbles, Saunders had come up with a gambit never before used in the corner game. He knew what could happen at the end of the game. Witness Ryan. The last thing he wanted to do was get stuck with a whole mess of shares, no money and no market in which to sell the shares. Or, even if there was a market, he wouldn't want to flood it. By offering about 25 per cent of the total holding now, before he was proclaimed the victor, he reasoned it might save him a lot of money when he finally claimed first prize. At the same time, he had to be careful not to sell any shares to the bears, giving them any ammunition in their fight to prevent his corner. So his gimmick was to offer the shares on the instalment plan. He wanted $25 down with three $10 payments spread over the next nine months. When the full $55 was paid, he would then turn the share certificates over to the buyers. That would not only help him pay his own debts to the banks – a large payment being due in September – but also keep those shares off the market until the end of the year.

It was totally unorthodox. The NYSE had never seen such a tack. Even Livermore admitted to being confused.

As the public was sceptically slow to take him up on his offer, he repeated it in March.

Now Livermore showed his concern. According to Saunders, Livermore 'gave me the impression that he was a little afraid of my financial situation and that he did not care to be involved in any market crash'. The two parted company.

By Monday 19 March, having taken full command of the Rebel troops, Saunders could claim 95 per cent of the Piggly Wiggly shares. His winning corner was a sure thing. So the next day he called for delivery of the shares owed him and set Wednesday afternoon as his deadline. The shares raced as high as $124 before closing at $82 on the rumour that the NYSE was about to suspend dealings in them.

Wednesday morning, before the opening bell, the NYSE did in fact announce the Piggly Wiggly suspension. They also automatically extended the share delivery date. Saunders explained, 'A razor to my throat, figuratively speaking, is why I suddenly and without warning kicked the pegs from under Wall Street and its gang of gamblers and market manipulators. It was strictly a question of whether I should survive, and likewise my business and the fortunes of my friends, or whether I should be licked and pointed to as a boob from Tennessee. And the consequence was that the boastful and supposedly invulnerable Wall Street powers found their methods controverted by well-laid plans and quick action.'

He ended his statement by saying that he would, regardless of any decision taken by the NYSE, extend his delivery date for shares owed by the bears to close of business Thursday 22 March. He proclaimed the price to be $150 until the deadline. After that the debt would be $250 per share.

The NYSE countered by permanently banning Piggly Wiggly shares, and allowing the bears until Monday 26 March to settle their affairs.

The Thursday deadline passed with very few takers. Most of the short sellers were running around looking for those widows and orphans who had $55 Piggly Wiggly shares under their pillows and would be willing to part with them for a profit. If enough came out of the woods, the bears knew they could pay Saunders back in shares and save their own skins.

On Friday, Saunders realized what was happening and did such an about face that it dizzied the market. The last thing he wanted was to have anyone pay him in shares. He needed real money. So now he said instead of $250 per he would actually accept $100.

The gates opened and the bears escaped. Some paid the $100, but many spent the same money buying what shares they could find and then handing him paper. For the bears that was the best of both worlds, combining convenience with nastiness, leaving Saunders in a considerably weakened position. As his own September deadline approached, he found himself owing the banks about $5 million. Having already given them what cash he had, the only thing left were Piggly Wiggly shares. Except now there was no market in which to sell them.

Once again, he went to the newspapers. He bought ads and made yet another $55 offer. The response was pathetic. Ever resourceful, he organized a charity drive to sell the shares door to door . . . as if they were Addis brushes . . . with boy scouts and matrons canvassing Memphis neighbourhoods. He appealed to civic pride. The Chamber of Commerce sponsored the campaign and even the American Legion joined in. 'A share of Piggly Wiggly stock in every home,' became the battle cry. But unlike 'a chicken in every pot', and 'Pikes Peak or bust', this slogan never made it into the first division. Local bankers were too suspicious and stayed off the bandwagon. At the same time, one Memphis newspaper wondered how come Saunders dared to spend money on the Pink Palace while half the town was working for him for nothing. The Piggly Wiggly charity drive ground to a halt.

With no market for the shares, Saunders started selling stores, hoping to meet the banks' demands. But by mid-August the writing was on the wall. It just wasn't to be. He had beaten the Yanks at their own game, yet somehow lost the war. With grace and honour, Saunders resigned himself to the fact that it was over, and gave up his presidency of the company. He also handed over all of his personal assets, including the deed to the Pink Palace. The company's shares were sold at public auction. They fetched $1 per. The Pink Palace was taken over by the city of Memphis, which completed the building and turned it into a museum. 'They have taken the body of Piggly Wiggly,' he told the world, 'but they cannot have the soul.'

And Clarence Saunders went bankrupt.

He spent the next few years trying to find a phoenix in the ashes. In 1926 a federal grand jury indicted him on a charge of mail fraud – they didn't like the way he had used the post office as a conduit for those $55 share give-aways – although the case against him was soon dropped. Two years later, with backing from several friends, he started another grocery chain with yet another ridiculous name, 'The Clarence Saunders, Sole Owner of My Own Name, Stores Inc.'. The stores caught on, he came back into the chips, sponsored a professional football team in Memphis known as the Sole Owner Tigers, and moved into another millionaire's mansion. Then came October 1929, the market crashed, and by 1930 the Depression had wiped him out. His stores went broke and again Saunders was a bankrupt.

Up twice, down twice, he tried for third time lucky.

He obviously didn't get the message with names like Piggly Wiggly and The Clarence Saunders, Sole Owner of My Own Name, Stores Inc. and this time came up with Keedoozle. It was another chain of self-service supermarkets, but with a variation on the theme of the Automat. Instead of the goods being displayed on shelves, they were hidden behind small glass doors. Each shopper was given a key with a ticker tape mechanism which opened the little glass doors while the ticker tape was notched with the item's price. At the check-out counter, the clerk would take the tape, put it into a register and add up the total of the purchases. As this was going on, the day's shopping was speeding along a conveyor belt, straight into bags or boxes for easy carrying out.

How surprised do you think Clarence Saunders was when the idea never caught on?

His next trick was Foodelectric, a supermarket that promised to do everything Keedoozle could do, with the added bonus of totalling the bill sans check-out clerk.

He died, without getting that one off the ground, in 1953.

* * *

More sensible in his choice of names was Richard Whitney.

No relation at all to William C. Whitney, Richard's forebears were counted among America's first families, sailing from England in 1630 on the *Arbella*, the ship that followed the *Mayflower*. The son of a Boston banker with longstanding ties to the House of Morgan – the legendary J.P. Morgan's investment bank – Richard was born in 1888, and possessed diplomas from Groton and Harvard. In 1912 he borrowed family money to buy himself a seat on the NYSE and formed Richard Whitney & Co. in 1916, his main business being bonds. His older brother George, one of the brighter, more respected partners in the House of Morgan, had cemented his own future by marrying the daughter of a senior Morgan partner. Richard took the cue and assured social standing by marrying into a well-established Union League Club family. With all the right connections, Richard quickly became known as 'the Morgan broker'. Unfortunately the title was worth more in status than it was in actual cash.

A tall, portly man, he was well groomed, impeccably dressed and fond of living big. There was a New York City townhouse during the week. And a 500-acre New Jersey estate for the weekends where he raised Ayrshire cattle, rode to the hounds and maintained a large staff. He was also known to sneak off to Baltimore occasionally for trysts with a lady friend he kept there in certain style. He once claimed that his monthly living expenses were in excess of $5000, even at the height of the Depression. And that figure could easily have been on the low side.

By his fortieth birthday, Whitney had become vice president of the New York Stock Exchange. But snobbish, boring, cavalier and egocentric, he was often described as 'the most unpopular man among rank-and-file members to ever hold that office'. Although he moved in powerful circles – there were White House dinners with President Hoover, and New York dinners with the Morgans, Bernard Baruch, General Motors' boss Jacob Raskob, et al. – his business acumen was considerably less substantial than his social connections would suggest.

To put it bluntly, Richard Whitney was basically a schmuck.

It seems no matter what he did he was never able actually to pay for the lifestyle to which he had become accustomed. The bulk of his problem was his incessant proclivity towards debt and bad deals. To keep his ship afloat he began borrowing from his brother in about 1921. Most of those early loans were repaid. But by the middle of the decade the sums were substantial and repayments were less frequent. In 1926 Richard hit George for $100,000 to buy a New York townhouse. Two years later the sum was $340,000 for investments that never came in. The following year George and a stockbroker friend loaned Richard nearly $600,000 to purchase shares in several high-risk businesses. None of those paid off either.

No one could ever accuse the guy of thinking small.

Among other 'pie in the sky' investments, he bought huge blocks of shares in a Florida-based fertilizer company, which quickly turned to fertilizer themselves. He sunk almost as much in a Florida minerals concern. Still nothing in return.

The habitual borrowing kept Richard fat. But with each loan George found himself more and more worried that one of the senior Morgan partners would soon discover that Richard was trouble. If that happened, George knew, Richard's reputation would go down the drain and, with it, his business. Needless to say, George rightfully felt he had a stake in his kid brother's future. When, in 1929, Richard asked George for nearly half a million dollars to buy another seat on the Stock Exchange, George penned a letter to Richard, lecturing him on how he should be dealing with his own finances. He was trying to protect his brother from the obvious. At the same time, he enclosed a cheque.

Whitney's personal financial situation continued to weaken throughout 1929. By the end of that year he was nearly $2 million in debt. That's when the president of the Stock Exchange, Edward Harriman Simmons, announced that he wanted Whitney to be the only candidate on the ballot when his own term of office came to an end.

The 'Morgan broker' was now officially heir apparent. With that came enough credibility to arrange for more loans.

As fate would have it, when the market crashed in October 1929 Simmons was conveniently on his honeymoon in Hawaii, having remarried late in life, reportedly also having sold a lot of shares before he left. It was acting president Dick Whitney who presided over the chaos. Almost bizarrely, with the market's rubble smouldering around his ankles, Whitney found himself touted as a hero. It stands to reason that after every disaster there are always heroes, as it is hero worship that can make disasters less horrific. But now here was the New York City press – at least the tabloids – saying that it was Dick Whitney who single-handedly saved US Steel on 'Black Thursday', 24 October. According to the press, it was Whitney who walked tall through the mayhem on the Exchange floor to buy large blocks of shares above their trading prices just to keep those prices buoyant. One version of the events has it that Whitney, on orders from a consortium of banks, spent as much as $250 million to help instil confidence in the market. Another, much later and perhaps much less emotional version, now suggests that in reality he did no such thing . . . that he tried to spend the money but never actually did.

But then where heroes are concerned the truth doesn't always matter. It's the legend that counts and legends are based on what people will believe. As long as the press heralded him as a hero, and as long as everyone believed what they read about him, it was easy enough for him to become a hero. Perhaps he was the only guy available to accept the award. Perhaps he actually did help to save US Steel. The point is that America wanted to believe it. As a natural self-publicist, Whitney took on the praise, while always managing to keep hidden the fact that the crash had deepened the hole in his own pocket by another $2 million.

In the spring of 1930, he succeeded to the throne, being duly elected president of the NYSE for the first of four consecutive one-year terms. Yet within a year he was in such dire financial straits that desperation set in. His firm, which had once dealt in millions, was said to be worth a pitiful $36,000.

Again Whitney *frère* thought that he could save the day with a $500,000 loan.

But, like most of the borrowings now, it quickly disappeared.

About this time Whitney came up with an investment scheme that almost made sense. He believed that Prohibition would eventually end. When it did, there would be a boom in booze. So he invested heavily in a New Jersey company that was going to clean up with a cider brandy called Jersey Lightning. Hoboken's answer for Château Latour. Home made in stills before

Prohibition. Whitney figured that, properly marketed after Prohibition, Jersey Lightning could become the national drink. If nothing else, he was perfectly right that Prohibition would eventually end. That came to pass in 1934. Within the first few weeks following repeal, Whitney's Distilled Liquors Corp. shares went as high as $45. He could have sold then and there, and actually made some money. But greed set in. So did America's taste for the real thing. Huge stocks of whisky had been sitting in Canadian warehouses ready to flood a thirsty America. The more Scotch that crossed the border, the faster Jersey Lightning was forgotten. The shares hit $10. And Whitney was once again a loser.

Forced to borrow simply to support the interest on his borrowings, he was caught in a classic squeeze. Now the best he could do was to play 'catch up'. What funds came into his company for clients' accounts became too tempting and soon found their way into Whitney's private accounts. In two instances he used clients' estates entrusted to him to secure loans. In 1936, as treasurer of the New York Yacht Club, he helped himself to $150,000 of the club's bonds, which he used as collateral against a $200,000 bank loan in his company's name. He followed that by taking charge of more than $1 million in bonds and cash belonging to the NYSE's Gratuity Fund and pledging that against loans.

First borrowing, then stealing, Whitney's was a vain attempt just to return to square one. Yet with each step forward there were two steps backwards. He mortgaged everything, bringing in a fresh half million dollars with his homes and race horses. Even that couldn't help. It was financial quicksand. The more he struggled, the deeper he got. Millions had been squandered. Now funds had been embezzled.

Between November 1937 and the end of February 1938, Whitney is believed to have negotiated over 100 loans totalling more than $27 million. New loans to pay off old loans. He owed his brother close to $3 million and owed other friends about half that. A good portion of the loans were totally unsecured. 'On my face', as he liked to call it. One account of his downfall notes that, towards the end, Whitney was actually walking up to total strangers on the Exchange floor and asking if they might loan him $100,000.

The sheer weight of it all finally brought the world crashing down on top of him.

On 8 March 1938, Richard Whitney & Company filed for bankruptcy.

Two days later New York City District Attorney Thomas E. Dewey – a man who very nearly became President of the United States – filed an indictment against Whitney. Expulsion from the NYSE quickly followed. It shocked America. A hero had fallen. The magazine *Nation* wrote, 'Wall Street could hardly have been more embarrassed if J.P.Morgan had been caught helping himself from the collection plate at the Cathedral of St John the Divine.'

Dewey's indictment was followed by a guilty verdict in criminal court.

Before April was out, Richard Whitney had taken up residence overlooking the Hudson River in Ossening, New York. His address for the next three years was Sing Sing.

After his release from prison, he retired to a quiet, if not humble life until his death in 1974. With his financial demise came the end of an era. But his story is an especially odd one because, in a day and age when anyone with money and social connections could almost effortlessly parlay both into more, when the NYSE was rife with insider trading and all sorts of now-illegal manipulations, the 'Hero of Black Thursday' managed to raise the definition of sheer stupidity to new heights.

The final reckoning showed that Dick Whitney had blown more than $6 million.

The British arrived at the 1920s with a good solid history behind them of great financial disasters.

First there was the South Sea Bubble.

In the late seventeenth/early eighteenth centuries, Parliament established a number of companies, granting them exclusive rights for exploration, trading, banking and insurance in exchange for assuming some of the government's debt. It was, as the legislators saw it, a means of increasing Britain's stature as a world trader while also helping to relieve the tax burden on the landed gentry.

In 1711, Robert Harley – whose family name is these days associated with the London street of private clinics and doctors' offices – was Chancellor of the Exchequer. It was his plan to help eliminate the national debt by forming a joint stock company called 'The Governor and Company of Merchants of Great Britain trading to the South Seas and other parts of America, and for encouraging the Fishery'. Through Parliament, he granted the company an exclusive charter to exploit the lucrative trading and fishing interests in the Caribbean, South America and the South Pacific. For these rights, the company agreed to assume £10 million worth of the nation's debt.

Popularly known as the South Sea Company, £100 shares were issued at par, although they traded through the coffee houses of the City of London for much less over the next four years.

While this was going on, a Scot named John Law had come up with an ingenious concept in Paris. He was a gambler who, in 1716, found fame and fortune by issuing bearer notes on his own Banque Générale that were also accepted as valid for payment of taxes. A slight fall in the interest rate sent shares soaring in Banque Générale.

Law followed that with his 'Mississippi scheme'. The plan was to merge the French Louisiana Company with the Canada Company, and therefore control all of the trading from the mouth of the Mississippi River in the Gulf of Mexico, north to Canada, branching out along the Missouri and Ohio rivers as well. Ambitious, to say the least, the share issue was oversubscribed. The fly in the ointment was that Law didn't have an absolute monopoly and, when a new company arrived on the scene to compete, his share prices started to slip. By that time however he had turned the Banque Générale into the Banque Royale, with notes guaranteed by the then 10-year-old King Louis XV.

Next, Law managed to bring the French East Indies and China Company into the framework of the Louisiana Company, calling the new conglomeration the Compagnie des Indes. This outfit was then permitted to mint and coin money, and in fact to manage the entire French economy as long as it also paid off the government's debt. Share prices continued to climb until 1720 when Law merged the Compagnie des Indes into his Banque Royale. It was an inverted pyramid, now top-heavy and starting to wobble. The public panicked. Within a few months the empire had toppled and Law had disappeared.

But the idea of taking charge of the national debt

had its appeal to Sir John Blunt, then a director of the South Sea Company. In 1719 he approached the government to make a deal. He said that, in exchange for additional subsidies and rights, his company would be willing to take on the remainder of the nation's £31 million debt. Many members of Parliament, in both Houses, realized that this was a way of eliminating tax burdens on their own land. At the time, the national debt was in irredeemable 99-year annuities, irredeemable 32-year annuities and very redeemable stocks of 4 per cent and 5 per cent. Blunt envisioned turning all of this into South Sea shares. What he didn't tell anyone in Parliament was that he and his friends were planning to clean up by cornering those shares.

The government went for the deal. Blunt hyped new issues of South Sea shares onto the market. The public was curious, share prices increased. As share prices increased, the public became even more curious. Then again, as share prices climbed, fewer shares were needed to pay the government's debt. Blunt and his cronies soaked up the excess. Between February and June 1720, South Sea shares soared from £129 to £890.

Much like the British Telecom issue of 1985, such excitement was created that nearly everything that followed was oversubscribed. South Sea madness swept through the entire British market. Greatly helping the situation was the fact that rules governing share issues were lax. And also that shares could be paid for over time. For instance, in June, the South Sea Company came up with a £5 million stock offer. They priced the shares at £1000, payable 10 per cent down with the remainder in instalments over the next five years. Who could say no? Even the smallest investor could make a profit out of this. However, in order to keep the scheme going, Blunt had to make certain that

more and more people would buy in. The problem was
that now every company in Britain began looking for
a similar deal. New issues were floated by companies
created a few days before with no business besides the
flotation of their own shares. That dried up some of the
investment capital that might otherwise have gone to
South Sea. With so much to choose from, the punters
became particular . . . they would buy only as long as
share prices kept going up. To keep those share prices
rising, and in turn bring more investors into the game,
Blunt and Co. had to declare larger and larger
dividends.

Unfortunately, they didn't have the money to pay
those dividends without selling more shares.

When the punters realized what was happening, the
slide began, and quickly turned into an avalanche.

By November, South Sea shares had toppled to £135.

When Parliament finally investigated, serious
wrong-doings, illicit payments and conflicts of interests were revealed. They passed the South Sea Suffer-
ers' Bill, which claimed back several million pounds
from directors' estates. But none of those measures
came soon enough. Any number of people were wiped
out.

Then there was Horatio Bottomley.

Raised in a London orphanage in the 1860s, he
trained as a court stenographer. But by the 1880s he
had eased his way into the newspaper business. In
those days debating societies met on a regular basis,
as much a social event as anything else. While living
in Hackney and taking part in the local debating
society, Bottomley was clever enough to see the opportunity to make some money by publishing the *Hackney
Hansard* as a record of the club's weekly meetings.

When that proved a success he created other debating society reports, all of which evolved into community newspapers. Before too long he even launched a rival for the then very popular *Financial News*. He called his upstart *The Financial Times*. How ironic that the FT was created by a man who escorted more companies into bankruptcy than anyone else in this century, and who was possibly one of Britain's most important financial crooks. No Bottomley. No comment.

After a split with his partner, who took over the FT, Bottomley somehow managed to land a printing contract for the real *Hansard*. Like the *Congressional Record* in the United States and the *Journal Officiel* in France, *Hansard* has been, since the beginning of the nineteenth century, the official record of the legislature's business. Needless to say, until Bottomley landed the printing contract, in spite of his village imitations, he and the original had absolutely nothing to do with each other.

But now, with the *Hansard* printing contract in his pocket, he merged four established printers and publishers into a consortium, which he named the Hansard Printing and Publishing Union. By adorning his main board with well-respected businessmen – he even paid some of them outright for the use of their names – the Hansard Union received a full stock market listing in 1889, capitalized at £500,000.

Bottomley's first move was to spend £430,000 purchasing paper mills and more printing works. The second thing he did was go to his board to ask that the share capital be doubled. They agreed. His next step was to declare a reasonably good dividend, which in turn brought new investors into the fold.

Sound familiar?

As long as he had a board with respected names on

it, as long as his books were showing a profit – £40,000
the first year – and as long as he was paying a healthy
dividend, no one much cared to look more closely.
What they would have seen, had they bothered, was
Bottomley borrowing against assets to pay those dividends, hoping to lure new capital into the fold so that
he could afford to pay even bigger dividends. In the
meantime, he was lining his own pockets. When the
debenture holders realized they had never been paid,
Bottomley tried to stall them. He had to because he
didn't have the money. After a while they got so fed up
waiting that they took over the business. That's when
they looked at the books and found that £600,000 of
the £1 million capitalization could not be accounted
for, that Bottomley had skimmed at least £100,000 out
of the business, and that the Hansard Union was
broke.

Faced with huge debts, Bottomley was declared
bankrupt and charged with fraud. The case against
him seemed watertight. However, his ability at the
bar soon became legendary. With his knowledge of the
law and a sixth sense for courtroom drama – all
acquired during the years he worked as a court stenographer – he defended himself. The trial lasted 22
days. The jury deliberated less than half an hour. The
verdict was not guilty.

That was 1893.

It was the same year that gold boomed in Western
Australia and mining shares became the vogue. As
Bottomley's trial had been so widely covered, he set
out to take advantage of his new-found fame. He called
himself a company promoter and sold mining shares
in companies that couldn't miss . . . but almost always
did. There were a pair of successful ventures that
legitimately made him a million pounds, but after a

while a fairly predictable pattern started to emerge with all the other Bottomley-promoted companies. Shares would look fine up through the generous first dividend. New investors would come in. Then he'd dissolve the company. One account of Bottomley's career notes that, out of 50 companies traced, no less than two dozen had been reconstructed, while 20 others had gone into voluntary liquidation.

Thanks to his clients, who were getting poorer and poorer, by 1896 Mr Bottomley was a multimillionaire, with all the trappings, like a house on Pall Mall, a country estate and race horses.

Over the next ten years, he started but eventually sold a newspaper called *The Sun*. It was an evening paper whose motto was 'If you see it in the Sun, it is so', and no relation at all to the current London paper of the same name; he got elected to Parliament as the Liberal MP for South Hackney; he started publishing a highly successful penny weekly magazine called *John Bull*; and he spent a great deal of time in court successfully defending himself against various charges of fraud, mismanagement and bankruptcy.

However, it was with *John Bull* that he became something of a hero of the people. The magazine was muckraking in tone, not afraid to criticize non-Liberal MPs and always in praise of the monarchy. It even had its own detective agency to seek out 'anything nefarious'. That led to a lot of libel suits but helped build a readership. Within a year *John Bull* was being heralded as 'the greatest success of modern journalism'. The quote, however, must rightly be credited to *John Bull*'s editor, Horatio Bottomley.

Partial to writing scathing editorials about sharks in the City, Bottomley himself should have qualified for a *John Bull* exposé because by this time he had invented a new ploy. When one of his companies went broke, he'd allow the shareholders to transfer their stock into a second company, crediting them with 75 per cent of the shares' supposed value. But the shareholder then had to come up with the 25 per cent difference, or lose everything in the liquidation. By folding a £1 million company, he could expect £250,000 to breeze in through his letter box.

It worked well until 1906 – the same year that Bottomley was served with 40 bankruptcy petitions – when his Joint Stock Trust and Finance Corporation was planned for voluntary liquidation, along with its largest creditor, Selected Gold Mines of Australia. Unfortunately for Bottomley, who stood to make a fortune on the two bankruptcies, a solicitor acting for a very small shareholder refused to be bought off and in turn insisted on an incorruptible receiver being appointed. Fraud was charged. The ensuing trial, where Bottomley again defended himself, lasted 28 days. It was another open and shut case for the prosecutor. Yet the verdict was, astonishingly, not guilty.

By the outset of the First World War, Bottomley had been relieved of his parliamentary seat, having personally gone bankrupt again, this time for £233,000. But it would only be temporary. He'd return in 1918 when he'd had that bankruptcy annulled, and serve for another four years. As it was, he spent the war years running crooked lotteries and Victory Bond swindles. Using the cash that came in from his confidence tricks he bought two money-losing newspapers, the *National News* and the *Sunday Evening Telegraph*, but they were a serious drain on his resources. Eventually the public, then the press and finally Scotland Yard found him out. In the spring of 1922 he was charged on 24 counts under the Larceny Act. Naturally, he defended himself. But 11 days later, after summing up the jury with the words, 'You will never convict me. The man is not yet born who would convict me on these charges,' his luck ran out. Found guilty on 23 of the 24 charges, he was sentenced at the age of 62 to seven years. The following year, Bottomley was judged personally bankrupt, one last time. He'd stolen and squandered upwards of £5 million, and served one year in prison for each million, being released on parole to spend his last years writing articles. He died in 1933, begging the government to supply him with an old age pension. His final humiliation was that they turned him down.

However, the minus millionaire who put the 1920s on the map in Great Britain was a tycoon in the modern risk-taker tradition called Clarence Hatry.

Just 17 years old in 1906 when his father's death left him to run the ailing family silk business, Hatry simply couldn't make a go of it. The business failed and he was saddled with £8000 worth of debt. Someone then told him that there was money to be made in insurance, so he found work in the brokerage business, and by the time he was 23 he had not only paid his debts but was earning in excess of £20,000 per year.

The first sign of his genuine flair for business didn't come until the post-Armistice boom, when Hatry supposedly became the owner of Leyland Motors . . . for a day. The way the story is told, he somehow purchased a block of Leyland shares for £350,000, although it's likely he never had to pay for them. Either he immediately found a buyer or already had one when he made the buy, and he sold the shares in just 24 hours, nearly doubling his money. These days at Leyland, they have no record of the transaction. Anyway, they say, Leyland then was owned by one family so there is some doubt that he could have had any sort of controlling interest. But it is possible that he bought a large block of shares and made big money by turning them around because by then he had a reputation for being a gambler and taking big risks. It is possible because that sort of a deal would be in character.

Anyway, he definitely earned big money somewhere along the line because in 1920 he set up the Commercial Bank of London, eventually changing its name to the even more sturdy-sounding Commercial Corporation of London. He was also the founder of British Glass Industries in 1919. Both companies were publicly floated, and by 1922 or so he was worth about £2.25 million. He lived in a mansion on Great Stanhope Street, around the corner from where the Dorchester Hotel stands on Park Lane. He maintained a household staff of more than a dozen. His basement was decked out exactly like an old English pub. There was a swimming pool on the first floor. He had a weekend mansion in Sussex, race horses, works of art and the world's second largest racing yacht. To keep that in the water he had a permanent crew of 40.

Although he owned the Drapery and General Investment Trust, which became part of the Debenham Group, and also controlled a municipal loan company called Corporation and General Securities, early on in his career he developed the habit of overextending himself and overestimating his financial prowess. The Commercial Corporation of London went into liquidation in 1923. Hatry staked some of his personal fortune on an attempt to save it, and lost £750,000. The fall of British Glass followed three years later. Around the same time he also brought Jute Industries to the market, and a major capital reduction scheme was necessary to save that.

But Hatry was never one to be burdened for long with failure. He bounced back as often as he was knocked down. The *Law Times* wrote of his return to success after early defeats, 'Few expected Hatry to come back after his first disasters and the completeness of his return is one of the most surprising things in history.'

For some years, while building that second fortune, Hatry had been formulating a plan to take over the United Steel Companies – they controlled some 10 per cent of Britain's steel industry – and turn himself into the British answer to Andrew Carnegie. In May 1927, with his main holding operation Austin Friars Trust, he began purchasing several hundred iron foundries and finally pulled them together as Allied Ironfounders Ltd. Using that as his base, in May 1929 he went after United Steel. Hard times had fallen upon the industry. In its heyday, United Steel had a market value as high as £27 million. When Hatry went after the shares, they were worth less than 20 per cent of that figure. In addition to serious cashflow worries, United Steel was looking at around £3 million in bank overdrafts. Dividend payments were late and there was a creditor's moratorium. But he believed that the company's main business was sound, so he agreed to pay the overdraft and buy the outstanding shares at a market value of £5 million. That meant he had to raise £8 million.

With some of his own money and some from friends in the City, he wound up £4 million short. But after meeting with Lord Bearsted at Montagu Stanley he left with the impression that the bank would join him for the remaining funds.

They were scheduled to talk again a couple of weeks later.

In between the two meetings, Great Britain elected its second Labour government. Stanley Baldwin was out, James Ramsay MacDonald was in. And the City reacted the way it traditionally does to Labour governments. The pinstriped suit brigade exchanged their bowler hats for battle helmets. Share prices dropped and the banks went liquid.

When Hatry returned to Montagu Stanley, Bearsted claimed in fact they didn't have an agreement.

Hatry was devastated.

He was also caught in a terribly awkward bind, with his reputation on the line. If he reneged on the deal, many of United Steel's 40,000-odd shareholders might have grounds for a suit against him. If he went through with the deal, he'd need backing quickly. But . . . Wall Street was out of the question, natively distrusting Labour governments, while the City was suddenly wary of possible nationalizations, and especially worried about getting involved in anything as fragile as the steel industry. The lone alternative was the merchant banks. However, they knew that Hatry had very little room to manoeuvre, so, even if he could somehow arrange backing with them, their terms might not be too favourable. Then again, if he couldn't get the bankers on his side . . . almost at any cost . . . that might be interpreted around the City as their vote of no confidence and his other interests could crumble.

Making matters especially bad, Hatry firmly believed that the then Governor of the Bank of England, Montagu Norman, was out to even a score. The two had never been on friendly terms and Hatry wrote in his diary that Norman, 'an old adversary of mine', was privately working behind the scenes to exert 'very

considerable influence' against his plan. 'I was, perhaps rightly, a dangerous upstart, an interloper in the
well-regulated affairs in the City of London. Now was
the chance to teach me a crushing and merited lesson.'

Aware that he was now playing against the odds,
Hatry called on every possible source of funding. And
money did come in. But when he added up the figures,
the bottom line was still £900,000 short. Then, at the
eleventh hour, Hatry and his associates cooked up a
scheme to raise some temporary money, just enough to
get them past the tape. They decided to issue unau-
thorized paper under the logo of Corporation and
General Securities as sponsor of a municipal loan
stock. They'd sell the paper, take the first instalment
of monies due, and immediately extend the registration date. That would delay the second payment and
the subsequent exchange of the paper for the munici-
pals. Having bought time, their steel project could go
ahead and once it did they'd have United Steel's cash
to buy back the fraudulent scrip.

Of course it was illegal. And of course they knew it
was illegal. There never was any municipal loan stock
for which the scrip could subsequently be exchanged.
But they convinced themselves it was just a stop-gap
measure, that it would only be for a few weeks.

By this point, word was out around the City that
Hatry might be in trouble. Shares on some of his
companies, especially Austin Friars Trust, started slip-
ping. To support his own share prices, Hatry was forced
to buy. It cost him nearly £1.5 million just to keep
Austin Friars afloat. Although they printed £1.6 million of the phoney scrip, they collected only about half,
and that still left him a long way from home.

Slightly panicked that the swindle hadn't worked,
in August 1929 Hatry swallowed his pride and went to

see Montagu Norman. Their discussion was said to have been very frank. Hatry tried to convince Norman that, with the central bank's support, the merger would come off and that United Steel, plus the rest of Hatry's £20 million empire, could be saved. Norman apparently didn't want to know. It seems he expressed the opinion that Hatry had paid too much for United Steel. Hatry must have had the sinking feeling that perhaps his opinion of Norman was right . . . that the Governor of the Bank of England was going to teach him a nasty lesson. The meeting ended with Norman's firm refusal to be of any assistance.

On 14 September, one of Hatry's closest associates, an Italian named Gianni Gialdini, left on what had been planned as a brief holiday. But instead of heading for Switzerland, Gialdini went home to Italy, where no extradition treaty existed with England. In his suitcase was £400,000 of Hatry's money.

Five days later, Hatry was called in to see Sir Gilbert Garnsey, a highly respected City accountant with the firm of Price Waterhouse. They had been asked to audit Hatry's books by Lloyds Bank.

With his own shares falling and his books being opened, there was little else he could do but admit to the phoney paper. He tried to explain that the scrip scheme had come about merely as a half-measure . . . it was only supposed to get United Steel into the Hatry empire and then all the debts would be paid off. But, by Garnsey's count, Hatry's empire was £19 million in debt with only £4 million in assets. And now there was also a matter of fraud.

Hatry suggested, the way a gentleman might, that Sir Gilbert accompany him to the nearest police station. To Hatry's astonishment, Garnsey . . . perhaps very much in keeping with the clubby gentlemanly ways of the City ... suggested there might still be a way to save the business. He said he would personally speak to Montagu Norman on Hatry's behalf.

So Garnsey rushed off to see Norman.

And Hatry rushed off to see his solicitor.

Later that same afternoon, when Hatry and his counsel met with Garnsey, Sir Gilbert reported that the word from the Bank of England was no. Norman had pushed the panic button. The Chairman of the Stock Exchange had been informed and trading on all Hatry shares was suspended. The following morning, Hatry and his counsel paraded into the office of the Director of Public Prosecutions and confessed to perpetrating a stupendous fraud.

That evening, Clarence Hatry was in jail.

He was still awaiting trial when the market crashed.

The case was finally heard in January 1930.

Clearly defeated, Hatry looked to the mercy of the courts. 'When I saw that matters were getting serious, I pledged every penny in the world that I possessed, my reputation and maybe my liberty, to avert what I knew would otherwise have been a terrible crash. I took grave personal risks, whereas I then could easily have let things go and have walked off a free man. The losses would then have fallen on thousands of shareholders all over the country instead of, as now, upon a comparatively limited few.'

He went on to state, 'Moreover, by having taken these risks I am now irretrievably and irreparably ruined. My name has become a by-word, and if I am found guilty, when I leave prison, whenever that may be, my punishment will begin all over again.'

After a few moments of thanking his friends and family for standing by him, he told the judge, 'I do not pretend to be a fool. I fully realized all this when I took the risks, and equally I had every reason to be convinced at the time that I was saving the situation and thereby protecting my creditors. Sir Gilbert Garnsey has already told you that not one penny of the money irregularly raised has gone into any of our pockets. So long as I am given the opportunity to prove, as I shall have no difficulty in doing, that, crazy as appear to have been my actions in the light of subsequent developments, I was actuated solely by a desire to do the right thing, and that my motives were clean and creditable, then sir I will take whatever punishment is in store for me without complaint.'

But the prosecutor would have none of it. The case was so complicated that it had taken him four days to explain the fraud to the court. Hatry had admitted that there were 'irregularities', so the Attorney-General based his summing up on that. 'Irregularities was a strange word to use in that sort of thing and if that was "irregular", what was a crime?' He said he did not doubt that Hatry and his pals had always hoped something would come along to save them, that somehow they would be able to pay for the false scrip before anyone noticed. 'I suppose that everybody throughout the course of history who had robbed the till in order that he might risk the money on some horse or something would have intended, if by some chance the horse had won, to put back the money into the till.'

Hatry was sentenced to 14 years . . . although it was not without complaint because he appealed, and lost. Released from prison in 1939, he wrote a book called *Light out of Darkness*, in which he advocated the theory that political and economic instability lay in the unfortunate distribution of population and the interdependence of nations, tried his hand at wheeling and dealing during the 50s with some minor successes, and died in June 1965.

Yet the king of them all – the dandiest minus millionaire of the era – was a rough-edged, tough-talking, slim, blond, lady-fancying, chain-smoking, ten Havana cigars a day, New Englander named Jesse Lauriston Livermore.

The bigger they are the harder they fall, and by the late 1920s Livermore was a Wall Street living legend.

Born in New England in 1877, he got his first taste of stocks and bonds at the age of 14 when he went to work as a $1 a week clerk chalking quotations on the board in a Boston brokerage house. And he might well have stayed there except for his uncanny ability to make instant calculations in his head. He quickly realized that he could come up with percentages, just like that, to show price fluctuations. When he began recording these percentages and the closing prices in a notebook every evening, he soon became aware that he could also see trends in some share prices.

In those days, Boston was filled with bucket shops . . . store fronts that were really nothing more than betting shops where a punter could wager on the price movements of shares. In England today there are several well-organized 'index' organizations that do exactly the same thing. The Ladbroke Index or the IG Index take bets over the phone from clients who think they can predict the rise or fall of currencies, the Dow Jones Index, the Hang Seng, the FT 100, and so forth. You play for so much a point – £5, £50, £500, whatever – and if the index rises 10 points you win ten times your stake. If the index drops 10 points, you lose ten times your stake. The modern 'index' wager operations have a small spread built into their prices – a buying price and a selling price – so that they can, like betting shops for the races or football games, hedge their own position. Interestingly enough, some of the 'index' betting services will quote slightly different prices for buying or selling. A shrewd punter can therefore buy one index and sell another and create a mini-arbitrage system where he in effect can't lose. The gain comes, like arbitrage in any commodity, from the difference between the two prices.

Livermore's talent for figures and his system of betting on the trends eventually got him banned from every bucket shop in the Boston area. Even disguises couldn't get him past the front door. So at the age of 21, with a $2500 stake in his pocket, he headed for New York.

Having cut his teeth in the minor leagues, he now turned his skills loose on Wall Street. And he kept right on winning. Where some people can juggle plates, or play Hamlet, it seems that Livermore had one of those God-given gifts for the stock market. He had a nose that warned him when a company's shares were overpriced, at their high, and when they would then start heading down. So he became a professional bear . . . and made his fortune by selling short.

He was good, and everybody knew it. But one night in 1906 he went from good to great. He and a lady friend were in Atlantic City – the promenade there was perhaps the most fashionable venue on the East Coast – and he stepped into a brokerage house just to have a quick look at the market. Shares were on the up. A definite bull market. Then one company in particular caught his eye. It was the Union Pacific Railroad. Their shares were very high. He felt they would have to come down and he put in an order to sell

3000 shares. They kept on rising. The next day he sold another 2000, dumped the lady friend and rushed back to New York.

It was 18 April.

Livermore was 5000 shares short. The Union Pacific Railroad shares were at an all-time high. And San Francisco was devastated by an earthquake.

The railway was left in a shambles. The company's shares took a deadly nosedive. And, before that evening was out, Jesse Lauriston Livermore was a millionaire.

Less than one year later, Livermore was short-selling again in the face of a rising market when the NYSE crashed. His daily profits during that episode ran in the hundreds of thousands of dollars.

He didn't always hit the jackpot. In 1908 he got caught in a cotton corner and blew an even $1 million. But the First World War brought him huge profits in steel and petroleum ... he was bullish for a while, rightfully feeling that the war effort would keep industry flush, and then went bear as soon as the Armistice was signed because he knew that all those returning soldiers would create unemployment, which would in turn toss a spanner into the overheated economy.

Although the SEC has long since imposed all sorts of rules on going short, in those days Livermore was so powerful a bear that mere rumours of his short selling could at times actually cause those shares to tumble.

By 1925, he was said to be worth in excess of $25 million. Certainly he had the usual trappings of wealth – a splendid Manhattan apartment at 817 Fifth Avenue facing Central Park, a private railway carriage, villas in Europe, a weekend estate on the north shore of Long Island ... and one almost unheard of trapping for the times, his own private airliner.

Of course, being that wealthy and that well known, he was also that much of a target. The press attacked him at every turn, calling him 'the boy plunger', berating him for being a professional bear, for aggressively selling short against market trends. Worse still, he was consistently successful against those market trends, and that, combined with his flamboyant lifestyle, bred considerable jealousy. By today's standards, he would definitely be considered a very tacky guy. That he kept mistresses in various villas scattered around the world is one thing. That he bragged about them, and let the world know what a stud he was, is another. His favourite evening pastime apparently was cruising the streets of New York in his yellow Rolls-Royce, trying to pick up girls. He constantly bashed the English language on the nose, a 'dems' and 'dees' man with a flat Boston accent. Yet in one breath he could quote the Bible, thanks to a strict New England Calvinist upbringing, and in the next he would explain in great detail the results of the previous night's catting. He was, however, considerably more discreet about his business activities.

His office was on the eighteenth floor of the Heckscher Building, at 730 Fifth Avenue, off 56th Street. The doorman downstairs was paid to tell anyone who asked that he had never heard of anyone named Livermore and no one by that name maintained offices there. When a caller said that he was expected, the doorman would refer to a prepared list of authorized visitors. A further security check was made by a bodyguard in front of Livermore's office door. Beyond that door, nearly five dozen people tended to the myriad of telephones, telegraphs and ticker tapes that were fed into the room. They also kept the huge quotations board current with the latest prices. It was a command post of the utmost sophistication for the era, complete with analysts to provide Livermore with immediate insights into market trends, and paid informants all over Wall Street to feed him with the latest intelligence.

Throughout the 1920s Livermore went in and out of the market on bear raids to increase his fortune. But when 1929 rolled around, with Herbert Hoover newly installed in the White House, Livermore felt that the nation's economic uncertainty had created a stock market like none he had ever seen before. It was almost too good to be true. One morning in March he shorted industrial shares, then switched to the railways, and, when word leaked out that he was on the warpath, he turned his attentions to the oil companies. The next day, as prices plummeted, he bought back the shares he had sold and found himself $200,000 wealthier for his three-hour foray.

Throughout the summer of 1929 and well into the autumn, the American economy rode high. Everyone was calling these times the good times. Funds flooded into Wall Street not only from across Europe – British money couldn't get into American shares fast enough because UK investors were desperately trying to protect themselves from the Labour government – but also from every corner of the United States. The stock market had become the nation's pastime. The price of admission was the price of a newspaper. A fantastically huge army of small punters had pulled their $100 – $200 – $300 savings out of the bank to play the market.

But Livermore tried to see through the general euphoria. By diligently scouring the financial press and combining that information with his own intelligence sources, he could see that American industry was heading for trouble, that the American banks were heading for trouble, and that the economy simply could not get hotter and hotter without bubbling over.

This, he started to believe, could signal the greatest bear market the world had ever known.

The first sign came in September 1929, when Livermore noticed in a newspaper that the British were worried about sterling. Word of the Hatry scandal reached America and Livermore wondered why the Bank of England hadn't come to Hatry's rescue. Perhaps they didn't because they couldn't. Intrigued, he asked his English 'spies' to find out what the Bank was thinking. They answered that the British were looking for a way of restoring faith in the pound. That could mean, as it traditionally does, an increase in the base rate. The American Federal Reserve Bank had upped the discount rate by 1 per cent, so the Britons, Livermore knew, had to follow. And if they did, then the funds pouring into Wall Street from England would dry up. There could also be a wave of selling by British shareholders getting out of Wall Street and going liquid at home. It looked to him as if prices might be falling.

At the same time, Livermore learned that an economist named Roger W. Babson was, for the third consecutive year, about to make the keynote address at the annual luncheon of the National Business Conference. Livermore knew Babson to be, like himself, a market bear. In fact, for the past two years Babson had been predicting gloom. In 1928 Babson told the NBC that if Al Smith and the Democrats came to power they would bring with them a great economic depression. Well, Al Smith and the Democrats did not come to power that year. Hoover and the Republicans did. So Babson's warnings were generally disregarded.

However, by keeping extensive newspaper cuttings on many people, Livermore noticed that, in the past, Babson did not receive a lot of coverage when he prophesied doom. And even if he personally discounted much of what Babson always said, he couldn't help but see that Babson might indeed suddenly start to make news.

Putting all his intelligence information together, two thoughts went through his mind. Over the past several months the press had stepped on each other's toes to sing praises for these best of times. That story was by now wearing a little thin. And, secondly, unless a big, late-breaking story appeared, this particular day could be a slow news day. If it was and if the press was looking for a different angle on its 'best of times' story, Livermore reckoned that Babson's luncheon speech might just receive some heavyweight national coverage.

He ordered his staff onto the telephones. Newspaper offices around the country received 'leaks' that Babson was about to make an all-important speech. Once the press was alerted and those wheels were set in motion, Livermore went into the market, using friendly brokers across the country to start selling.

With Babson at the speaker's rostrum, Livermore shorted shares for a total of $300,000.

Within half an hour of Babson telling the assembled press 'Sooner or later a crash is coming which will take in the leading stocks and cause a decline from 60–80 points in the Dow Jones barometer', the press agencies were reporting across all of their wires, 'Economist Predicts 60–80 Points Stockmarket Crash.'

Livermore kept going short.

Just about every afternoon paper in the country

carried the story. Just about every radio news programme in the country carried the story.

He continued selling the market until the close of trading, by which time other economists had come up with rebukes and retorts to Babson's over-publicized speech. The next morning, Livermore closed all of his positions, buying back the shares he had shorted. Within a few days the market was all right again. Back to where it had been. In the meantime, Jesse Livermore had made yet another stupendous killing.

Then came October.

The first explosion smashed the market apart on Thursday, the 24th.

The second finished it off on Tuesday, the 29th.

Fortunes disintegrated in the mushroom clouds.

But Livermore, like a handful of others, had long since sold.

With more than enough money to last several lifetimes and see him through an extravagant old age, he stayed in the game.

Sadly for him, his innings were over.

By 1930 something had changed. Whatever it was, whatever happened inside his own head, Jesse Livermore started to lose his touch. He had problems at home and maybe they got to him. Or maybe, like any great athlete, there is a peak and once you're past it the downhill run is suicidally fast. Who knows? It doesn't really matter. Just that suddenly he was the great bear gone into hibernation.

By the end of 1931, half his fortune was gone.

By 1933 the other half was gone.

Some $30 million had been squandered on sure-fire winning deals that couldn't lose . . . deals like he used to make in the old days, but that now came in only second.

The SEC had by this time changed a lot of the rules surrounding short selling. Where before it was a 'let the buyer beware' game, now it was a 'let the seller beware' operation. And Livermore was in deep trouble.

By 1934 he was a drunk. A shadow of his former self, he had been beaten and bloodied by the markets and left for the vultures by his old enemies. He was destitute. On 4 March 1934 he filed a petition of bankruptcy. His debts were listed as $2.26 million. His assets were a questionable $184,000.

Only just managing to get by, in 1940 he published *How to Trade in Stocks*. But it was obviously a dozen years too late. When he was up, it would have sold millions. But no one loves a loser. The book was a flop. In November of that year he walked into the men's room at the Sherry-Netherland Hotel, pulled a pistol out of his pocket, and blew his brains out.

The note he left read, 'My life has been a failure.'

5
Alec Herbage – Very Conspicuous Consumption

Once upon a time Alec (a.k.a. Alex) William Herbage had a castle in Scotland, and the Sutton Manor estate in England, and land with cattle, and access to people in high places, and a fabulous art collection.

Now there's nothing left.

Or, if there is something left, it's been hidden.

Whether or not anything is ever found depends on the British courts and the American courts and the myriad of people who are looking for it.

At stake is upwards of $69 million.

They call him the fat man because at various times he weighs 350 or 400 or 450 pounds.

That's 24 or 28 or 32 stone.

He is the founder of the *IMAC Economic and Financial Review*, of the so-called Sutman Institute for Strategic Economic Studies, and of the Caprimex Group of companies.

His game was commodities.

At least that's what he says.

However there are doubts.

Born in 1930, Herbage is fast to point out that he is the victim. That, $69 million later, all of his problems stem from the fact that he has always been a thorn in the side of the establishment.

'Being the product of a good public school the attitude has always been that I should join with the establishment and not, as they say, rock the boat. On the other hand, I've always had a burning thing to fight the establishment. I was rather bitter after I left college where I studied music, that I couldn't make a living conducting, which I wanted to do.'

Although he attended Whitgift, records there show he did not graduate. Nor is he necessarily remembered for any obvious talents, musical or otherwise. After leaving school he found his way into the record business, landing a job as a salesman with Decca. Then, at the age of 21, he started his own label. 'That's when I had my first brush with the establishment because I discovered that Decca and EMI owned a company called Phonographic Performance and so if you wanted your records broadcast you had to sign your royalties over to them. And I just decided it wasn't going to happen and I broke it. They then told me I'd never work in the record industry again. I sold out and two years later came back representing Deutsche Gramophon. I started that for them in the UK, which of course made everybody very bitter.'

Another version of the story, obviously not his, suggests that he and Deutsche Grammophon couldn't agree on his 'silent partner' style of book-keeping so they rather impolitely let him go.

He popped up next in Bournemouth, England, with a creation called the Merchant Guaranty Trust.

'I started a small finance company. It worked very well for five years. Then my biggest customer went bust and that was it. That was about 1963. And that's when I had my first big trouble. Merchant Guaranty went down for about fifty grand, of which I covered about forty.'

Other records show that Merchant Guaranty went broke leaving debts of £200,000.

1963 was also the year he started the Bank of Valette. With an office in London's West End, he

offered piped music and free coffee to attract customers. Wrapped around his banking activities was a
company called Eurotrust Ltd, through which he
offered his banking clients the possibility of investing
in 'leading European and British growth stocks'.

The bank went out of business in 1964.

And so did Eurotrust.

'I had a very bad time. I was ill. I had a complete
breakdown. Whilst in Guy's Hospital they served
notice that they wanted an annual general meeting
held of the company (Eurotrust). Good timing. The
hospital said I couldn't do it. Unfortunately, they told
me when I was coming out of the hospital. They wrote
me. I said, look, I've made arrangements to go to Spain
to recover. I would deal with this matter when I got
back. It was only a £5 fine. Went off to Spain. Whilst I
was in Spain, corresponded with the solicitor, said will
you set this whole thing up, I'm coming back in about
nine months' time. And they said, well we don't know
whether you should or not, they've issued a warrant
for your arrest as a fugitive offender. In due course, I
came back and I am the only person who has ever been
inside for not holding the annual general meeting of a
company.'

Court records show he was sentenced to six months.
But they also show that there were in fact three
violations of the Companies Act. In addition to his
failure to hold an AGM, he was guilty of failing to
publish balance sheets and profit and loss accounts. He
served four months, was fined £50 and ordered to pay
£300 costs.

Although he followed his banking experiences by
founding the London Dance Studios – that folded in
1965 – he was facing a mountain of debt. So in 1965 he
declared bankruptcy.

'I came out of prison and I couldn't get a job. Every time I got a job the official receiver would move in and I'd lose the job. I started a business newsletter. I heard he was after me, so I went to the Channel Islands, which are outside the jurisdiction. They couldn't do anything to me there. It started building up. I got a flat. I got a little office. I began to see things well. Been there about six months and one day I got a phone call from the bank. They said, the official receiver has frozen your account this morning. Which he couldn't even do. It's illegal. But he'd done it.'

Actually it can be done, legally, with the agreement of the local authorities.

'I realized then that things were getting out of hand. The next thing was *The Times* ran a great big article against me; sort of, here was Alex Herbage, undischarged bankrupt, running a business in Guernsey. Well, there was nothing illegal in that. It's outside the jurisdiction. But I decided I'd had enough with bloody England and everything else at that stage, so, with about a couple of grand which I'd made, I packed up, went to Zurich, got myself a fourth-floor one-room office, and extended my activities which I had started in dealing in commodities.'

At that point, he says, he hooked up with Stavros Niarchos and his crowd, and introduced them to commodities. 'Nobody knew anything about commodities. I was making money in the commodity business at that point and doing well in cocoa, copper, silver, that sort of thing. Those Greeks were marvellous. They were wonderful clients. They had a lot of money and just gambled like mad. It's a good business being a broker. And I got on well with them. I always get on well with Mediterranean types. I'm now talking about '67, '68. A marvellous boom time. Bernie Cornfeld was

booming. Everybody was booming. I knew Bernie quite
well. I decided I was going to take a leaf out of his
book. And I grabbed on an idea that there were all
these people getting locked into mutual funds, which
was crazy, because what you wanted to do was to
unlock them. I wanted to set up a stock exchange for
mutual fund clients in Germany. I decided to invest
£25,000 in an advertising campaign.'

His ads ran in newspapers and within a few days
mailbags filled with responses were dumped into his
office.

'We went from those offices in nine weeks into an
11-storey building with 200 staff. But that was the
mutual fund business. We were doing something like
taking 2 or 3 million dollars a day back off Cornfeld's
clients. Because that was just the time too when all
those no-load funds were coming up in the States and
so we were saying, look, you know you've been crazy
to spend 8.5 per cent to go into this thing and we can
switch you into a fund which is a better performer and
has no front-end load. And all we want is a 1.5 per cent
brokerage fee for doing it.'

It was, he brags, a fantastic business. 'It really was
extraordinary. Everything was absolutely marvellous.
That's when I met my present wife. I'd been married
twice before. And everything went very well until the
day Cornfeld decided to crash. Or the boys decided to
pull the rug out from under him, which is more to the
point. We would have survived. We scaled down and
started cutting and all the rest of it. That was coming
up to the end of 1970. But the NYSE went down about
250 points and there was just total heavy selling by
everybody, and everybody who had any form of mutual
fund wanted out. One makes one's money from putting
people in, not from getting them out.'

Then in January 1971, while in England looking at a yacht he had hoped to buy, he slipped on the gangplank and slid to the bottom of the hold. 'After 11 operations, and three months later when I came to, of course, everything had gone. My lawyers, quite rightly, had said to my wife don't worry, you look after him and we'll move in. They moved in and they just closed everything down and started liquidating like mad. And everybody got paid off. In fact we finished up with a certain amount of surplus.'

Not quite. What he conveniently forgets to say is that the Swiss police raided his Zurich offices and the company collapsed, leaving debts reportedly in the range of £50 million.

He also conveniently forgets to say that, over the next four years, another seven Herbage companies were formed and folded.

'We finished up in '71 with a certain amount of capital and quite a large payment from the insurance company for the loss of my leg. I was sitting in a wheelchair, having been told I'd never walk again for the rest of my life. And that I'd never work again. I discovered that I could drive the car, so we just spent our time driving around Europe with a wheelchair in the back. We also had a boat in Marbella and I suddenly had a thought one day that if I used the boat I could teach myself how to walk because there are always things to hang on to. And I did. It took me a year but I taught myself how to walk again.'

He returned to England at the end of 1973 because, by this time, his money was running out. 'I couldn't work, I could only take three or four paces, didn't know what to do, and that's when I said the only thing I could do to make some money was to start writing again. And I'm going to write a newsletter on commodities. That was the start of Caprimex. It started in England. We bought a duplicator and my wife said, what's a newsletter, what do you do with it. I said you write this thing, print it, sent it out and people send you money. She said, you're crazy. I rapidly found that none of my ex-friends in the City could be bothered to spring for 35 quid, which I thought they would, so we then got an out-of-date Telex directory and looked up commodity firms and started sending out 100 copies a week, which was all we could afford to post. We ran the thing for 12 weeks and on the 12th week I was very depressed. My wife said, this is crazy, let's stop it, we can't afford it. And that's when we got our first subscription. This letter came in from Abu Dhabi. I remember it came in around breakfast time and we were both in tears about it. She said, isn't it wonderful. And I said it's fucking awful because now we've got to write the bloody thing for a year.'

With the Inland Revenue now asking about his residency status, Herbage felt it was time to leave England again.

'I decided I wanted to get out, that England was no good to me. I wish I had remembered that. I wanted to go back to France. But I decided we couldn't possibly afford that because we didn't have that sort of money. The only place we could think of was Andorra.'

He realized all his assets, bought a second-hand car and set off for the one-village country stuck in the mountains between France and Spain. With nothing more than a short-wave radio for news, a telephone that used to break down a lot and a Xerox telefax machine to send his newsletter to the printers, he built up his newsletter's circulation while also dabbling in commodities on the side.

'I'm a political economist, if I can put it that way. I

mean, I predicted every major move of everything that was happening at that time. The Shah of Persia going, the fall in the pound, the fall in the dollar, and very, very accurately, within 2 or 3 cents.'

In spite of his dismal business record, throughout 1976 Herbage managed to find a loyal readership for his *Commodities Research Digest*.

'The big break came when I decided I wanted to get into the States. Our market was the Middle East but what I suddenly found was that we were beginning to get subscriptions from the States. I couldn't make out why. Then of course I realized that these were people like geologists who were going back and telling their friends. I thought, well, how do we get into the States. So I picked out what I thought were about half a dozen of the leading newsletters, and I wrote to them all very carefully, saying they wouldn't know anything about us, we were a funny little firm publishing in Andorra, which is a funny little place in the Pyrenees, and could I swap with them, or could they do anything to advise me or help me or perhaps give me a little write-up. Six of them, from the *Professional Investor* downwards, came out with about three pages on us in the same month. Of course they never spoke to me again after that. But I mean the publicity was fantastic. And Americans are very generous in this sort of thing. Suddenly we were overwhelmed for business, as you can imagine. That's really when Caprimex started.'

After a year he and his wife moved to France. And for the next three years they developed their client list and continued publishing their newsletter. They also opened an art gallery in Cannes. But then they got into a real estate tangle that wound up in the French courts, and that cost them a great deal of money. Reacting to those pressures, his health deteriorated. 'I was very, very ill indeed. I got more and more depressed. I was nearly dying. It was all very unpleasant, the whole thing. That's really why, in 1981, I decided to come back from France to England.'

Returning home, now flush with cash, he bought Sutton Manor, Lord Rank's former estate, for £460,000 and supposedly sunk another half million into it. In a brochure he wrote and published about the manor, he explained that the house and grounds were acquired by the Fondation Herbage, a private Swiss charitable trust, endowed by Mr and Mrs Alec Herbage, whose aims included the development of economic aid to the Third World, medical research and encouragement of the arts. At Sutton Manor he also established the Winchester Corn Exchange, Wincomex and a company called Imex.

And at the same time he established Trier Investments with an office in Holland.

Now all of the pieces were on the board.

And now the game could begin.

Herbage ruled Sutton Manor like a feudal lord.

Investors who met him there claimed he held audiences in the throne room.

He surrounded himself with a fabulous contemporary art collection. The sculpture garden alone took up the estate's entire back yard. Among the artists represented were Moore, Miró and Picasso.

'By this time I was investing very heavily in art, dealing in art. I was one of the biggest art dealers in Europe. The collection we built up alone was fantastic. Buying in and selling out all the time.'

In July 1984, the auction firm Sotheby's were asked to do an evaluation of the art collection. Their 46-page report is entitled, 'Sutton Manor – Inventory and evaluation of bronzes, drawings, paintings, prints and outside sculpture, the property of Mr A. Herbage taken for the purpose of insurance.'

They valued the collection at 12 million Swiss francs.

Herbage now claims that all of the art was bought for clients as commodity investments. His creditors claim he squandered their money buying himself a collection.

But he insists, 'The art belongs to the bloody clients. That's what nobody will accept. This is Caprimex's art. This is just one of the stories which they've loved to stir about the whole thing. You know, about the property and things. But every single thing belongs to the clients. They were all bought in different nominee names for tax reasons. But I've never laid claim to any of these things. You know, at its height, we had something like £7 million worth of art just lying around Sutton Manor, which we were dealing in. I find that nobody seems to be able to understand that art is a commodity just as much as armaments. Let's be honest, you go and buy a Matisse and you spend 3.5 million francs for it and then sell it for 7.9 million francs and it's a good business. So I consciously made this thing that I would invest the clients' money in art and that if we wanted to build up the value of it we would have to show it. We got fantastic planning permission to turn Sutton Manor into an international art and conference centre. We started putting a lot of money into it, but it belonged to the clients. It was a highly valuable property. At its height I had it valued at £3.5 million. I paid £460,000 for it. But this is what I'm good at. This is my commodity flair, whether it's property, whether it's art. Whatever it is. I was highly successful at all this.'

Yes and no.

Sutton Manor, according to the liquidators, was never worth £3.5 million. It has since been sold for less than £1 million, although under better conditions it might well have gone for slightly more. But certainly not 3.5 times more. Based on the Sotheby's audit, the art collection was worth £6–7 million, but a lot of the works have since disappeared. Some were sold. That is known for certain. Some have probably been stored somewhere, hidden from the receivers. At least that's what they believe. What's left has netted only about £1 million. But then, as one of the liquidators said about Herbage's ability to distort figures, 'If he didn't live in a fantasy land he wouldn't have wound up in Pentonville Prison.'

Besides art, he was also a collector of names.

He used his newsletters and his Sutman Institute for Strategic Economic Studies to invent associations with some of England's most respectable people. Pictures of Herbage and British notables frequently appeared in various issues of his *IMAC Economic and Financial Review*, his *Caprimex Group News* and his *Commodities Research Digest*. There he was alongside former prime minister Edward Heath, shaking hands with the Queen's cousin, Prince Michael of Kent, posing with the Deputy Secretary General of the Commonwealth, discussing matters with leading merchant bankers.

Accepting the Horatio Bottomley philosophy that one is often judged by the company one keeps, Herbage knew that there was profit in being seen with all the 'right' people.

And that's what 'Winchester 83' was all about.

The Winchester Conference, held at Sutton Manor in July 1983, was billed as a forum for investment

strategies and political freedom. It was co-sponsored
by the Sutman Institute and the Centre for International Studies – a wing of Sutton Manor – together
with the International Newsletter Association – a
group of investment advisory publishers which, by
coincidence, was also founded by Alec Herbage.

While there were some other newsletter publishers
in attendance, the large majority of 'conferees' were
subscribers to Herbage's own newsletters and investors in his IMAC Currency Hedge Account Fund.

For the three days and two nights, there were
luncheons, banquets, panel discussions, awards, and
excursions to Stonehenge. One afternoon there was
even a medieval jousting match. The conference brochure listed all sorts of speakers who have to be called
minor attractions . . . basically editors of small, unimportant American newsletters. However, also included
were the recipients of the Thomas Paine Awards for
1983 – former West German Chancellor Willy Brandt,
US Congressman Ron Paul and entertainer Danny
Kaye. Unfortunately, Messrs Brandt, Paul and Kaye
were unable to attend.

The foundation of the empire was Caprimex.

It was a network of companies through which Herbage claimed to service investment and financial
requirements for clients in 93 countries.

The main Caprimex Holdings was registered in
Luxembourg with group offices in the Cayman Islands.
Caprimex-Trier was based in Amsterdam, while the
Imex Computer division was in Winchester, England.
There was also a company called Wincomex Money
Brokers with an address in Geneva. Several Herbage-
owned and/or -managed companies were registered in
Great Britain. Among them are Wincomex Ltd, the

Winchester Corn Exchange Ltd and Trier Investments Ltd.

Incorporated in the UK on 2 March 1982, the object of Trier, as listed with the British authorities, was as dealers in stocks and shares. But the company never posted annual returns. It was a £100 company, with 100 £1 shares, all of them allotted for cash. The shareholders were Chemische Treuhand AG, of Broad Street, Monrovia, Liberia (50 shares) and the Sutman Trust Co. Ltd, also of Monrovia, Liberia (50 shares). The one director was listed as Dr Peter David Beter, whose occupation is given as a lawyer and whose address is listed as 5101 Brookeway Drive, Bethesda, Maryland, USA.

Interestingly enough, in a later Herbage fund prospectus, Dr Beter is described as 'an international financial and legal consultant based in Washington DC. He was legal counsel with the Export-Import Bank of the United States and has been in business in Kinshasa, Zaïre as Director, Treasurer and general counsel of Sodesmir SPRL, a project development company. Dr Beter was a former director of the Citizens' Crime Commission Metropolitan Washington and formerly General Counsel American Gold Association, Washington. He is a member of the Federal Bar Association, American Judicature Society, Royal Commonwealth Society (London), and is a member of the DC and United States Supreme Court Bars. He won a class case against the United States Department of Justice in the United States Court of Claims, involving awards of over $1 million in 1955. He is author of several books and articles on gold, including the book entitled, "The Conspiracy Against the Dollar". He is married and has three children. He is listed in the Who's Who in the East, USA.'

At the Royal Commonwealth Society he states his occupation as 'international legal and financial consultant'. They don't list him as a lawyer. Nor is he listed under the Washington DC or the Maryland bars in Martindale and Hubbell, the official guide to attorneys in the United States. Nor does he appear to be a member of the American Bar Association, the main body of lawyers in the US.

The full extent of his association with Herbage has never been made perfectly clear. One former Caprimex employee notes, 'Beter runs his own financial newsletter. He was also a licensee to Caprimex. He's of Lebanese extraction and an absolute right-wing crank.'

From correspondence with Herbage, it's evident that he has done financial dealing either for Herbage or some of the companies. In one letter from Beter in Spain to Herbage in England dated 24 March 1985, he adds a PS, that a certain deal is *now* in London with Bank of America.

At first glance it looks as if he's written the 'AU' deal. Who knows what that could stand for. Or it might be the 'ALL' deal. Which doesn't make a lot of sense either. But when you look closely, it could also be the 'AG' deal. AG as in Chemische Treuhand, AG.

Less than a month later, on 21 April, he wrote to Herbage on his own stationery, presumably from Maryland, 'The big 1000 T deal has now been moved from B of A to Chase for closing.'

In gangster slang, a 'T' is a ton ... 100. Could this suggest that Beter has had something to do with 100,000 dollars or pounds? Or could the 'big 1000 T' reference here mean 'big T' or 100,000, which multiplied by 1000 is 100 million?

* * *

The Herbage empire now appears to span some 66 companies worldwide.

In addition to controlling and/or maintaining beneficial interest in various companies with the name Sutman, Alec William Herbage had control and/or beneficial ownership of several companies using the name Trier. He is, for example, titled Managing Director for Trier Investments International Services, Bureau for Caprimex, with the Caprimex-Trier address in Amsterdam. On those documents, next to the words 'Restriction of the authority' is the word, 'None'.

On the official documents for Wincomex Ltd, Herbage is listed as a director. The company was registered on 3 February 1983, the objects being commodity brokers, with the same registered office address as Trier. Wincomex is also a £100 company. Two subscribers' shares are in the names of registered agents. Herbage lists other directorships in Capamin Ltd, Sutton Manor Herb Farm, and one illegibly written. It appears to be either McColl or Malcoll Estates. Here, too, no annual returns have ever been filed. Although, in this instance, the company secretary is noted to have resigned on 10 July 1984.

The most complete listing at Companies House in London is that for the Winchester Corn Exchange. Incorporated on 2 April 1982, the company was called Voyagevale Ltd until 29 July 1982. Its objectives were as brokers and dealers in commodities. The registered office was, like the others, Harmon House in Winchester. However, unlike the others, here there is an annual return, dated 31 December 1982. It shows administrative expenses of £51,113. That's broken down to salaries and state contributions, £17,230; advertising, £1511; entertainment, £85; motor vehicles, £4506; travel and accommodation, £13; equipment leasing and rental, £13,413; light, heat and power, £266; rent £2896; repairs and maintenance £323; insurance £506; printing and stationery £832; telephone, telex and postage £8160; sundries, £372; audits and accounts, £1000. Under the heading 'loss on ordinary activities, tax and transferred to reserves' is the figure £51,113.

Yet another £100 company with registered shareholders, there were two original Winchester Corn Exchange directors. Alec Herbage was one until 6 April 1983 when he resigned. The remaining director is Herbage's wife, Maria. Both of them listed their additional directorships as Davos Ltd, Harpvale Ltd, Eftavia Ltd, Imex Ltd, Sutman Security Ltd, Capamin Ltd, and the Winchester Corn Exchange Ltd.

By 1984, even as some investors began complaining about Herbage's inability to refund their monies, he was offering three different types of account under the Caprimex logo. The first was called the Standard ... minimum investment $10,000. The second was called the High Performance ... minimum investment $35,000. The third was called the IMAC (International Metals and Currency) Currency Hedge ... minimum investment $1000. Apart from the usual brokerage charges on all of the accounts, Caprimex also took a 15–25 per cent 'management fee' off the profits realized.

According to papers alleged to be Herbage's own accountings of the monies in those three funds as of 31 August 1984, there was $8 million in the Standard Fund, $21 million in the High Performance Fund, and over $35 million in the Currency Hedge Fund.

Discreetly advertised but heavily subscribed in the

United States, the three funds promised profits of over 30 per cent, with monthly statements sent in plain envelopes. They offered the usual secrecy associated with the Cayman Islands, where 'account holders are not subject to any profit, capital gains or other taxes', and where 'managers will not under any circumstances release any information about holders or their accounts to any third party whatsoever'. They also offered cash settlements anywhere in the world. The hint was obvious. If you don't want anyone in America to know you're making money on this . . . anyone such as the Internal Revenue Service . . . don't worry because we're on your side.

Of course that sort of advertising attracted all sorts of punters, any number of whom were more than pleased at the prospect of keeping their investment profits away from Uncle Sam's hands.

But that kind of deal is a double-edged sword.

If you can't tell the IRS where it came from or how much you've been making on it, who can you complain to if it goes walking out the back door?

The writing on the wall should have been clear to any truly astute investor. For example, in brochures for the Currency Hedge Fund dated August 1979 and June 1983, there are some interesting discrepancies. The first lists the investment advisers as IMAC, S.A. and the managers as CAPA S.L. with an address in Andorra. A note says, 'Imac–Capa act solely as independent investment advisers and managers. The companies do not act as brokers or agents and do not directly handle clients' investments all of which are effected through the company's clearing brokers who are required to be members of the New York Stock Exchange or leading commodity exchanges.' No mention is made of who those brokers are. Nor is there any explanation of the relationship between IMAC and CAPA. That brochure was printed in England by CAPA.

In the second brochure, bearing the same logos and design, the investment advisers are IMAC S.A., the managers are CAPA S.A. (not S.L. this time) and a head office address is listed as Caprimex, Inc. in the Cayman Islands. The international service bureau is Trier Investments Ltd with the Amsterdam address.

Both brochures clearly note, 'not available to residents of the United Kingdom'. And that's important because Herbage knew he could not appear to be doing any business at all in the UK.

The second brochure also notes, 'The Caprimex Group acts as investment advisers and managers and, whilst acting as brokers, transact all clients' business through their correspondent floor brokers in New York and Chicago who are required to be members of either the New York Stock Exchange or leading US commodity exchanges.' Still no mention of who they are. But this time Herbage says they do act as brokers – the first time he said they didn't – while the statement definitely ties Caprimex, IMAC, CAPA and Trier into the Herbage flock.

Now, in those heady days of Winchester 83 and jousting matches, Herbage was making good on his bills . . . although he was fast getting a reputation for paying late. One agent in the United States, who had solicited up to 400 clients for the various funds, admits that his average commission at that time was $10,930 per month. One letter from Herbage to another agent offers commissions of 0.75 per cent on all transactions arising from the agent's introductions. At that figure, a $10,930 average monthly commission would represent transactions totalling $1,748,800. The agent now says that cheques from Herbage did come in, but through 1983–84 they got slower and slower, until they eventually just stopped. That same agent, with a client list of nearly 400 people scattered across the United States, claims that during the months January–May 1984 he was personally responsible for clients' deposits to Caprimex for $300,000.

Many of those cheques were written on an account at the Western Bank, Westwood Branch, on Westwood Boulevard in Los Angeles. The account was in the name of Sutman International Inc., with the address given as Trier Investments Ltd in Holland. Several cheques to investors written on that account through the summer of 1984 were returned marked 'non sufficient funds'.

Clients began objecting.

One American investor from Oregon requested his money by telephone and a letter from Caprimex signed for Alex Herbage was sent on 13 August confirming that a cheque was enclosed. That cheque was returned from the bank marked 'Account Closed'.

Obviously not an isolated case. Herbage wrote to his clients on 24 August, 'Recently we forwarded you a cheque in settlement of your outstanding account. If this has been returned to you unpaid, we shall be grateful if you would advise us immediately and return the unpaid cheque to us, in order that we may issue you with a draft drawn on our European bankers. Should your cheque unfortunately not have been honoured by our American bankers we will of course compute and add interest to the amount payable to you for the time lost since you should have received the original payment.'

According to copies of returned cheques, the Westwood account was closed between 7 August and 29

August. Yet cheques continued to be written on the account until as late as October. The signature on the bottom of those cheques appears to be that of Alex Herbage.

Finding himself in the middle of a constant barrage of letters from clients demanding their money, he tried another tack in September.

On Caprimex letterhead, with the Trier Investments Amsterdam address, Herbage wrote, 'After many months of intensive study, we have now established a new entity "the International Currency Fund" to which I shall act as sole adviser. My trading policy for the "ICF" will be carried on in exactly the same manner in currencies, bullion, financial instruments and options and stock indexes, as the present "Currency Hedge Fund". However, unlike the present fund, the Administration will come directly under the day to day control of our Auditors and Accountants who will issue regular quarterly and annual audited balance sheets that will be available to all members of the Fund. As an added protection we have also incorporated strict control into the new Fund whereby all clients' funds will be maintained in special fiduciary accounts from which no movements of any monies of any kind may be made without the joint signatures of our Accountants and the Management Company. Finally, this new fund will allow me to considerably enlarge the net asset base of the trading unit, as the first tranche to be offered in early October will be for US$125,000,000. The first offering is particularly geared for the institutional investors, being an opening 50,000 shares of US$25,000 each.'

Here comes another parallel to Bottomley.

Remember how he offered his clients shares in a new company rather than refund anyone's money?

Herbage said in that letter, 'Before the end of the year, we shall be making available to our present IMAC clients an opportunity to swap their IMAC holdings into the new "International Currency Fund" by means of a holding in a special "Shareholders' Holding Company" . . . where investors may purchase fractional units of shares to be held in trust for them by a Fiduciary Company of international standard. As such, their holding will also be controlled under the supervision of Auditors and Accountants. Clients will lose none of the present rights when swapping IMAC to ICF. Indeed I believe that the protection of their privacy will actually be enhanced. I will be writing to you shortly when we are ready to start accepting switches of investments from IMAC Fund to the new International Currency Fund and will forward you more details of the new fund.'

Reading between the lines, and with the benefit of hindsight, what he's saying is that IMAC and Caprimex are about to go broke. If you don't transfer your funds, you lose everything. If you do, you can't sue Alex Herbage anyway because the money you invested is tied up in some worthless fiduciary account managed by someone else.

A letter accompanying the prospectus for the ICF uses Trier's Amsterdam address but makes no reference to either Trier or Caprimex. It comes from someone with an illegible signature representing the 'information office', and not from Herbage.

As described in that letter, the ICF 'is primarily intended for investment by institutional clients who seek to hedge and protect their possible US Dollar exposure on the world currency markets.' For this purpose, the letter says, the fund has retained 'Sutman Management Ltd of the Bahamas who have undertaken to provide the services of Mr Alex Herbage to direct the trading policy of the Fund.'

That letter gives Herbage's credits as a consultant to several central banks as well as many commercial banks and multinational corporations. 'Mr Herbage also advises various Government Ministries as well as Embassies worldwide . . . '

Which ones?

No one bothers to say.

It all sounded good.

On paper it even looked too good.

In reality it was all just a lot of crap.

Some of Herbage's victims wrote to Trier at the Amsterdam address. But letters and returned cheques sent to that office were forwarded to England. Many of the office memos from the Amsterdam staff to England were addressed to Mrs Herbage.

Many of the people who received bouncing cheques tried to contact Herbage directly. And in early October at least one client noted, 'Mr Herbage does not respond to my phone calls or wires. I have decided to try legal action.' To that he added, 'My sources indicate that investors have not been able to withdraw funds for at least three months.'

In at least two cases, angry American investors actually travelled to England.

One of them reported, 'On the 13th of October I journeyed to Sutton Manor along with X (name withheld) in an attempt at gaining an interview with Alex Herbage, director of the IMAC currency hedge fund. After a journey of some 2½ hours' duration, X and I arrived at Sutton Manor. We were immediately met by two security guards who breathlessly asked us what they could do for us, whereupon X asked to see Mr

Herbage. After waiting some 15 minutes in a very dingy rear waiting room we were shown into the office of Herbage's girl Friday, Jenny Wheeler. She informed us that Mr Herbage was very busy and quite possibly could not see us. I then informed her that I had come over 3000 miles and I would stay right where I was until next week if need be, but I was going to see Alex.

'That brought about the response I was hoping for because we were immediately shown into Alex's office. It was obvious from the start that he (Alex) was annoyed at our being there, but to give the devil his due, Herbage was very cordial. The usual amenities were observed and then we got down to business. Alex immediately launched into a diatribe on how busy he is and how tired he is and how poorly he was feeling.

'When I again tried to bring the conversation to the matter at hand Alex blew his cool so to speak, not at me but at X. It is to the credit of both of us, X and I, that neither one of us joined him in that luxury. We were then compelled to listen to the history of Alex Herbage for five hours, interrupted by a sparse lunch.

'The upshot was that he promised to cover all the requests by the 17th of November at the latest. At the moment of our arrival Herbage was in the process of drafting yet another letter to all of his clients explaining his dilemma, so I won't go into his excuses at any great length. Suffice it to say he is one smooth article and bears watching.

'I was able to get Alex to give me a token cheque in the amount of $5000 for a small lady client of mine. That cheque was made out on his personal bank. It bounced. I called Alex and he went into his usual monologue, all to no avail, the cheque still bounced.

'Herbage still insists everybody will get all the money coming to them on or before the 17th of November. It remains to be seen. In any event it doesn't do any of us any good to bring him down without giving him the allotted time he asked for. If he can arrange his affairs so as to come up with the money we all win. If not, we may get our pound of flesh, but we will lose all our money by forcing him into Bankruptcy.'

On 8 November, Herbage wrote to his clients in a form letter, 'Since March of this year, one particular group of American investors have, with others, endeavoured to make a deliberate "run" on the Company. It was only in June that I became aware of their tactics, and their efforts to place pressure on the Management of Caprimex. These actions have been a deliberate campaign, instituted with the intention of trying to take over the Caprimex Group at a discount and consequent loss to investors.'

He added that at the same time, but quite independently, his accounts department had suffered computing problems. Yet, he assured his investors, 'Over the last few months, the Company has continued to pay out substantial sums, to meet redemptions requested by clients.'

He claimed that in spite of the continuous pressures exerted against Caprimex he was not prepared to undertake a 'forced sale' of assets, which would only have been made at a loss and to the detriment of all account holders. So 'Following on the establishment of financing guarantees with a leading London Merchant Bank, it is our intention to liquidate positions in an orderly manner, *which will ensure that we meet all clients' redemptions in full. Additionally, as payment is made, interest will be added at 12½% to compensate for the delays suffered, from the date the redemption should have been made, to the actual date of payment*.'

Here, he promised 'payment in full, to all clients who have requested redemptions and whose investments do not exceed US$5,000 within the next 21 days . . . Following these payments, we will then resume, during November, payment of all other outstanding redemptions on a "paripassu" basis, so that *full payment of all outstanding redemptions will be made by the end of December 1984.*'

The italics are his, not mine.

After reminding his clients about the ICF, and the opportunity they would have to transfer their funds into that account, he appealed 'to all our clients and friends to be patient for just a little longer throughout this period.'

Some were.

Most weren't.

Neither were the police.

It was the middle of 1983 when Herbage actually decided to form the International Currency Fund.

'I said to my professional advisers, what we've got now is just something that's grown up higgledy-piggledy, which you can't have in this business. It's got no structure. I want a new thing, structured properly by lawyers and accountants from the start. I said to my auditors, Finnie's (Finnie and Co.), who are a very respectable firm, you will come in and be the auditors to this. You must be the fiduciary agents with the Dutch accountants. And I don't want any responsibility for anything. I want the money to come in to you, I want you to put it in the bank, it's under your signature, your control, and you tell me what we're doing. You say we've got so much in the bank and I say all right, send so much to our dealers. We were dealing with various American firms, directly in the markets, floor brokers. But my idea was to have a system where I wouldn't touch any money in any form whatsoever.'

Once the fund could be put in place, he planned to sell off the offices and all of the computers. He said there would then be an enormous saving in overheads. He wanted to reduce it so that he had a staff of four or five people in new offices based in Frankfurt. 'We would start absolutely clean. I put the planning of all this into the hands of an American lawyer named Robert Citroen and my English solicitor Richard Stewart, who worked for me full time on the staff. Citroen was the biggest agent we ever had, he brought more business than anyone else, and the idea was that he was going to be the chairman of the Fund. It was all agreed we were all going to meet up in Amsterdam in February '84 to finalize the thing and get going.'

When they did meet, Herbage says he had an enormous row with Citroen, who suggested that Richard Stewart, Aislinn McKibbon, who was the director of the Amsterdam office, and Soroush Rousta, who was a broker in Geneva, run the business. Citroen would be chairman while Herbage looked after his health and went off on a cruise.

His response was an angry one. 'I kicked them out. All of them resigned. And I thought there might be trouble. I started getting a bit liquid. We had a lot of liquid funds. And certainly, redemptions started hitting us. We started paying them out, and every time we paid them out another wave would come in. We sat down and discovered that the clients who were liquidating were very carefully selected. We contacted a few of them and they said, oh yes we've had telephone calls from someone in Rotterdam who has advised us that you're going broke, to get out. We checked back and discovered that a complete set of all the computer records of the whole company, everything, had disappeared. Another agent came to see me. This was in June when all of this was coming to a head and we realized what was happening. He said, there's a scheme to break you. Someone is trying to bring you down. We could work a deal. If you told your clients that they're not going to get their money back from you but that they could get 75 per cent from me, then you and I could split the rest of it. I kicked him out. I then discovered that he was double-crossing the other partners because he was the one who was ringing around everybody telling them to get out of the thing. He was an American agent who had teamed up with Interconsult.'

Now, once upon a time, bounty hunters might have been considered a romantic breed.

The whole idea of riding the plains, sleeping out under the stars, sneaking up on the bad guys and herding them back to the sheriff at Dodge City is the stuff of Louis L'Amour.

In modern times, bounty hunters are a much less attractive lot.

A group calling themselves Interconsult and Partners in Rotterdam found out about Herbage and saw a chance to make some money by taking the angry investors' cases into their own hands.

Head of the unofficial posse was William Van den Hoek, a Finn who speaks fluent Dutch. Riding with him was an Australian businessman named Graham Ayre . . . who at one point in a telephone conversation claimed to be an international lawyer, which he is not. He worked for AGIP, the Italian oil company, and began investing with Herbage in the summer of 1981. Ayre purchased 514 units in the IMAC Currency Hedge Account, which by December 1983, he claims,

was worth $319,064.78. In January 1984 he opened a
new account with Herbage, this one the Caprimex
High Performance Fund. He claims that by August
1984 the combined value of both accounts was now
$538,964.88. But he says, in an affidavit to Intercon-
sult, when he contacted Trier, Caprimex and Herbage
to try to get his money out, none was forthcoming.

So he and Van den Hoek joined forces.

Not only did they both see a chance to get Ayre's
money back, but they also worked out a scheme to
make some money at the same time. They put out the
word that for a down payment of 3½ per cent of any
investors' claims, against a further 6½ per cent of the
monies recovered, they'd do whatever it took to seize
Herbage's assets.

A very large, muscular blond young man opened the
door of a converted house in South Rotterdam. He
rather sternly wanted to know who was ringing the
bell and what they wanted. When the two callers
explained that they had an appointment with Mr Van
den Hoek, he said, 'Wait here,' and closed the door to
check.

The appointment confirmed, he returned to say that
Mr Van den Hoek was not at this particular address
but he would take us to him. With some reticence, we
climbed into the young man's car. A miniature set of
boxing gloves dangled from the rear view mirror. He
drove quickly through the bleak streets of Holland's
largest port and finally deposited us at a restaurant.

It was long past the luncheon hour and the place
was deserted, except for Van den Hoek and three other
men sitting at the bar.

Van den Hoek was a short, wiry fellow who always
carried a portable telephone.

With him was a tall, thin, very nervous American man.

The other two – both burly fellows who were actually larger than the young blond boxer – left as soon as we came in. They saw us, Van den Hoek gave them a nod, and they quickly made their exit.

The nervous American man turned out to be a Herbage investor who was paying Van den Hoek and Ayre to help recover close to $100,000.

In perfect English, Van den Hoek explained that he had gone to sea as a young man, worked his way through the shipping trade until he could afford to charter a vessel and first started making money by running that vessel between Europe and Lagos.

He wouldn't say what his cargoes were.

Interconsult and Partners, he led us to believe, was just one of his many businesses.

He wouldn't discuss any of the others.

Van den Hoek did, however, claim to have a document, several hundred pages long, which would tell the entire Herbage story and show him up as a fraud. He also claimed to have seized various Herbage bank accounts, and to have obtained computer print-outs of Herbage's entire worldwide operation.

The computer print-outs were acquired, he bragged, through 'our own means'.

The story as he told it went like this. Sometime in November 1984, Van den Hoek, Ayre, the young boxer and the two burly guys who had been in the restaurant, all dressed in black and raided Sutton Manor. Herbage was not in residence at the time. They 'neutralized' the staff – his word – and helped themselves to whatever records and documents they could find. Among the items they claimed to have taken were computer print-outs of Herbage's activities up to the end of August 1984. They also said they found a hand-written list of Herbage's expenses at Sutton Manor, dated 31 October 1984. Included were notes of bank accounts with Grindlays, National Westminster, Coutts and Midland. Among the items on that hand-written list were: Writs – £10,526.26, Replacement Cheques – £7425.55, Solicitors' Letters – £4674.85, Very Very Urgent Inland Revenue – £35,128.44, and Light Refreshment – £2545.75. The total on the first page alone was £110,803.

An account at Grindlays entitled 'Sutman Pound Sterling' showed such items as *The Times* – $820 (in those days it only cost 20p per day and 40p on Sundays), and the Royal Opera – £1110. The 'Sutman Multicurrency' account, also at Grindlays, showed the word 'Fund' with the figure $100,000. Under the heading of 'Nat West SME No. 1' account were items such as British Telecom – £271.04, Lloyds Bank – £3360, and City of Winchester – £5546.17. There are references to Nat West accounts in the name of Harpvale and another in the name of Davos. The Coutts 'Caprimex' account shows a cheque for £2000 to Lloyds Bank. The Nat West 'Light Refreshment' account has a listing for a cheque to Horton's Ice Cream for £168.02.

With evidence based on those documents, and claiming to represent nearly 600 investors with interests totalling nearly $15 million, Interconsult filed a civil action against Herbage and no less than 18 companies associated with him. On 6 December 1984, a Dutch judge granted their request to freeze five bank accounts in Holland and allow them to seize assets up to a total of 1.288 billion Dutch guilders, about $350 million. Van den Hoek said that Interconsult was also planning to take similar action against Herbage and the named companies in the UK.

Back at the converted house in South Rotterdam, the Interconsult offices were as odd as you might have expected. First, there was a bar. Not just a room with a bar, but a room that was a bar ... as if someone always wanted their own private pub so they went and built one in their spare bedroom. The Interconsult bar even came complete with two ladies sitting on stools, drinking beer, talking away in Dutch. Down a hall and around a corner, past a small kitchen and a stairway that led to bedrooms, Van den Hoek's office was a long, narrow room, with a safe and a conference table and a couple of desks.

Sitting down at the conference table, he produced the document he had previously referred to as being several hundred pages long, which would explain everything. It turned out to be a folder filled with photocopies of the papers they had stolen from Sutton Manor, plus newspaper clippings and some court documents. It was neither several hundred pages long, nor did it explain everything.

'They're nasty,' Herbage is fast to say about Interconsult. 'They beat me up outside the law courts. They physically attacked me on the steps of the law courts. There's a film of it. Southern Television. Van den Hoek set the whole thing up with them. Had the cameras right there. They filmed whilst I was being beaten up in front of it.'

In the end, the Interconsult's business looks as if it might have been a decent one for Van den Hoek and possibly also for Ayre. What they did for their clients is however questionable. Their plan of attack was to start by getting a Dutch receiver appointed to wind up Trier Investments in Holland. Then they brought action in Holland against Herbage and Caprimex even though there was no jurisdiction. They got a judgement

. . . it was unopposed by Herbage . . . which they then
tried to enforce in England. Of course, there it failed.
In all, they managed to spend upwards of £100,000 in
legal expenses. But then, by their own admission, they
were representing clients who had lost $15 million.
Their stated fee was 3.5 per cent up front. Multiply
that by $15 million and you get $525,000. For the sake
of round numbers, call the £100,000 an even $125,000.
Then subtract that from $525,000. That leaves an
extra $400,000.

By mid-November 1984 there was a very strong run
on Caprimex. But, Herbage says, by now the ICF was
ready. 'I knew that the moment the fund started to roll
we could advise the clients and stop the run. By this
time we knew it was Interconsult who was behind the
thing. We closed a lot of bank accounts. People like
Interconsult were going around making troubles
everywhere they could. They got the complete computer print-outs of everything. There were a lot of
muddles. There was money which got stopped in
transit. I mean the whole thing . . . you've no idea
what a mess it was at that point . . . but it was put-
able right the moment that ICF came on.'

The International Currency Fund Ltd – with the
same address as Trier Investments in Amsterdam –
was registered in Turks and Caicos Islands in the
British West Indies. It was to be a part of the International Currency Fund SA, registered in Panama. The
investment advisers were Sutman Management Ltd of
Nassau Bahamas.

According to the shiny gold-covered prospectus, no
monies could be got to by anyone without the signature
of the independent auditors. Those auditors, an established firm of London-based accountants, immediately
posed a number of questions about the fund and,

because of their objections, trading was never begun. Nicely enough, listed as a director of the International Currency Fund Ltd was Dr Peter David Beter.

Then, on Thursday 6 December 1984, the Hampshire police arrested Herbage at Sutton Manor. That same day, Dutch police, acting on a request by the British authorities, raided Trier's Amsterdam office and seized all of their records. But on Friday afternoon Herbage was released on his own recognizance. No specific charges were lodged and he was freed on 'police bail' ... meaning that no money had to be put up for his release, he still retained his passport and merely had to make himself available while the police continued their investigation.

'The police came in,' Herbage recalls, 'they seized everything and nothing much happened. I had a nervous breakdown, went to Scotland on the 8th of December. I came back on the 20th of March because I was going into a clinic. I arrived in London and was served with a warrant for all the documents. It cost my wife £100,000 because I had everything frozen. She sold all her jewellery. After five weeks and £100,000 down the drain, the solicitors pulled out and left me holding the baby, plus another warrant, which had just been launched.'

Eventually he was charged with false accounting and stiff conditions were set for his bail.

Enter here, Gerald Chappell.

An extremely astute, London-based lawyer, Chappell had been contacted by an American from Texas, a Caprimex investor who claimed to be owed about $53,000. He wanted Chappell to put Herbage out of business.

The American had invested in Caprimex through the Trier address in Amsterdam, which presented

Chappell with his first problem. Unlike the bumbling attempts of Interconsult, Chappell knew that, to bring an action against Caprimex and Herbage in England, he had to prove that both were doing business in England. He also realized that Herbage would claim that Caprimex was a Cayman Islands company and that the money was invested in Holland.

Chappell was able to prove that Caprimex in the Cayman Islands was nothing but a post office box where agents simply forwarded mail to Herbage, usually at the Trier address. He then set about trying to establish the Caprimex business base in the UK. He managed it by compiling various correspondence from Herbage to overseas investors, mainly in the States, plus correspondence from Trier to those clients, plus inter-office memos showing that Herbage operated from Winchester and Sutton Manor.

'These documents, all read together,' Chappell says, 'indicated that Herbage was the directing mind of the company and was giving instructions either to the Trier offices in Holland or in some cases writing directly to clients. We were also able to get transcripts of meetings held at Sutton Manor which clearly demonstrated that Herbage was running his business affairs from there.'

So, on 22 March 1985, Chappell filed a petition against Caprimex in the British courts. A hearing date was set for 13 May. Three days after filing that petition, Chappell applied for the appointment of a provisional liquidator to Caprimex. He felt that Caprimex's affairs were highly irregular and that the creditors' interests could only be protected by the courts. He argued that, failing the court's intervention, assets would be dissipated before the hearing. The court agreed.

In an unusual step, Chappell then requested that the provisional liquidator be a private firm, instead of the government liquidator, because he felt they had to deal with this special case very quickly.

Again, the court agreed.

On 13 and 14 May, hearings took place for the winding up of Caprimex. Chappell produced notices of support from some 200 other investors claiming £12,793,941.11. He argued that Caprimex could not meet those debts. Herbage resisted but to no avail.

Investigations of this sort are a maze. The liquidators began untangling the business by first getting inside Caprimex. They then followed the trail of dispersed monies through Trier and into three specific bank accounts. First there was Grindlays in London. Money there was used to pay administrative expenses. Then there was the Bank für Handel Effekten in Zurich. A lot of money there was dispersed either to Herbage personally or to other Herbage companies. Then there was the Western Bank in Los Angeles, which was used mainly to repay investors when Herbage was pressed.

Once inside Caprimex the liquidators also discovered Sutman International Inc., another Cayman Islands company. That company, operating as Herbage's private bank, had been lent about $10 million by Caprimex, so the liquidators of Caprimex could now ask for the winding up of Sutman International. Once inside Sutman, they discovered that monies had been forwarded to Sutman Settled Estates, a Panamanian company that owned Sutton Manor. The liquidators applied to wind up that one as well.

While this was going on, the Secretary of State for Trade and Industry took action to wind up four other Herbage companies, 'in the public's interest'.

At the same time, Herbage violated his bail.

First he tried to contact some of his 3000 investors with a circular explaining that there had been terrible problems at Caprimex and urging them to transfer their money into the International Currency Fund. Then evidence was submitted that he was trying to sell works of art. That was followed by a request for extradition from the US District Court in Orlando, Florida, which had indicted him on 25 counts of fraud. Finally, evidence was presented to the courts that Herbage might now attempt to flee.

Herbage was ordered to be detained in Pentonville Prison, awaiting further action.

While in jail, in February 1986, unable to pay a £24,500 bill for legal services, another court ruled him personally bankrupt.

Caprimex was also declared bankrupt for £3.5 million.

Pentonville, just north of the City of London, is basically a holding operation, filled with young punk kids either awaiting trial or sentenced to under six months. It was built in the nineteenth century to house 400–500 prisoners. There are, these days, more than 1200. You walk in through heavy locked doors. The walls all need paint. The guards have a tired and bored look in their eyes. To get to the hospital wing, where Herbage was a guest of Her Majesty's government, you go through two courtyards and no less than five more locked doors. The hospital wing is one corridor, with cells the size of small horse stables. Each has one bed, one table, one chair and one lamp. There are no toilet facilities. And the stench is awful.

With a jaundiced complexion and having lost some 50 pounds, Herbage was led into a small room at the end of the hallway where he sat in a chair between two tables so that he could rest his arms.

This was about as far away from the splendour of Sutton Manor that anyone could get.

'First of all,' he said, 'I'm up on remand. They'd claimed I'd breached my bail conditions, which I hadn't. They said I'd committed perjury so they put me inside at Winchester. They thought that was the end of the matter so I went on fighting it from Winchester. I put an application in for bail to be heard on the 2nd of October, and when I arrived there the DPP was there and he said, I shouldn't bother because tomorrow we're withdrawing the English charge against you and we're going to have you extradited to America. I was brought up to Bow Street and thrown in this place. Into the lunatic asylum. I was kept without my medicine so I went into an absolute and complete physical decline, DTs and all the rest of it. So they restored the medicine. On the 23rd of October, when the Divisional Court heard the rest of my judicial review, of course the DPP got up and said this is no longer relevant. Mr Herbage is not under restraint at Winchester so this matter should be dismissed. He is now under restraint for an extradition warrant. It was dismissed. What they didn't tell them was five days previously they had used the same reasons for denying me bail at Bow Street. The situation is that they are determined to bring me down somehow.'

Interviewing Herbage is an odd experience.

That he is an intelligent man is obvious. He speaks well. You can see in his eyes that he knows what he's doing.

Yes, his weight is a serious problem. It can't be easy going through life at 400 lbs. But he has learned to play on that, and on his general ill health. There is laughter and there are tears. They come startlingly close to each other. There is a moment of concern for his visitor's comfort, an apology that there is nothing to offer in the way of coffee or tea. Then there is the resignation of a man who sees himself a victim. And after sitting with him for a few hours there is a strange feeling of sympathy for the man ... sympathy for a fellow human being who has got himself into this awful mess.

His visitor's sympathy is not an isolated reaction. Those who know him are easily divided into two distinct categories. There are his former clients who want their money back and think he's a crook. But then, too, there are some – former clients included – who feel he is indeed the victim he claims to be and that, given a fair chance, he will repay his debts and maybe even make more money for them in the future.

It's either total dislike or blind loyalty.

There doesn't seem to be anything in between.

Although, when he starts talking about his secret political connections, at least one visitor snapped back to the moment and started wondering whether or not he has any touch with reality.

What he says here may be true.

On the other hand, it may be nothing more than lunatic ravings.

There is, unfortunately, no way of proving any of it.

'I was deeply involved in politics. Within the course of the year 1983–84 I was on the edge of all sorts of extraordinary deals. I mean, they (names withheld) had a deal going to run an expeditionary force out of Oman to relieve the Seychelles again. I was mixed up in some very peculiar negotiations with the Chinese. When (name withheld) was supposed to be on the other side of the world, he was actually climbing up the back stairs of the Dorchester to see me. We were organizing political interference. We got mixed up with the Foreign Office and (name withheld) to try to do a deal with the Argentines. I was getting mixed up in all these deals.'

Moving away from politics, when you say to him that there do not seem to be any records of commodity trading during these years, he responds, 'Oh balls.'

So, you ask, who were you trading with? And he answers, after a long pause, 'We were dealing with a lot of firms in America. There are records of that. The police have had all the records in their hands now for over a year. They refuse to hand them over, or copies, which is quite illegal. It's contrary to a ruling of the Court of Appeal. They refused to even make an inventory available, although they promised one last February and eventually we got it out of them this January. It just happens to leave off the 6000 clients' accounts. I mean the whole thing stinks from top to bottom.'

But even after the police handed over what records they had, there was still no proof of commodity trades. Herbage answers, 'What can you do when you're one person against the system and you get locked away in a place like this. I've got people who believe in me. People like the BBC. There are certain people who know what it's all about. And the only hope I've got is to keep going into the High Court.'

Again, who were you putting your trades through in the United States? Again, long pause. 'Chicago Board of Trade firms. But, you know, this was known before. The money can all be accounted for. There should be millions but I don't know where it is because everything has been seized. I haven't had control of a single thing since December 1984. I haven't got control of a single piece of paper.'

During his extradition hearing, counsel for the United States government claimed that Herbage had defrauded some 3000 clients out of more than $46 million. Herbage himself says that at the height of the Caprimex business, investors' assets had been valued at $69 million. But when you ask how much money is left, Herbage tells you, 'A lot of liquidations were paid off. Millions and millions went out. But nobody ever thinks of that fact. No, I mean, I'm just resigned to the fact that I've been fitted up and that's the end of it. And I'm going to go on fighting as long as I can.'

A former Herbage employee who worked at Sutton Manor from June 1983 to August 1984 paints a different picture. 'There was a minimal amount of trading being done while we still had our Geneva office open. But once Geneva was defunct, there was a hell of a row in early '84, once that was defunct there was no commodities trading going on at all.'

The former employee says that, with the sophisticated computer system they had installed, it was easy for Herbage simply to make up gains and losses by looking at the newspapers after the fact, then program those into the computers that tallied all the clients' accounts.

A lot of money, the former employee continues, was subsequently spent on all of those events at Sutton Manor and up in Scotland. 'He was also trying to buy his own executive jet and we lost I think $450,000 on that. He reneged on the deal. We used to lose money all over the place. The money came from Caprimex.'

According to that former employee, Herbage maintained a staff of about 140 people. There were 33 in the security force alone. Then there were gardeners and maintenance people on the two estates. There were three offices in England, one in Scotland, one in Amsterdam, a small one in the Caymans and they were just about to open one in Frankfurt.

'As long as the money kept coming in we could get away with it. We were robbing Peter to pay Paul. And with the ICF being set up, which was the new one, he was figuring we'd get enough there to pay off all the people who were screaming about Caprimex and we'd be okay.'

Asking the former employee who knew what was going on brings forth the admission, 'Quite a lot of us. You couldn't miss it after a while. It started to blow up in about February '84, and there were so many people screaming for money back and we knew we couldn't do it because the money simply wasn't there.'

But then why, if some employees knew, didn't they immediately get out? Now the former employee confesses, 'Difficult to explain. He paid us very well, although he had his 110 per cent out of us. We all had extremely good jobs with him. The guy has got a charisma that keeps you working for him. How does anybody get caught up in this type of thing?'

The Herbage extradition motion was heard in March 1986. The verdict was not what Herbage wanted to hear. The judge ruled in favour of the Americans.

After two years in Pentonville, Herbage was shipped off to Orlando, Florida, where he was charged in a US District Court with defrauding nearly 3000 investors through crooked schemes involving gold, silver and agricultural commodities.

Legally bankrupt and apparently destitute – although much of Herbage's acclaimed art collection has never been found – he managed to plea-bargain, accepting his fate on three charges of fraud in exchange for two dozen additional charges being dropped. The Justice Department reasoned that it would cost the American taxpayer hundreds of thousands of dollars to prosecute him on all the charges, as witnesses would have to be flown from Europe and housed during the trial. Anyway, the three guilty pleas would prove to be enough.

In November 1987, the 'fat man' – who had by this point shed nearly 200 pounds – was sentenced to 15 years.

Maybe the lesson to be learned, if there are any lessons at all, comes straight out of a Caprimex brochure. Herbage wrote there, 'We can prove to you "go-go" management is one thing, but constant proven profits are another. After all, it's the bottom line which matters, isn't it, in the end?'

$69 million later, it certainly is.

6

Commodities: The Fastest Way to Lose a Million

Commodities have never been for the faint-hearted.

They are even less so these days.

The world's commodity markets generally deal in foodstuffs and raw materials . . . sugar, soybean products, wheat, potatoes, jute, coffee, eggs, timber, frozen turkeys, frozen pork bellies, live pigs, live cattle, cocoa, oil, rubber, cotton, orange juice, aluminium, copper, tin, lead, nickel, zinc, silver and gold, among others.

The bulk of the world's commodity trading takes place in three cities – London, New York and Chicago – although there are dozens of smaller markets scattered over the globe where the action is just as frantic.

Yet no matter what the product is or where the market is, the game is always the same. Sellers and buyers come together with only one thing in mind . . . the sellers want the highest price while the buyers want the lowest price. It's your basic freshman-level Economics 101 supply and demand curve. More supply than demand, the price goes down. More demand than supply, the price goes up.

In practice, the market is divided into two categories . . . actuals and futures. When you deal in actuals, you're looking for eventual delivery. You buy 1000 bushels of wheat because you need 1000 bushels of wheat today, or will need them before too long. When you deal in futures, you're merely taking a position on the price of the commodity somewhere down the line. Winding up with 1000 bushels of wheat on your front door is the last thing in the world you really want.

ABOVE LEFT:
The man who coined the phrase
'minus millionaire',
Jim Slater.
© *Popperfoto*

ABOVE RIGHT:
Juan Maria Ruiz Mateos.
Spain's richest man ran up
against the Socialist
government and quickly became
one of Spain's poorest
fugitives.
© *Financial Times Photography*

RIGHT:
Property magnate, William
Stern, had the dubious honour
of finding himself in the
Guinness Book of Records as
the world's largest bankrupt.
© *Len Burt*

ABOVE FAR LEFT:
The relish and ketchup
king, H J (57 Varieties) Heinz,
was a minus millionaire
long before his name became
a household word.
© *H J Heinz Ltd*

ABOVE LEFT:
Charles Goodyear died broke
despite his world famous
patents.
© *Guy Bown, Magna Pictures*

FAR LEFT:
French businessman Jacques
Borel swore he would never
make a financial error.
He did.
© *J Haillot, Camera Press*

LEFT:
Freddie Laker went broke when
his airline fell (or was yanked) out
of the sky.
© *BBC Hulton Picture Library*

ABOVE:
35-stone Alex Herbage lived
big with other people's
money in his pockets.
*Photo taken at the 1984
Conservative Party Conference*

ABOVE:
Sir Clive Sinclair and his fated C-5 back in the days when he thought he had something to smile about.
© *Popperfoto*

LEFT:
False starts busted Henry Ford several times, although he quickly made enough in the car business to sponsor a nationwide campaign against cows. © *Popperfoto*

ABOVE:
John Z De Lorean went from cars to courtrooms and dropped
millions along the way.
© *Popperfoto*

BELOW:
The Schlumpf Brothers, Hans (l) and Fritz (r) with a few
of their friends.
© *Bueb-Reumaux Strasbourg*

ABOVE FAR LEFT:
Norah Docker, with a string of
pearls for each fortune she
went through.
© *Camera Press*

ABOVE LEFT:
Rock star Mick Fleetwood blew
his fortune on houses and toys.
© *Sam Emerson*

FAR LEFT:
Hollywood legend Doris Day
had her millions taken away.
© *Bob Willoughby, Camera Press*

LEFT:
Film director Peter
Bogdanovich lost his fortune
when Playboy Playmate
Dorothy Stratten lost her life.
© *Jerry Watson, Camera Press*

ABOVE:
Texas wildcatter,
Glenn McCarthy, then and now.
© *The Houston Post*

ABOVE LEFT:
British millionaire, Clarence Hatry, helped spark off the Wall Street Crash.
© *Popperfoto*

ABOVE:
Horatio Bottomley, MP, publisher, investor, swindler.
© *Topham*

LEFT:
An artist's rendition of the mysterious Eli Pinkas, whose picture is only slightly less difficult to find than the $300/$600 million he is purported to have had.

To understand actuals, take the example of companies like Nestlé, Hershey or Cadbury, all obvious buyers of sugar. If sales were suddenly to increase, they might find themselves in a situation where they needed to buy sugar right now. If so, they'd go through a broker and into the market to buy actuals. But let's say the chief sugar buyer for one of those companies has heard that next year's crops may not be very plentiful. A scarcity of sugar runs prices up and in turn increases his production costs. If he has to raise prices to the consumer, he risks falling sales. So he goes into the market to buy futures – sugar not yet produced – at a set price, for delivery in perhaps four, six or eight months. If the price stays the same, he's even. If the price goes up, he's ahead because the seller has agreed to let him have that future sugar at a fixed price, regardless of the actual price in the market at the time of delivery. If, however, he's got it wrong and the sugar crop is a bumper one, causing prices to fall, then he's paid too much for his sugar and he could be in trouble.

Could be . . . except he probably isn't because commodities markets are also an arena for hedging risks.

As he can buy or sell futures contracts – in other words, go short or go long – that chief sugar buyer keeps a careful eye on the market so that he can always cover his position. He might sell futures when he's buying actuals and buy futures when he's selling actuals. The bottom lines – plusses in one column and losses in the other – should just about cancel each other out. In his case, hedging helps to create a more stable business environment, which is basically what he wants.

But then there's that other aspect to futures trading. Enter now the punter.

Commodities have always had an attraction for private investors because of the speed of the game and the enormous sums that can be won while the stake is very small.

The reason the entry fee is low is because, sometime around the sixth day, God invented leverage.

Often called margin, it means the punter can buy a futures contract generally for about 10 per cent of its face value.

Again, sugar.

To oversimplify, let's say it's January and there's a 50 tonne contract for March sugar at $160 per tonne. Traded in dollars, even in London, that's $8000 per contract, or $800 down. Ten weeks later, or ten days later or even just ten minutes later, the price shoots up to $170 a ton. Each contract is now worth $8500. Someone's just made $50 per contract.

If that sounds gentle, how about the fellow holding 100 contracts. He's made a fast five grand. Or 1000 contracts. He's just made fifty grand. Of course, it's also possible that sugar can fall by $10 a ton just as quickly. When that happens, a broker gets on the phone to ask the punter to top up the account, which means he's got to cough up five grand or fifty grand, or whatever, just to stay in the game.

Adding to the excitement is the concept of pyramiding. Accounts are settled on a daily basis, meaning that the profits are put into a punter's account and the losses are called in. When someone is long, and riding a bull market, money is – in principle – going into his account every day. That money can then be used as margin on more contracts. Same thing if he's short in a bear market. So, in the case of the punter who's just made $50,000, that money can then be used to buy him another $500,000 worth of contracts, without his having to take a single penny out of his own pocket.

When it works, the world is your oyster. When it doesn't, you can't afford yesterday's cockles.

Unlike shares on the stock market, commodities are a 'zero-sum' game. That means, for every winner there is a loser. Every time someone rings up a profit, that's a loss to someone else.

Also unlike the stock exchange, commodity exchanges set down house limits. Where your General Motors or BOC shares can vary each day, depending on nothing more than the whims and fancies of the free market, there are upper and lower limits on each day's commodity trades. Take, for instance, the Chicago Board of Trade's limits on soybeans. It's 40 cents either way of the final average closing price from the previous day's trading ... that average closing being halfway between the buying and selling prices. Forty cents may not sound like a lot of money, but soybeans are traded in bushels and each contract is 5000 bushels, so 40 cents is $2000 per contract. In a really volatile market, it's not unheard of to see the limit reached in the first few minutes of trading. The fellow trying to get out might not have time. Or, the fellow trying to get in might not have time. If the market is volatile enough, the limits might be hit every morning at the opening bell for two or three or four days. Now consider the stomach palpitations of the fellow who's just not fast enough off the stick to get out while fooling around with 100 contracts.

At this point add in the strategy called arbitrage.

The price of a particular commodity quoted in London does not necessarily have to match the price of the same commodity as quoted in Chicago. It often happens that the two might differ by a few cents.

Selling soybeans at $5.25 a bushel in London and buying at $5.22 in Chicago may look like a very tiny percentage. But then, 3 cents on 5000 bushels is $150 per contract. Multiply $150 by 100 contracts and then take 10 per cent of that. A few minutes on a trans-Atlantic arbitrage phone call can be a fast $1500. The idea is that when the amounts are large enough the small percentage can add up. All you have to do is get in on the game when the percentages are running in your direction.

It goes without saying that $1500 does not a million-aire make . . . unless of course you're doing that several times a day, five days a week. Although private dealing on the floor is rare in Europe, you do find players in the US exchanges trading for their accounts. They'll take $1500 here and willingly accept an $800 loss on the next trade because where they're concerned it's strictly the bottom line that counts.

For most players, the easiest way into the game is through a broker. You pick up the phone and tell him what you want to buy or sell. Then you stay in constant touch with the broker, although you manage your own account. The problem is that the dealers on the floors are first in and first out, and you're getting news of the trends second-hand. The usual way to overcome that is through a discretionary account. In other words, you give the broker a sum of money and he plays the markets for you. What you get at the end of every month is a statement telling you where your account stands.

That may sound like the most painless method. But it requires confidence in the broker handling the account because it's ridiculously simple if he decides to fudge the papers and turn your winnings into losses for his own benefit.

Now it must be stated here, clearly and plainly, that most brokers are honest. Most brokers are content to let you take the risks while they merely take their percentage off your action. Most brokers take pride in making money for their clients.

However, there are exceptions.

In England, in the early 1980s, there was a commodity whizz-kid named Keith Hunt who as a very young man started a company called Exchange Securities and Commodities. His gimmick was to offer his commodities skills – basically his insights into the gold markets – in exchange for a percentage of his clients' profits. Between 1978 and 1982 he bragged about 93 per cent average annual returns. He also invented the 'index' bet, these days a popular pastime in the City of London, where instead of going through a broker you deal with a bookmaker. Buy gold or sell sterling, a specialized bookie takes your bet. You play for so much per point. The attraction is that winnings are treated as gains from gambling and are virtually untaxed. Winnings on a commodity flutter through a broker wind up as capital gains.

By the spring of 1983 Hunt's empire was flush. Clients' funds were reported to total £18 million, with another half million coming in through the post every week.

That was about the time some gentlemen from the Department of Trade came knocking on his front door, asking to see contract notes for certain specific trades. He was unable to produce those contract notes, or in fact any contract notes for the past six months because there hadn't been any trades for the past six months. Seems the authorities were on to him. So, knowing that discretion is always the better part of valour ... Hunt disappeared. As did £10 million.

In 1984, a group of investors in the United States alleged that some $15 million had evaporated in a sugar arbitrage scheme run by ContiCommodity Services out of their Pearl River, New York, offices. A wholly owned subsidiary of the privately owned Continental Grain empire, ContiCommodities is usually considered to be the third largest brokerage house in the United States, annually generating some $100 million or more in commission revenues. The investors said in their complaint that Conti had gone beyond the agreed trading limits and also traded cocoa. A spokesman for Conti agreed at the time that their arbitrage programme was mainly sugar but he said that it aimed at being one in which several commodities could be traded. If in fact they were trading cocoa at Pearl River, it's not surprising that they ran into difficulties. The cocoa market collapsed only a few months before the complaints began coming in.

To invest in one of Conti's discretionary accounts, punters put up a sum of money, sometimes as much as $50,000–100,000. That's all it took. No skill. No imagination. No experience necessary. Then the clients sat back and relied totally on the brokers at Pearl River to wheel and deal for them.

Before punters opened an account, Conti always insisted that they sign risk disclosure statements as mandated by the US Commodity Futures Trading Commission (CFTC), which reinforces the ultra-risky nature of the commodities game. It's like a health warning on a packet of cigarettes. The manufacturer puts it there. Then you either believe it or you don't.

Early in 1984 some Conti investors began complaining that they were not getting full and/or comprehensible statements of their accounts, that their accounts were not being closed out as soon as they had ordered them to be, that Conti executives were not returning phone calls, and that the final tallies on their accounts were, to say the least, disappointing.

Just to belabour the point of what can happen when things go wrong in the commodities game, one investor who had put $97,000 into the programme, and had been repeatedly told that he was ahead, wound up with a mere $43,000. Another, who invested $50,000, was eventually told by Conti that it had all been lost and, adding insult to injury, that he owed them an additional $17,000. A third – this one a stockbroker who perhaps should have known better – claimed that he sent Conti $85,000 and that they agreed to put most of it in Treasury Bills so that he'd earn at least Treasury Bill interest and maybe even 10–20 per cent or more on regular commodity trades. Over the next several months he drew $14,500 out of his account, believing that his statements still showed a balance of $85,000. He thought he was merely taking his interest and profits out of the account. But when he finally got someone to confirm his balance, about eight months into the programme, he was told it was now only $41,000. He closed the account then and there, ordering an emergency liquidation of any contracts. The following day his account was worth just over $17,000.

Almost bizarrely, one of the Pearl River traders, a chap named Terry Ballard, once worked for a London-based operation called SNW Commodities. The company changed its name in early 1984 to Sunshine Mining of London Ltd, a subsidiary of the Sunshine Mining Corporation, which a few years before had played a role in the Hunt brothers' attempt to corner the world's market in silver. Since then Sunshine have closed their London and New York offices, given up commodity dealing and retreated home to Texas to concentrate on the mining side of their business. Anyway, in 1981 a group of angry investors – mainly from England, Northern Ireland and West Germany – levied charges against SNW that several million pounds had gone missing from their discretionary accounts. No charges were ever brought against anyone by the police as no evidence was ever found to substantiate the charges. The official explanation was that Ballard ran into a losing streak on several sugar deals, and that was that.

Too bad it happened to Ballard more than once.

Oh well, such is the nature of the game.

In spite of what commodity traders would have the public believe, controls on discretionary commodity trading are not necessarily very strict. The CFTC in the United States has some power over commodity traders, but not nearly as much as, say, the American Dental Association has over dentists. Even the 1986 so-called 'big bang' modernization of the City of London and the self-regulatory changes that came hand in hand with it are far from adequate to protect the public from thoroughly unscrupulous traders. Again, most traders are honest. There is big money to be made in commodities but, where colossal gains are there for the taking, colossal losses are also part of the high risks involved.

It's just that it would be so very easy for any trader who really knows the business to turn scores of his clients into minus millionaires.

This is how he might do it.

The trader works for Crooked Commodities in New York and handles discretionary accounts. He has a friend, plus his own private account, at Sleazy Commodities Ltd in London, and another friend, plus another private account, at Shady Commodities in

New York. Because this is zero-rated – for every loser there is a winner – all the Crooked trader has to do is to put his own account at Sleazy on the opposite side of his clients' trades in London and have Shady do the same thing in New York. He sells on one and buys on the other. With the arbitrage numbers in his favour, his clients always lose while he's always on the winning side at both ends. It's just that simple.

Somewhat ironically, it was ContiCommodities that not long ago, while trying to lure new punters into the game, ran a series of newspaper ads listing the rules of the game.

Among them are basics such as:

- Don't trade on rumours.
- Standing aside is a position.
- Don't overstay a good market – you're bound to overstay a bad one also.
- Most people would rather own something (go long) than owe something (go short); it's human nature. The markets aren't human. So you should learn that markets can (and should) be traded from the short side.

And, probably the best of all:

- Recognize that fear, greed, ignorance, generosity, stupidity, impatience, self-delusion, etc., can cost you a lot more money than the market(s) going against you, and that there is no fundamental method to recognize these factors.

The world is, perhaps understandably, awash with commodity minus millionaires.

And has been for centuries.

There was gold in the California hills and in 1849 all of America heard the cry, 'Eureka'.

Like tens of thousands of others, Isaac Friedlander went west in search of instant wealth.

He was a very large young man – they say he stood 6 foot 6 and weighed nearly 300 pounds – who was born in Germany, who came to the States as a child and who was raised in South Carolina. He was also obviously a very bright young man, because as soon as he arrived in San Francisco he assessed the situation and realized – much the way Rowland Macy did – that, with everyone else panning for gold, there was probably a lot of money to be made in areas otherwise overlooked. One of them turned out to be bread. Miners coming in from the hills with gold dust to spend didn't seem to worry much that prices were high. So Friedlander manoeuvred himself into business as a middle man, slowly but surely tightening his grip on the market at every turn.

In 1852, having cornered the supply of flour into San Francisco, he was able to force bread prices high enough that he could now lay claim to being a millionaire.

To consolidate his position . . . or at least he thought he was consolidating his position . . . he built flour mills and grain storage silos. As the suddenly booming grain trade opened between California and the United Kingdom, he became an exporter and a trader and a producer. He cut himself in at almost every step of the way from farm to ship. And when he found that the shipping business from San Francisco to England was less than satisfactory to meet his own needs, he also became a shipping magnate. In fact, he soon had such a strong position in grain shipping that he could dictate freight rates. The moment any competition appeared on the scene, he had no problem bidding them out of business.

But all his chips were riding on grain.

And one day in 1877 grain fell out of bed.

Friedlander found himself caught in a squeeze. He had too many eggs in one basket. Prices went against him. He was sitting on too much grain at too high a cost. He was over-committed. His ships were over-chartered. The grain market stopped and everything else he controlled ground to a halt with it. The pyramid toppled. And, just like that, Friedlander went bust.

Exactly 20 years later, another commodity wheeler-dealer made a name for himself by blowing a fortune.

Joe Leiter was the 28-year-old son of Levi Leiter, co-founder of Chicago's Marshall Field department store, and he had it in his head to corner the country's wheat market.

That autumn, with $1 million of his old man's money, he dived in head first. It looked to him like a basic enough game to play. $1 million in real money could get you $10 million in futures. All he'd have to do was hold on to the contracts until he forced prices up, then sell. How complicated could that be? So for the next three or four months he bought every wheat future he could.

Right off the bat his timing seemed to be perfect. Europe and India reported poor crops. Wheat prices on Chicago's Board of Trade couldn't help but rise. Luck was on his side. He kept right on buying.

He was betting on winter.

And anyone who has ever been to Chicago in winter knows first hand that's the best bet in town.

Chicago in winter is cold. Very very cold. And windy too. The wind comes off Lake Michigan . . . the local black slang for the wind is 'The Hawk' . . . and if you're walking along the lake shore you'd better hold on to the rails they've put there because the wind is fierce enough to blow you into the water. Then there's the snow. Mountains of it. The cold and the wind freeze the snow, crippling Chicago by turning it into a gigantic block of ice. These days road-clearing equipment is fairly sophisticated, and yet when there's a storm everything still shuts down. Imagine what it must have been like before the turn of the century.

During the first few months of 1898 it looked as if Leiter couldn't lose. The Great Lakes froze over, as usual. Barge traffic was stuck until spring, as usual. Wheat couldn't possibly get to Chicago till spring, as usual.

Prices skyrocketed, as usual.

But, once again, where commodities are concerned, one man's profit is another man's loss. And in this case, Leiter's profit was coming directly out of Philip Armour's pocket.

The Armour family business was meat, meat packing and cereals. It was then – as it is today – a very important business, with important commitments. Armour could see what the weather was doing to wheat prices and knew how costly it would be if he just sat in his office waiting for the thaw. So he aimed to at least cut his losses. Whatever wheat he could get was better than nothing. He ordered the captains of vessels carrying grain to dynamite their way through the frozen lakes. He also offered those captains incentives to make it worth their while.

Each ship that got to Chicago took money back from Leiter.

The price of wheat dropped to under $1 a bushel. Leiter forced it back up to $1.83. Then suddenly, out of the blue, the government announced that the spring wheat crop would come in at record levels. Leiter should have listened to Meyer Rothschild's famous advice, 'You can never go broke by taking a profit.' He had been way ahead. Now, wheat prices tumbled. Leiter was left holding huge amounts of overpriced wheat. He dropped a cool $10 million.

There is, by the way, a nice little PS to this story. Leiter's sister Mary married a Briton named George Curzon who later became Lord Curzon, Viceroy of India. In those days it was expected that the Viceroy would have the private means to support himself. Mary counted on family money to see them through. But Joe had blown away a huge chunk of it and very little was left. Curzon almost had to refuse the post.

Another grain magnate who took a very heavy fall was Edward W. Cook.

Called Ned by just about everybody, he was a cotton broker from Memphis, Tennessee, who worked for his father at Cook & Co. until the early 1960s when he managed to convince his old man that it was time to steer the company away from cotton and into soybeans. His first venture was the purchase of 12,000 bushels, on which he rather clumsily produced a $14,000 loss. Just shy of his fortieth birthday, he dug in his heels and scrounged around to learn the grain trade. When his father retired from the business in 1967, Cook put $12 million worth of chips on the table to build a grain elevator along the Mississippi about 30 miles north of New Orleans. It strained his cash flow, being a £10 million company with a $12 million grain elevator, so he went looking for a way to solve the problem.

He found it right there in Memphis and it was called E.L. Bruce and Co.

Notorious in its own right, E.L. Bruce was in hardwood flooring. Less than ten years before, its shares had been sitting at a cosy $17 per share, when, just like that, the shares took off. It was the spring of 1958

and almost overnight they reached the dizzy heights of
$190. On one particular day they actually increased a
full $100. It came about as the result of a take-over
battle which had inadvertently created a near-corner
in the shares. Almost like Stutz and Piggly Wiggly
more than half a century before, but not quite.
Anyway, within four or five months the shares quietened down and they stayed quiet until 1962 when E.L.
Bruce again hit the headlines. It seemed that the man
who controlled the company, a fellow named E. M.
Gilbert, had decided rather quickly on a Brazilian
holiday. And just to tide him over while sunning
himself in Ipanema, he took $2 million with him.

When Cook came along and looked at E. L. Bruce,
the company was on its uppers but still worth three
times as much as Cook & Co. Best of all, it had some
cash. He therefore arranged a complicated take-over
which created Cook Industries, a company he took
public in 1969.

The first year they lost money. The next year they
made some . . . not a lot, but some. The year after that
they broke even. Unorthodox in style, Cook once called
four executives into a meeting, each of them a candidate for the same promotion, and asked them to write
a memo recommending one of the other three for the
job. Yet he was heavy on Southern charm and in 1972
he pulled off a coup. He made a sale to the Russians
that totalled $225 million and included up to 40
million bushels of soybeans. The Soviets had bought
grain from the Americans before, but this was the first
time ever that they had purchased soybeans. Although
Cook's cut of the deal was only somewhere between 1
and 2 per cent, it was the deal itself that put him on
the map.

Cook Industries' earnings shot up from $3.6 million in 1972 to $46.2 million in 1974.

For a while he could do no wrong.

Soybean prices rose from $3.40 a bushel to $13 a bushel in a few months. One estimate is that Cook made $10 million on that alone. At the same time he had contracted for elevator capacity when rent was in the neighbourhood of 10 cents a bushel. He had it to sell when rents leapt up to 75 cents a bushel.

His pre-tax profits headed towards the $75 million mark.

Then the market turned sour.

Unlike Friedlander and Leiter, Cook had diversified into other fields, including insurance. But, at exactly the worst possible moment, a whole lot of grain exporters got caught with their thumbs on the scales. It's never been proved that Cook himself was involved, but Cook Industries was. So was Conti. So was Bunge. It turns out to have been standard practice for the elevator operators to help their companies cut costs by short-changing the customers and also at times misgrading shipments. It seems instructions had been given to load ships bound for modern ports to within one-eighth of 1 per cent of the manifested amount. A negligible percentage but it would of course add up handsomely over several shipments. On cargoes destined for Third World ports, where weighing equipment wasn't very accurate, grain elevator operators were skimming off as much as 1.5 per cent. The United States government lowered the boom on all of the heavy-thumbed exporters. The companies concerned pleaded 'no contest' and took their bruises. Some of the culprits who had been actively engaged in these thefts were indicted and later sent to jail.

That's when the lawyers swooped in for the kill. Law

suits were filed against Cook Industries, including one for $24 million by the US government. Shares fell to less than half their book value. Trading losses spilled all over the books ... they totalled $27 million in just three quarters. Cook was forced to sell assets, including E.L. Bruce. In a desperate attempt to recoup, he turned to the futures markets. He went short. And he lost. So he went short again. And he lost again. He couldn't catch up. The heavier he played, the heavier he lost. When the dice aren't with you, there's nothing to do but quit playing. But he didn't. He kept on playing. No matter how short he went, he merely got deeper and deeper. No one really knows how many millions he dropped in futures but it was enough so that after a while there was clearly no way out.

In June 1977 Ned Cook asked that his shares be suspended from trading. He'd lost a king's ransom, and bankrupted the company.

The night that news was announced, a rather bizarre telephone conversation is said to have taken place in Dallas. A reporter supposedly phoned millionaire Bunker Hunt to ask what he thought about Ned Cook having gone belly up. Hunt wanted to know if his comment was to be on the record or off. The reporter said on. Hunt answered, 'I think Ned Cook's a fine gentleman, and I'm real sorry this has happened to him.' Then the reporter asked what Hunt thought, off the record. This time Hunt is supposed to have replied, 'Tough shit.'

But then it wasn't too long before a lot of other folk were saying that about Mr Hunt.

In the early 1970s, before the Arabs pulled the plug on the world's oil prices, silver was gently riding along at around $2 an ounce. As silver is a primary component of both the electronics and photographic industries, Bunker and his brother Herbert thought it might be both amusing and highly profitable if they could quietly corner the market.

Their father, H.L., was an oil speculator and a gambler and almost undeniably the model for *Dallas's* Jock Ewing. The main difference was that old H.L. was richer than any Ewing could ever hope to be. Probably one helluva lot meaner, too. He died a billionaire in 1974 ... at a time in America when there just weren't a lot of billionaires. Twelve years later, the list of the five wealthiest people in the United States – all of them in the billionaire category – included two Hunts. Adding in the next five Hunts gave just seven of H.L.'s fifteen children a combined asset value of over $3 billion.

Just before H.L. died, Bunker and Herbert began buying silver. It's said that Bunker found a book called *Silver Profits in the Seventies*, and that was the basis of his interest. That silver would some day become more valuable than gold – as the book predicted – certainly couldn't have deterred Bunker and Herbert, no matter who or what put the idea into their heads.

From $2.90 an ounce in December 1973 – with the Hunts holding contracts for some 35 million ounces – the price started climbing. Less than two months later it had reached $6.70 an ounce. The Hunt brothers thought they had, rather effortlessly, managed their squeeze. What they didn't know at the time was that the Mexican government was sitting on 50 million ounces of silver, all purchased at under $2. From Mexico City the world at $6.70 looked rosy indeed, so they decided it was time to take their profit. The Mexicans flooded the market. The price of silver tumbled back to about $4.

Having got their feet wet ... and their taste buds

activated . . . the brothers spent the next four years quietly acquiring silver.

During some of those years they were more active than in other years.

They also still dabbled in other commodities and there was a period when they turned their attention to soybeans.

But by 1979 the Hunts – together with the Royal Family of Saudi Arabia as their partners, and brokers like Conti and Sunshine on their side – owned or controlled, through various companies, several hundred millions of ounces of silver.

The price stood at around $6 an ounce when they made their big move.

Now they jumped in head first, going all the way, putting constant pressure on the markets. By October the consortium actually owned more than 25 per cent of all the silver shares on the New York Commodity Exchange and five out of every eight silver shares at the Chicago Board of Trade.

By the end of 1979, they had forced the price of silver up to $19 an ounce. They had more than tripled their money. But that wasn't enough. So they borrowed a staggering $1.3 billion between February and March 1980 – once said to be nearly 9 per cent of the entire total borrowing in America over that 60-day period – just to sink into silver, and kicked the price as high as $49.

Because severe price fluctuations always worry the men who make markets, a meeting was held at the New York Commodity Exchange to see what could be done to help bring some stability back to the market.

Throughout the Hunts' buying sprees, the margin calls were as little as $1000 per contract. Each silver contract represents 5000 ounces. At $2 an ounce, $1000 down is 10 per cent. At $49 an ounce, it's ludicrous. So they decided to raise the margin requirements. The Board of Governors saw this as a drastic situation and, even though they proceeded slowly in the beginning, the margin requirement eventually went as high as $60,000 before they instituted a 'liquidation only' rule. That meant no new contracts could be taken up. The only business on the floor could be the closing out of contracts already held. And that effectively put the brakes on silver.

It also effectively put a squeeze on the Hunts.

Silver prices began falling.

As prices slipped, cash calls came in to the Hunts. They had been buying silver with borrowed money, then using that silver to secure more borrowings. Now, because their collateral was diminishing in value, the banks wanted more collateral. On 25 March, the New York investment house Bache Halsey Stuart Shields sent the Hunts a call for $135 million.

But the Hunts couldn't meet it.

Bache ordered the sale of Hunt silver reserves to satisfy their commitment.

The floodgates opened. Silver poured onto the market. And prices disintegrated.

The Hunts were sitting on thousands of long contracts. Simply to meet those debts they were forced to turn over 8.5 million ounces of silver, plus oil and gas assets, for a total of nearly $400 million.

Facing ruin, Bunker and Herbert now decided to play hardball. They went to Washington to meet with government officials to try to arrange a loan that would save their own bank accounts. Such things are, of course, not usually done. Just try ringing the Treasury and asking them to come up with a few coins to tide you over because you happen to be a little skint this month. That's basically what Bunker and Herbert were doing. Except in exchange for a handout they were willing to be nice guys. First, they said, we're still sitting on 63 million ounces of silver and if we dump all of that onto the market at one time, sheer havoc will be the result. Second, they said, here's a list of major American banks that will absolutely go under if we don't pay our debts with your help.

The United States government came up with an unprecedented long-term $1 billion loan to keep the Hunt family afloat.

Some lessons come expensive to everybody involved.

Others cost even more.

In October 1985, an organization that most people had never heard of ran out of money.

It was called the International Tin Council.

Who? That's right.

Made up of 22 member countries, they were a kind of buying and selling cartel whose only purpose in life was to keep tin prices high. And during the 1970s they were very successful doing just that.

When the 1980s came along and tin production far surpassed tin demand, they came into the market to support those over-inflated prices. They maintained what is known as 'buffer stock' . . . supplies of tin they could add to quickly if prices were falling, and then unload slowly enough so as not to disrupt the market.

Dealers on the London Metal Exchange – the world's primary tin market – knew that the ITC was owned and managed by the member governments (including Great Britain), and therefore felt secure about tin prices. After all, everyone knows . . . or at least used to believe . . . governments do not renege on their debt responsibilities. And certainly, even if some of those funny Third World tin countries try to renege, HM government does not renege on its responsibilities.

So, with 22 member governments holding the foundations, the LME went happily about their business, being the stage for trading in tin. If prices slipped, dealers knew they could always flog the ITC some long contracts and there would be nothing to worry about.

Then came October 1985.

That's when the ITC came clean. They were sitting on £900 million worth of debts to banks and LME dealers, and they couldn't pay.

But the ITC is just a grouping of governments, the LME dealers argued, so the governments will pay.

Not quite.

All sorts of proposals were put forward. But none of them could work because some of the governments involved said no, too bad, sorry, but we're not paying.

A contract is a contract, the dealers argued. Your word is your bond.

Maybe it is, the governments shrugged, maybe it's not. No soap. No money. Bye.

The average price when tin trading was suspended in October was just over £8000 per tonne. A settlement price was finally agreed by the LME to resume trading in March 1986 at £6250. And that was a tough pill to swallow because right there, from one price to another, through no direct fault of anyone at the LME, 13 LME members were being asked to take a healthy £140 million loss. A further 11 non-LME trading companies had to make provisions for another £40 million loss.

And those figures were calculated at the £6250 price. Commodities being what they are, as soon as the settlement price was announced and trading began again, tin prices dropped to below £4800 per tonne.

Looks like where commodities are concerned you sometimes can't even trust governments.

Carlos Bianchi left Italy around the turn of the century and came to the New World where he changed Carlos into Charles and Bianchi into Ponsi.

By the end of the First World War Ponsi was called Ponzi, had already done time in a Montreal jail for cheque forging, was now living in Boston and had just discovered the wonderful world of international postal reply coupons.

Still in existence today, the coupons are a way of paying postage in one country with the currency of another. It's the international answer to self-addressed stamped envelopes. Because someone in Germany can't buy stamps to pay for postage from his correspondent in France, he buys a coupon worth a fixed amount at his local post office, and sends it to his correspondent, who exchanges it at his local post office for the return postage.

What Ponzi discovered, sometime around 1919–20, was that an international postal reply coupon he received from Italy was actually purchased in Spain. Because these coupons are priced at fixed rates of exchange between the governments involved while currency rates are allowed to fluctuate, this particular coupon had cost only around 15 per cent of the actual value of the US stamps Ponzi could get by exchanging it. In other words, he could make more than six times his money by going into the international postal reply coupon business.

Like so many con men who think that a legitimate-sounding company name breeds confidence, the operation he formed for his coupon game was called The Securities and Exchange Company ... the 'S.E.C.'.

His idea was to ask investors to give him the money to buy international postal reply coupons at exchange rate discounts such as in Spain. He would then exchange them by the thousand for stamps in the States which could be wholesaled to businesses with large mail requirements, and in return he could promise his investors 40 per cent profit in just 90 days.

Money came in, slowly at first, but enough to get the scheme off the ground. Within a couple of months he upped the promise of 40 per cent profits to 100 per cent.

Now he couldn't count the money fast enough.

On good days, several hundred thousand dollars came into the S.E.C. He became so rich, so quickly, that within six months he not only purchased a large stake in the Hanover Trust Company – today known as the Manufacturers Hanover Trust Co. – but had also taken over the Boston import–export firm of J.R. Poole & Co.

However, at the end of July 1920, a local newspaper started asking questions. They claimed that Ponzi couldn't be buying as many international postal reply coupons as he said he was because that many hadn't been sold or turned in. The investors who now queued at his front door wanting their money back were given Hanover Trust cheques for the amount of their investment plus interest. Ponzi assured them that all was well. He eventually confessed that the postal coupon story was really just a red herring to protect his actual scheme.

By August the newspapers were saying that Ponzi was actually millions of dollars in debt. Ponzi's house of cards was starting to shake.

Through it all Ponzi maintained a calm and assuring exterior. He filed a $5 million suit against the *Boston*

Post for libel. In the same breath he announced a $100 million international investment syndicate.

Then the Massachusetts State Banking Commission closed down the Hanover Trust for clearing Ponzi's cheques. The Boston papers printed stories of Ponzi's earlier scuffles with the Canadian authorities. Auditors fine-tooth-combed the S.E.C.'s books only to discover that legitimate transactions were negligible . . . a grand total of $30 . . . and that Ponzi never bothered at all with his international postal reply coupon idea. Ironically, that probably would have worked.

The net result was that Ponzi was a minus millionaire to the tune of about $3 million.

He went to jail for a few years in Massachusetts, was allowed out on parole, skipped and headed for Florida, and set up a real estate scheme, which earned him another trip to prison. In 1930–31 he was deported to Italy, made his way to Brazil and eventually died there, penniless.

But his legacy is the 'Ponzi Scheme'.

The ghost of Ponzi lives on.

Sometimes it comes through the post looking like a chain letter.

'Dear Friend,
This chain letter really works. For the past 25 years, literally tens of thousands of people like yourself have made a small fortune simply by investing £1 and keeping the letter alive. All you have to do is photocopy this letter ten times. Put your own name on the bottom of the list of names, send merely £1 to the first name on the list, and then mail this letter to ten friends. Each of those friends will in turn send the letter to ten friends, while adding their name to the bottom of the list and sending £1 to the name on the top of the list. Within only a few weeks, you should receive in the post no less than £100,000. It really does work. So please don't break the chain.'

At the bottom of the letter are five names. You cross off the top one and add yours to the bottom, meaning that your name gets sent to 10 people. Those ten then send out ten copies of the letter, which puts your name, number 4 on the list, to 100. Then it's times 10 again, times 10 again and when you hit number 1 there should be 100,000 copies of the letter in circulation.

The problem with chain letters is that too many people break the chain and the names on the bottom more often than not wind up with nothing. Which is why in some places, such as the United States, such Ponzis constitute the federal offence of mail fraud.

One way around that, changing the face of Ponzi's ghost, is through a distributorship.

One fellow calling himself a mink oil distributor has the right to sell ten distributorships. Those ten sell ten more. Nowhere along the line does anyone actually have to sell any mink oil ... whatever mink oil is or does ... although every 'distributor' is supplied with mink oil sales promotion booklets and testimonials for the product. The product might even exist should one of the 'distributors' actually ever sell any of the stuff, presumably to someone with a squeaky mink. But the gimmick is obvious. As long as the chain keeps going, the folks at the top of the list make money. It's when no one else is left to buy a mink oil distributorship that the losers sit around wondering why such a wonderful investment isn't showing any returns.

Because the first theory of investment says that return is in direct relation to risk, and because commodities offer such a high return, there are always people willing to take big risks for the big kill at the end.

And that's why the commodities game is a perfect one for variations on the Ponzi.

As P.T. Barnum said, there's a sucker born every minute.

In the early 1970s, Ponzi's ghost appeared in the form of Harold Goldstein, late of Goldstein, Samuelson Inc., of Wilshire Boulevard, Beverly Hills, California . . . a neighbourhood where you find only banks, brokers and psychiatrists.

Billed as America's best commodity options trader, the sole owner of Goldstein, Samuelson Inc. offered his clients a spectacular return on their investments. And in southern California, where there is plenty of money ripe for the picking, Goldstein had no problem lining up clients. On good days as much as $800,000 to $1 million came in with the morning mail.

Nicely enough for Goldstein, there wasn't any Mr Samuelson, or anyone else, to share it with.

His records revealed that in 1972 he sold $42 million in options, and nearly that much again in just the first two months of 1973. The trouble was, most of the options were phoney.

Goldstein became a multimillionaire with an original and very believable commodities gimmick. Having heard all the scare stories that are forever being told about commodity futures and understanding that many people are always wary of the high risks that are an integral part of the game, he came up with a 'foolproof' scheme. He offered his clients the possibility of insuring their investment against a loss. His product was the perfect no-lose investment. And his sales pitch was frank and to the point: at the very best you make big money on your investment, or, at the very worst, you come out even by having hedged it with insurance.

On paper it seemed almost too good to be true.

With so much money coming in every day, Goldstein

didn't have to worry about paying Paul because he could always rob Peter. After his arrest he admitted that at least in the beginning he was indeed doing some trading. 'But when you're doing more silver trading than the exchanges, and more coffee than the coffee exchange, you rely on new premiums to pay off the old ones.'

As for the insurance bonds on each contract ... surprise, surprise ... they never existed.

He milked Beverly Hills and 75 other communities across the country through his offices there of some $76 million.

All of this before his twenty-ninth birthday.

In 1973, facing $50 million in law suits, he managed a plea bargain on nothing more hefty than three counts of mail fraud. It brought a 15-year sentence – as opposed to the possibility of 80 years in jail as the Grand Jury had originally suggested – plus a $3000 fine. The 15-year sentence was astonishingly reduced to 18 months. He served his time, and within a year was in the dock again, this time for a gold fraud scheme.

Great minds think alike and while the enterprising Harold Goldstein was doing his thing in Beverly Hills, 100 miles to the south in San Diego, the party was still going strong.

The city of San Diego is said to have the best weather of any spot in the United States. Depending on how you count the population, San Diego sometimes shows up as the nation's eighth largest city. It is first and foremost a Navy town. The huge base dominates San Diego socially, economically and in every other conceivable way. But it is also a thriving metropolitan area with splendid beaches and probably boasts more golf courses per capita than any other area of the country.

Jerry Dominelli was 38 years old when he showed up on the San Diego scene in 1979. He had spent the previous years bouncing around brokers' offices leaving only a mediocre impression of himself.

Nancy Hoover was three years older, a broker with Bache in their La Jolla office, where she and Dominelli met, fell in love, started having an affair, arranged her divorce, and went into business together.

He took offices in the basement of a Mexican restaurant, while she stayed at Bache to trade for his clients.

They called themselves commodity advisers.

They called the firm J. David & Co.

To get clients to invest in discretionary accounts, Dominelli began advertising his skills. He claimed that, while trading in 1977, he had turned $5000 into over $50,000. The following year, he bragged, a $10,000 pot was turned into $84,000. The year after that $15,000 became $39,000.

Little by little some clients came in and he had his first few accounts. But nothing too spectacular took place until Dominelli happened to meet an author who was in the midst of doing a book on commodities. Dominelli bragged about his track record, the author believed him and mentioned the Dominelli success story – albeit not his name – in the book.

Suddenly everything started booming.

Dominelli became one of those 'best kept secrets'.

People with money to invest found out who he was and invested it with him.

Expansion came like an explosion.

Money poured in. Millions were spent on offices, homes and cars. The fellow who wrote the book calling Dominelli a genius wound up on J. David's board.

Dominelli created subsidiaries and established a network of freelance sales people who shilled for him, taking their own large commissions off the top.

Claims of uninterrupted 40–50 per cent profits now ranged over a three-year period.

By 1982 Dominelli turned his sights on London.

The J. David Banking Corporation opened an office in Plantation House on Fenchurch Street, in the heart of the City. With their perfect address, Dominelli planned to funnel money from British investors who wanted to jump on the bandwagon of his perfect three-year profit record. But now the Bank of England smelled a rat. They've got no sense of humour along Threadneedle Street when companies that are not banks begin calling themselves banks. They issued a cease and desist order, telling Dominelli in no uncertain terms that J. David could not use any word in their title to suggest that they were a bank or a trust company.

Without missing a beat, he turned his act into a company called J. David International.

Under that umbrella he applied for membership of the London International Financial Futures Exchange. And LIFFE turned him down. That was odd because Dominelli applied at a time when LIFFE was actively soliciting members. Undeterred, within a year he tried to buy a seat for £65,000. And for the second time LIFFE said no. Under their by-laws, LIFFE has the right to deny membership if they have sufficient reason to believe that the prospective candidate lacks experience, a sound reputation or sufficient funds. Well, they've never said why they twice black-balled Dominelli, but there is a very strong possibility that a call came from the Bank of England saying forget this guy. Such intervention, while not unheard of, is however only usually reserved for extreme cases.

This turned out to be one of those.

By 1984 the good days were over. It happened the way it always happens with these kinds of frauds. In spite of his claims and shiny brochures that promised big profits from high-risk funds in world currencies, he hadn't actually been doing any trading. He was just spending the money on his own lifestyle, and reluctantly paying whichever clients put the squeeze on him to close their accounts. When money stopped coming in there was nothing left to pay out. Cheques started bouncing. Word spread that Dominelli was in trouble. There was a run on his resources. Creditors wanted their money back. He couldn't pay them. The cops arrived to close him down.

Jerry J. David Dominelli, a man who once had up to $60 million of other people's money to play with, went broke.

On 21 March 1985 he pleaded guilty to two counts of mail fraud, one count of bankruptcy fraud and one count of tax evasion owing to his failure to pay $10.7 million in back taxes.

7

Glenn McCarthy – King of the Wildcatters

Everyone has their shining hour.

For Glenn McCarthy it was 1949.

An earthy, hard-drinking six footer with wavy black hair and a thin moustache, he looked a little bit like Errol Flynn.

Or, maybe, like the way riverboat gamblers used to be in Hollywood films circa 1935.

He was just 41 years old and he had $60 million to his name and he was known throughout Texas as 'King of the Wildcatters'.

Now he wanted to become the hotel king as well.

He had chosen a site a few miles from downtown Houston. Everybody said he was crazy building that far out of town. But he was crazy like a fox because he knew that one day the town would come out to him.

Ground had been broken on St Patrick's Day, 1946. Glenn McCarthy and actor Pat O'Brien did the honours.

Now it's St Patrick's Day three years later.

The place is called The Shamrock.

'One of the most lavish buildings the hotel business has ever seen,' says *Life* magazine.

Eighteen storeys high. 1176 rooms. Designed so that there would be six corner rooms on every floor because lots of people like corner rooms.

It will change the face of Houston for ever.

Because he's so especially proud of his Irish heritage, McCarthy decorates The Shamrock in 63 shades of green. There are also green floodlights to shine across

the outside of the hotel at night and green ink in the
pens at the registration desk.

Because this is The Shamrock, and because The
Shamrock is McCarthy, everything has to be just
perfect. He wants elaborate lawns to cover the
grounds, so when a local company refuses to sell him
enough grass because it's all the grass they own he
buys the company. He wants his guests to feel the
height of comfort, so he puts air conditioners in every
room – a rare treat – and includes piped music as well.
Televisions are also installed in every room . . . and
this long before they're a common fixture in every
house. Afternoon tea is served in the lobby where a
string quartet plays softly in the corner. The restaurant features 'French cooking', which means filet
mignon that costs $11 . . . this at a time when many
restaurants have a fixed-price filet with all the trim-
mings for $2.50. The 165 foot swimming pool is lyre
shaped. The ballroom can easily hold 1500. The lobby
is panelled with 22,000 feet of Brazilian mahogany.
The columns are imported rose travertine marble. No
one ever has to knock on an apartment door because
every apartment door has an electric chime. The bath
towels – 52" x 30" – are said to be the biggest bath
towels in the world. And the nightclub brings in name
entertainers such as Edgar Bergen – Candice's father
– and Dorothy Lamour – of 'On the Road' fame.

Downstairs there is McCarthy's very private Cork
Club, aiming to be one of the most exclusive clubs in
the country. Kind of like an early version of that place
where J.R. Ewing keeps bumping into Cliff Barnes at
lunchtime when they're both there to swing a deal or
just to drink bourbon and branch water. Except the
Cork Club, named for County Cork and not what gets
pulled out of a champagne bottle, costs $500 to join . . .

an astronomical fee . . . and $15 a month. Unheard of. And by 1950 the membership fee and the monthly dues will be doubled and the membership list will pass the 800 mark.

Upstairs, rooms start at $6 a night and the big suites are $45.

Even New York's Waldorf Astoria is cheaper.

To bring his hotel into the world with style, McCarthy foots a $1.5 million bill for an opening night party. He's covered the lobby in 2500 shamrocks brought in expressly for the night from Ireland. Filling out the crowds of local and state politicians, dignitaries, business luminaries, society ladies and general freeloaders are a horde of movie stars, flown in on two private Constellations and brought by rail on the Super Chief. MacDonald Carey. Ellen Drew. Van Heflin. Charles Coburn. J. Carrol Naish. Ward Bond. Andy Devine. All big names. And, of course, Errol Flynn. And, of course, Dorothy Lamour. And, of course, Pat O'Brien.

The next morning, with many of the 1400 notables still partying, the festivities will be described in the press as, 'The most exciting features of a subway rush, Halloween in a mad house and a circus fire.'

Thirty-seven years later that night is remembered by an older generation as the greatest party in Houston's history.

But now The Shamrock is no more.

And with it the legacy of Glenn McCarthy has faded into the legend of another time.

Peter Aloysius MacCarthy of County Cork married a woman named Lane, also from County Cork, and with promises of a better life and streets paved with gold they left Ireland to sail to the New World.

Somewhere between the west coast of Erin and downtown Cincinnati MacCarthy became McCarthy.

Eight children followed. One of them moved to Texas to work in the oil fields. He was William Peter Aloysius McCarthy. He married a girl of English ancestry named Leah Townsend, and the two of them brought Glenn Herbert McCarthy into the world on Christmas Day, 1907, in the then small town of Beaumont, on the road that went two miles further along to the oil field known as Spindletop.

That was the most famous oil field in Texas because it was the first oil field in Texas.

It's where the Texas oil boom was born.

On 10 January 1901, an Australian named Tony Lucas brought in a well after four dry holes. He said he was an engineer. But then he also told people he had been a captain in the Aussie Navy. Maybe he was. Maybe he wasn't. Nobody would have cared. It didn't matter because in the end he turned out to be a wildcatter who believed so strongly that there was oil under the huge salt dome near Beaumont that nothing in the world could discourage him. All those previous dusters at Spindletop were warning enough for most men. Anyone with half a pack mule's sense would have seen that there was nothing but sun-baked mud and, under that, quicksand. But Lucas obviously didn't have half a pack mule's sense, so he set up again and drilled with new equipment until he reached 1020 feet. And this time the well erupted. First there was mud shooting everywhere. Then there was water. Then there was gas. And then there was a geyser of thick black oil. And within a few weeks Beaumont was a sea of tents and shacks, wildcatters and their roughnecks, rushing to stake their claims for $1 million an acre on the salt dome, in the oil boom at Spindletop that would make Texas famous.

McCarthy's father sometimes worked in the field. He crewed and roughnecked. McCarthy sold water there when he was a kid. And sometimes he went to watch his father work. But when the work dried up the old man took his family out of Beaumont and eventually they settled in Houston.

A strapping kid, who played football on several school teams and was never one to miss out on a good fight, he always had his eyes open for a good business deal or at least an odds-on chance at a good bet.

As a boy of 14, with only a nickel in his pocket and two hamburgers in front of him that cost a total of 10 cents, he bet his nickel with the soda jerk, double or nothing, heads or tails, and won himself the second hamburger. Once when he wanted to rent a small office and the landlord told him the price, he explained that he could only afford half that. The landlord shrugged because, obviously, that wasn't his problem. McCarthy then somehow convinced the man to allow him to rent the office for half the asking price on the promise that he would use only half of the room. Another time when he and his young bride were down to their last $2.65 he put $2 on a long-shot nag that actually did come in and fed them for several months. On still another occasion, he got into a crap game with some 'good ol' boys' in Galveston and walked out with $28,000 of their money. His response to such good fortune was, 'Well, I needed it.'

For a while he called himself a plumber. But he didn't know a lot about plumbing, so he'd find a good job then sub-contract it to someone who really knew the plumbing business, and keep a percentage of the deal. While he was at school he ran a dry cleaners, where he nearly went broke because the shop was at the back of a building and no one could ever find it. One day a fellow walked in . . . it was one of the few days when McCarthy actually had a lot of dry cleaning to do . . . and the fellow said he'd be interested in buying a busy going concern, so right then and there McCarthy sold out and made a profit. After he dropped out of school to get married, he worked as a petrol pump attendant for a while, running a station for the Sinclair Oil Company, impressing the management by the way he could make money. One day someone assured him a cold winter was on the way. The almanacs agreed so he stocked up on anti-freeze. When the bad weather hit, his was the only station for miles with anti-freeze. And the line of customers went all the way down the block.

He won scholarships to play football and thought about trying to make the pro's, but an injury ruined those chances. Then he went to medical school for a while because he thought he wanted to be a doctor. But he was born on the road that went up through Spindletop, with the sound of pumps ringing in his ears day and night, and oil was in his blood.

So he parlayed one of the petrol stations into two, and after a time he sold the second one to buy himself his first stake as a wildcatter.

With a drilling rig held together by string, bailer twine and a prayer, he dug into a claim in Hardin County, not far from Beaumont, and stuck it out for six back-breaking months.

It was dry.

Then he rented a better rig and staked another claim in Montgomery County's Conroe Field, due north of Houston.

It was his second duster.

He followed that with another dry hole at Conroe.

Now it was 1933. He was 26 years old. It was the height of the Depression. Along the way he had acquired a young family to support. Most wildcatters, he knew, died broke. Most young men would have given up a long time ago and hurried back into the anti-freeze business.

But that's not what Glenn McCarthy is made of.

'Naturally you get discouraged but you keep on going. I never considered quitting. Wildcatting is a series of ups and downs. It's just plain hard work to keep the business going. Any chance you have is a possible break of some kind. I never thought about not succeeding.'

He went after his fourth well, this one east of Houston, at Big Creek in Chambers County.

And this one came in.

'I remember that first hit. Of course I do. You might think I thought it was a great feeling. Well, in a way it was. But it was more a feeling of relief.'

He hit for $700,000 and the first thing he did was order a builder to start work on a $700,000 house. Then he bought a million dollars' worth of new equipment on credit and borrowed another $700,000 to sink into new leases. And now he was in the oil business.

That's when disaster struck.

One well blew out. The fire took several days to get under control and in the end cost him a quarter of a million dollars.

At another site a derrick collapsed.

He couldn't pay his crews and had to beg them to stay with him. He hired his father and his brother because they'd work for nothing. Then there were days when the sheriff would come out to the rig, with a warrant for McCarthy, to seize his assets because bills weren't paid. And McCarthy would have to hide until the sheriff went away before he could go back to work and hope that this well would come in.

It didn't.

None of them did.

All five new wells came in dry.

The day he moved into his brand new house, Glenn McCarthy was fresh out of money . . . flat broke . . . and close to $2 million in debt.

They used to call him 'Jelly Bean'.

Not to his face, of course.

They called him Jelly Bean behind his back because if they had called him that to his face he would have rolled up his sleeves and punched a few of them on the nose to teach them a little respect.

But behind his back he was known as Jelly Bean McCarthy because when he first started wildcatting he'd come to work on the rigs with two-tone shoes and loud shirts and his hair all greased back with hair oil. He kind of looked like a shiny little jelly bean, so they called him Jelly Bean.

But not to his face.

In those days everybody had an opinion about him.

It would have been impossible to meet him, or know him, and be totally indifferent.

Not everybody liked him.

But the people who did, liked him a lot and the people who didn't, at least they respected him.

As one man was quoted in those days, 'Just don't call Glenn lucky. To us, luck is what happens when preparation meets opportunity. His so-called good luck came from his utter defiance of bad luck. He resents being called lucky. He thinks the best weapon to use in beating the competition is hard work.'

Today the familiar moustache is gone. His hair isn't wavy black any more. It's white. And thinned out. But he's still broad shouldered, and big enough so that you know how tough he must have been, and the famous diamond ring is still on his left hand.

His hands are very large and seem strong. Like hands that would make big, solid fists, or could take a sure grip on a well cap and twist it shut.

And the slow, Texas drawl is there. A little more gravelly now. But as slow as they say it always was.

'The way you found oil in the old days was to follow the trends of the salt domes. You could see them a mile or two away. You see, oil migrates. There are faults in those salt domes, fractures in the land and that stops the oil. Every dome had oil under it if you drilled deep enough. The problem was that you didn't always have the technology to drill deep enough.'

His office is a long, narrow room in downtown Houston. It's smaller than his offices used to be. You can tell that because all the furniture he used to have is there and it's crowded into the room, with tables covered in maps and geological charts. There are bronze scale models of oil derricks and bronze scale models of oil pumps too. And the walls are covered with pictures. Him. His family. Oil derricks. Roughnecks standing close together in a faded black and white photo.

In his secretary's office there is a movie poster – Edna Ferber's *Giant* – because he was, supposedly, her model for Jett Rink.

'I met her once, when she crashed a cocktail party at The Shamrock. I didn't even know who she was.'

The next thing he knew there was James Dean in his final role, with Rock Hudson, Elizabeth Taylor and

Carroll Baker in the 198-minute movie that was supposed to be his life.

He shrugs, obviously not wanting to talk about that, yet again. Everybody always asks and he's just grown tired of answering. He's often said he didn't care much for the book and even less for the film. He didn't like the way some people thought he was Rink because Rink was nothing more than a tough guy. At other times he's said that maybe Edna Ferber used the rowdy McCarthy image for Rink and the softer, quieter, lesser known side for Bic Benedict.

In spite of that, McCarthy did go to Hollywood for the film's 1956 opening. Some people, he says, were expecting him to be very critical of his own characterization. Instead, he showed up wanting Miss Ferber to explain 'how she could get those cattle so fat on tumbleweed instead of grass'.

These days all he says is that Edna Ferber didn't do a very good job painting either side of him. 'I especially think she was unfair to Jimmy Dean. He deserved a better part.'

Next to the poster is a portrait of him looking more like Errol Flynn than ever before.

'I knew him. He was a friend of mine. But I wasn't anything like him.'

Back in his own office, the once-gleaming brown Moroccan leather furniture that so impressed a *Time* magazine reporter he even mentioned it on a story, is no longer shiny and soft. But then, neither is Glenn McCarthy. They're both faded and worn in some spots, and stiff in a few places the way good leather can get stiff when it's been left too long without being saddle-soaped to keep it supple.

But at least they're both still hanging in there.

'I guess a lot of people think wildcatting sounds

romantic. Yes, I guess it was. You'd go out there and find a spot and drill a well and bring in oil and all of a sudden people from distant cities would hear about it and there would be a boom. There'd be people trying to dig wells everywhere. Listen, there are still wildcatters today because there's still oil to be found. But it's much more scientific nowadays. Used to blow out a well to get the oil up. Now they use energy to bring the oil up to the surface. I guess you'd say it's much less romantic.'

He pauses for a moment before he insists, 'But it was never anything like they show it in the movies. I mean, there was never any dancing around the well, shouting Eureka and getting covered in a gusher of oil. It wasn't that romantic.'

Now he reaches for a small thin cigar, lights it and takes a few puffs. He puts it down and eventually it goes out. And there it sits until he decides to relight it and take a few more puffs.

'You know, some people think we were called wild-catters because we were crazy. It should mean, I guess, that we were wild, like independents. But you don't have to be a wild man to find oil.'

So the creditors wanted their money.

And Glenn McCarthy knew he could pay them if he could only get another stake in the wildcatting game.

As good fortune sometimes has it, just when everything seemed to be the bleakest, along came a fellow who didn't have the slightest idea what the oil business was all about.

'He was from Minnesota. I guess he was pretty old then. Of course I was pretty young then so maybe he just seemed old to me. But he had this idea of drilling a well off the Galveston Highway. He was a fine man, and I hate to say it, but his geologist was a fake. Everybody thought that land over there was just sand. But this fellow came down from Minnesota with the fake geologist and he wanted someone to sink a hole.'

McCarthy needed the money and wasn't in a position to say no to a contracting job. He took it and the other contractors in the area started calling him 'the boy plunger'.

'Well, I went to the site and stood there kind of amazed as this fake geologist pulled out a glass-topped box with a string and ball hanging down from under it. He called it an "oil finder". I guess he thought he could find oil the same way you can find water with a divining rod. Anyway, he stood over his box and watched the ball swing on the string and counted out loud, and did some calculations and finally he said to me, you drill right here and go down 9000 feet.'

As a contractor, McCarthy seems to remember he was charging something like $5 a foot at the time. So this wasn't going to be a cheap experience for the fellow from Minnesota who believed in the phoney geologist.

'He was paying so I set up a rig and started drilling. I guess this was sometime around 1934 or 1935. Well, one day I'm driving past the derrick on my way to a club in Galveston where they had really good steaks, and I don't know why but I stopped and went up onto the floor of the rig and asked my guy there how it was going. He said that we had gone to the contracted depth and there was nothing but sand. So I could have stopped right there and the fellow from Minnesota would have lost his money. But just then I looked at a piece of the drill bit and felt some muddy earth and I guess my old Irish nose can just smell oil.'

He says they cored the well below the 9000 foot

mark and came up with a core barrel containing 10 feet of oil sand.

'We did everything the fellow from Minnesota had asked us to do and we didn't hit oil. He had already gone home because he knew there was nothing in that well. And I could have called him that night and probably bought his leases for a buck an acre. I could have kept my mouth shut and made maybe $10 million right there.'

Except he didn't.

He rushed to a phone and called the fellow in Minnesota and convinced him to keep drilling.

A few days later the well came in.

The man from Minnesota showed his appreciation.

McCarthy's creditors were paid off within a year.

And for the next 15 years there was no stopping him.

Wherever he pointed his Irish nose he smelled oil.

He opened new fields ... Cotton Lake, Chocolate Bayou and Palacios, Lovell's Lake, Bailey's Prairie and Blue Lake, Collins Lake, New Ulm and North Big Hill. At the same time he went into established fields and stretched them. There was Anahuac and Coleto Creek, Hankamer, Fannette, and Pierce Junction.

But the best of them all was the legendary field called Winnie-Stowell.

That find, on the line between Chambers and Jefferson counties, south west of Beaumont, was so rich that he built his first refining unit there, an absorption plant to extract hydrocarbons from the gas and distillate wells. It took him heavily into the natural gas business. A second absorption plant was quickly built at Winnie-Stowell. And then came a $9 million chemical plant that was supposed to take him heavily into the production of petrol and petroleum by-products.

'We didn't succeed like we thought we could. But I had no regrets for trying.'

During those days he pioneered the science of deep drilling. Where many wildcatters simply stopped at certain levels, McCarthy sometimes drilled twice as deep. For a while it was as if everything he touched turned to money. Every well he drilled brought up oil. He was on a roll, the likes of which the oil business had never seen before. He kept finding oil and gas everywhere.

'Each time I did, I came out with more money. But you don't just drill and quit. You don't ever finish. You keep on working. You run into problems and sometimes you come out lucky, and sometimes you don't.'

In all, he brought in an unbelievable 38 East Texas fields. Some were small. Most were average size. One was bigger than Manhattan Island. In his lifetime he probably drilled close to 800–900 wells . . . he has no idea how many, but people who have followed his career reckon that sounds like a reasonably accurate figure . . . and brought oil or gas out of maybe as much as 90 per cent of them. Most wildcatters would have been thrilled with one big field and a batting average half that size.

He made a fortune, even though oil was, for most of those years, only $2 or $3 a barrel. There were times when it was down to under $1 a barrel and in those days he didn't make as much as he did when the prices were higher, but he still made money. For a while he was almost certainly among the wealthiest men in America. If he had the same success today, with oil prices where they are now, he would probably make the list of the world's wealthiest men.

Over the years he gave a lot away, to various charities. He was never shy when the truly needy came knocking on his door. But over the years most of the money he made in oil was spent on comfortable living or put into other ventures. He paid $2.25 million for the 22-storey Shell Building, in the heart of downtown Houston. He bought a chain of neighbourhood newspapers. He bought a Houston radio station. He bought a Houston bank. He formed the Jefferson Pipe Line Company to transport natural gas in the Port Arthur–Beaumont–Orange area. He formed the Neches Natural Gas Company to sell and deliver dry gas as a fuel to various industrial clients. He bought a chunk of Eastern Air Lines, and for a while sat on its board with his old pal, Eddie Rickenbacker. He even took on a distributorship for a well-known brand of shoes simply because he liked to wear them and give them to his friends. 'Too bad', someone once said about McCarthy's shoe business, 'that he doesn't have enough customers like himself. If he did he'd make a lot of money in shoes, too.'

When he had a lot of money, he spent a lot of money. He bought a 15,000 acre ranch.

An hour's flight from Houston by small plane, there was, of course, a private landing strip. While such things are not uncommon in Texas, McCarthy's landing strip was 3000 feet long, large enough for multi-engine aircraft, and relatively close to home . . . being only four miles from the ranch house.

That ranch house was six rooms, with a living room big enough for two dozen deer heads, an antelope head and several stuffed birds to hang on the walls. The dining room table sat 22. The three bedrooms, oddly enough, slept 20. The master bedroom was for McCarthy and his wife. The other two – one for men and one for women – were dormitory style, with single beds lined up in a row.

Coyotes, panthers, ringtail cats, jackrabbits, whatever threatened the cattle or the prairie land, could be shot. So there was McCarthy, speeding along in a jeep, steering with one hand, aiming his rifle with the other, plugging jackrabbits as he rode home on the range.

There was fishing too. Crystal clear lakes that he stocked with big mouth bass, channel cats and blue gulls.

He also bought aeroplanes.

Over the years he owned several.

Although he didn't fly himself – he started taking lessons but his instructor pilot got killed and McCarthy called it quits after that – he bought a twin-engine Beechcraft in 1945 for $60,000. In those days that was considered a huge extravagance. The following year he bought a DC-3. When that proved too small, in 1949 he purchased a Boeing Stratoliner from Howard Hughes, reportedly for $500,000. But then it was often said to be the plushest private aeroplane in the world.

And then he bought his way into the movie business.

McCarthy became a film maker because he felt Hollywood wasn't doing a very good job.

'I want my kids to see some movies with real Americanism,' he announced before footing the bill for *The Green Promise (Raging Waters* in the UK). 'None of this gangster and shoot-em-up stuff. My object is to educate people into good morals and out of hating each other.'

The setting for his first film was a farm. The story involved a young girl who, as a member of a 4-H club (kind of like the Scouts but for kids who want to be farmers), doesn't like sharing everything and wants a lamb to call her own. You can just hear the strings playing the theme song. To find the right girl to love the lamb, McCarthy put out a casting call in 43 states for under-13-year-olds, looking for that special ingénue 'with a quality of stillness'. Supporting her was a lamb . . . less of a casting problem there . . and an actor named Robert Paige, whose next film appearance was four years later in *Abbott and Costello Go to Mars*.

When Glenn McCarthy had big money he spent big money.

But most of all, he bought himself a hotel.

Wildcatters are a special breed.

They are to the oil business – especially in the dry, flatlands of Texas – what stage robbers or the Earps in a gun fight at the OK corral were to the great American cowboy legend.

They're a rugged, sweaty, hit-and-miss special sort of loner who never know if they're a foot away from a million dollars or a million feet away from one dollar. They're often heavy on the boozing and heavy on the fist fighting and heavy on the gambling, too. Over the years, stories ran rampant about McCarthy's exploits. The drinking bouts. The barroom brawls. The $1000-a-throw crap shoots.

As Glenn McCarthy grew up in the oil business, all sorts of stories grew up around him. There he was driving his Cadillac convertible at 110 mph along a dusty road, a bottle of bourbon at his side.

Or there he was, the super-tough businessman with a super-soft centre. 'In a big business deal,' one friend has since been often quoted, 'Glenn will take the shirt right off your back. He's as cold blooded as he is calculating. Always lets the other fellow do the talking. But in a personal deal, it's all different and he's as soft as that banana cream pie he likes so well. When he's trading with a friend, he'll take the shirt off his own back.'

Someone else long ago described him simply as 'an earthy type fellow who don't want nobody to even try telling him what to do. Goes against the grain to take orders.'

But that's all part of the spirit that you might expect from a man who'd be willing to bet everything in the world that there was oil down there somewhere, just below his muddied boots.

Few people have ever written about a wildcatter as well as the man who will always be considered to have been one of America's finest war correspondents, the late Ernie Pyle.

Come to think of it, few people have ever written anything about anyone as well as Ernie Pyle.

He was a syndicated columnist for the Scripps–Howard chain of newspapers, and showed up in Houston one day, back in the 30s, where he met McCarthy.

The way McCarthy tells it, Pyle wanted to go out to an oil field with him, so the two spent several days together. At one point they ran into a fellow from Lake Charles who asked McCarthy if he still had the diamonds he'd borrowed money against. McCarthy told him yes. Pyle wanted to know the story. So McCarthy related it to him.

'This man had borrowed some money from me and gave me these diamonds as security. So he told me he'd come back and get 'em in 30 days and he didn't come back in 30 days. Then I called him and told him I'd let him have the diamonds if he'd bring the money in another 30 days. Finally, after about six months, he told me I could keep the diamonds because he couldn't raise the money. It wasn't but about $3000 but there were 32 carats in diamonds involved. I gave one of them to my brother and one to my father and several to my mother and some to my wife.'

You can't help but notice the one he still wears. The ring. It's just a shade under seven carats. It's a diamond as big as The Shamrock.

Pyle loved the story, and the way he told it was as 'Diamond Glenn McCarthy'.

'If I were in the oil business,' he wrote, 'I'd never sleep a wink. An oil man can go broke quicker than a tourist at Monte Carlo. You may have ten million today and nothing tomorrow, nothing that is but the oil fever. You have to know these men to know it isn't money they're after. Maybe it is at first, but once they've got it, then it's the oil fever. They want to be big. They want to be smarter than the others. Make bigger finds. Drill deeper wells. See what's under that ground. Out gamble the other fellow.'

Pyle observed, 'A man with the oil fever will never tell you what he's worth. He's probably afraid he'll go broke before he gets back to the office. But he'll always tell you how poor he used to be.'

And then he described McCarthy, a man he had come to know with a terminal case of the oil fever. 'A perfect physical specimen. If his $20 million slips out on him some night, he's equipped to go right back in the field and put his broad shoulders to the business for a fresh start. With five children and the oil fever, what else can he do?'

In the chips or out, through the 1940s and well into the 1950s, always the promoter, Glenn McCarthy had a natural gift for his own PR.

Just before opening the hotel, he had a plane named The Shamrock entered in the Bendix California to Cleveland Air Races. It caught fire in mid-air and the pilot had to bail out. McCarthy found himself with front-page publicity across the country. The next time he entered three planes and they came in first, second and fourth. It didn't matter that the race had cost him $300,000. The publicity that followed was, he knows, one of the best advertising campaigns ever.

'It didn't make much difference how you got into the newspaper. But it had to be worthwhile or it wouldn't carry a headline.'

To get people into his hotel, The Shamrock offered free honeymoons to newly weds. That made the papers and brought in hundreds of couples from across the nation. One Fourth of July he put on the biggest fireworks display Texas had ever seen.

'There were 400,000 people lining the streets in front of the hotel. And the mayor, after we had it the first time, said to me, "For God's sake, don't ever give any more of those." We did have it other years, but not with the same mayor. People said it was kind of silly to spend all that money on fireworks. But I couldn't have bought a full-page ad in every newspaper in the state for less than that amount of money. And I got full-page coverage that was news coverage.'

With a nose for oil and his flair for publicity, he was a reporter's dream. Wherever he went, there was sure to be good copy.

'Paris: Glenn McCarthy, the Houston, Texas millionaire oil operator has offered to buy 51 per cent of the shares of the Egyptian National Petroleum Company's oil concession rights.'

'Houston: Oil man Glenn McCarthy sought $11 million today in a suit against Dresser Industries, Inc., a Dallas company.'

'Guatemala: Texas oilman Glenn McCarthy said tonight he is seeking permission to open a big gambling casino which would make Guatemala "the Riviera of the Western Hemisphere".'

'Houston: Glenn McCarthy, the fabulous oil million-

aire, may be ready to "forgive and forget" the elope-
ment of his 17 year old daughter.'

'Los Angeles: Glenn H. McCarthy, the Houston oil
man who has entered a souped-up P-38 in the August
30 Los Angeles to Cleveland Bendix race, offered
yesterday to put up $500,000 that his plane will win.'

'Houston: Oil wildcatter Glenn McCarthy was sued
yesterday for $60,000 by a Massachusetts doctor who
alleged the now-and-then millionaire attacked him on
an airliner bound for Peru.'

'Hollywood: Oil millionaire Glenn McCarthy, invad-
ing Hollywood with his wife, five children, four pilots,
three limousines and two airplanes, went to work
today to reform the town.'

Legends are often made of lesser stuff.

Then again, getting your picture on the cover of
Time is instant stardom.

The 13 March 1950 cover featured Glenn McCarthy.

'If it were possible to cap the human ego like a gas
well', the story began . . . sadly unsigned because the
prose is so good . . . 'and to pipe off its more volatile
byproducts as fuel, Houston's multi-millionaire wildcatter Glenn McCarthy could heat a city the size of
Omaha with no help at all.'

The anonymous journalist went on to say that the
combination of McCarthy's bull-like determination to
become Houston's first citizen and the tough, no-
nonsense way he runs his business, makes him seem
like something of a throwback to the lustier days of
the last century.

'In an age when most businessmen allowed themselves to be governed by politicians, unions, directors,
psychiatrists, the threat of ulcers and the precepts of
Emily Post, McCarthy holds himself only accountable
to McCarthy.'

That *Time* magazine cover story made him internationally famous.

It was also the first hint that there might be trouble coming over the horizon.

'His big chemical company, which is reported losing money, and his endless drilling ventures have been great financial drains. Last week Houston was alive with a titillating rumour, that its most flamboyant citizen was strapped for cash.'

To keep himself afloat during the late 1940s, McCarthy had borrowed upwards of $50 million from insurance companies, using his 100–200 million barrel oil reserves as security.

That's the way oil men always raise money. Except that the oil was still in the ground. Even then there never would have been a problem had the price of oil not started to fall and had the Texas Railroad Commission not suddenly imposed severe production quotas to try to stabilize prices.

It was precisely the worst thing that could have happened. Overnight, with his revenue sliced into shreds and his production costs still as high as ever, his cash began to evaporate.

Ever aware of the public eye, he gave an interview to the London *Daily Express*.

'In the first few minutes of our meeting,' wrote the *Express*'s man in New York, 'McCarthy did what he has seldom done before. He gave an estimate, he does not know exactly, of what he is worth. At current prices between £150 million and £200 million.'

Remember, this was April 1950 when a pound was really worth something . . . like $2.90.

'"You can't go broke with all that, can you?" he asked. Yet a few minutes later he all but admitted that the rumours were true. "I mean I am an independent oil man," he said. "And we independents are being killed off. My income was cut overnight 50 per cent by government orders to prevent an oil slump, they say."'

It was then revealed that in December 1949 McCarthy had asked the Reconstruction Finance Corporation, a government body, to loan him $70 million.

Speculation ran wild as to why McCarthy needed the money. But, with the benefit of hindsight, the reasons are clear. Demand for petroleum had fallen and profit margins narrowed. Then, the Texas Railroad Commission didn't help matters with their quotas. But McCarthy, unlike lots of other oil men, had some additional problems. His chemical plant at Winnie-Stowell had been losing money. Even The Shamrock, which supposedly brought him a first-year profit of $1.25 million, was not turning out to be the investment he had hoped it might.

Quietly, towards the end of 1949 he started selling some assets, among them the 22-storey Shell Building.

'Most people who have followed his career figure he'll make out all right,' wrote *Business Week* at the time.

'It's my bet that McCarthy will survive,' chimed in the *Daily Express* man.

Even *Time* magazine was somewhat encouraging. 'McCarthy's zest for chance, life, personal combat and the power of wealth seems undiminished. He still likes to rub his hands together in thick, crude oil and mutter, "This is oil." He still has grandiose ideas. Last month he tried to buy a professional football club for Houston. Last week he paid a princely $15,400 for an 890-pound prize Hereford. Where was Glenn McCarthy going? Houstonians say, "He's going to kill himself, go bankrupt or get to be the richest man on earth. You figure out which."'

But the RFC $70 million loan did not come through.

Trying to fight his way off the ropes, he managed to hold the creditors off for over a year.

He also managed to keep it quiet for nearly two.

The story broke when someone at *Newsweek* spotted something in a company report. And they told the world about it on 10 March 1952.

'There have been times when Glenn McCarthy has enjoyed the proverbial luck of the Irish. There have also been times when the Texas oil millionaire hasn't. Last week fortune wasn't smiling on the colorful, freespending Texan. At least not for the time being.'

The Equitable Life Assurance Society explained in their annual report for 1951 that McCarthy hadn't been able to meet amortization requirements on loans to him totalling $34.1 million, although he had been paying the interest. To protect themselves, Equitable had called in the collateral, and taken over the management of McCarthy's oil, gas and hotel holdings.

On top of that, it turned out, he owed $6 million to Metropolitan Life . . . other versions of the tale say it was $15 million . . . and that was the end of his money-losing chemical plant.

The Shamrock was also sold. Equitable did a deal with the Hilton chain.

McCarthy was left with his home, his newspapers, his radio station, some real estate and his ranch.

Little by little all of these disappeared from his grasp as well. Although some took longer than others.

'I was disgusted at being curtailed like that. In 1950 I had a lot of oil in place. But the Railroad Commission quotas hurt everybody. They stopped you from getting the cash you needed to do the job. Well, to be honest I guess I had overspent myself. So I started selling things that weren't productive, like newspapers. I had too many employees. Eventually I even had to sell 5000 acres that used to be called Sharpstown that is now right in the middle of downtown Houston. I never wanted to sell. But I had to.'

His three-storey colonial $700,000 mansion wasn't sold until the 60s, and then it only went for $1.5 million. A developer wanted the land to build a high-rise block of flats.

And at the very point when Glenn McCarthy could have saved his empire, being told what to do flatly went against the grain.

There is a common belief in the oil business, whenever the legend of McCarthy is mentioned and whenever there are enough good ol' boys sitting around who remember him, that McCarthy could have saved everything by simply incorporating himself. Or, they also say, he could have saved everything if he had accepted an offer from Harry Sinclair . . . the very same fellow whose name was on the front door at Sinclair Oil Company and who had owned the petrol station where McCarthy once sold anti-freeze and worked as a pump monkey.

The way the story goes, Sinclair was willing to give McCarthy $100 million for his holdings plus $50 million more to pay off his debts. That would have left McCarthy with something like $75 million after taxes. But that's not the way McCarthy ever played the game. He was a loner right from the start and loners, no matter what the risk, go it alone.

Mere profit isn't what he's after. It's the game. The gamble. It's being right. It's being ready to risk your own money to be proved right, and just as ready to accept your losses when you're proved wrong. It's almost as if the wildcatter – true to the romantic legend — is the ultimate gambler for whom only the game matters. Whatever is won, no matter how big the pile of chips, it's just tossed back into the pot. Whatever is lost, well, you write that off as the price of admission.

Anyone who has ever met a real wildcatter — especially one of the few left from McCarthy's days — merely has to look into the man's eyes whenever the word oil is mentioned. That's how you know for sure that, if they knew they were going to lose nearly everything before they started, not a single one of them would quit.

It isn't profit.

It isn't money and power.

It isn't even the oil.

It's finding it that matters.

Within six months of Equitable's seizure of his major assets, McCarthy was on his feet, raising his gloves to fight again. He created Glenn McCarthy Inc. and wanted to sell 10 million shares of himself on Wall Street. But the Securities and Exchange Commission had other ideas. They blocked him, saying he hadn't spelled out to his potential investors just how risky this might be. He rewrote his act and found a broker willing to handle the placement. But, the day before he was set to make his market debut, a Dallas-based industrial group, claiming to hold McCarthy's IOUs for $2.5 million worth of chemical plant equipment, filed suit. The SEC immediately withdrew their permission.

A year later McCarthy turned up in Bolivia, trying to do a gas and oil deal there. He got himself 970,000 acres leased from the government. And for a while it looked as though he was on the come-back trail.

He started drilling Gran Chaco and hit on his first well.

But the political climate in Bolivia was not always healthy for gringos. And his Gran Chaco wells were surrounded by jungle too thick to get oil trucks in or out. The money that he had raised for drilling was not enough for a pipeline too, so he got in touch with a Persian rug dealer in New York, from whom he had bought carpets, and asked him to help raise $2 million for a pipeline. The rug dealer and his friends came through for McCarthy ... because it was McCarthy ... but costs rose faster than anyone could get the pipeline down, and he came home with a lot less for his efforts than anyone would have bet.

The Cork Club had long since been moved out of The Shamrock to a new location, so he spent the next few years running that.

By 1963 he sold his interests there and quietly faded out of sight.

But old wildcatters never die. They still smell every salt dome their Irish nose can lead them to.

When Hilton Hotels announced that they were selling The Shamrock and that it would be turned into something else, the first thing the manager did was take down the portrait of Glenn McCarthy that had hung for 37 years in the lobby.

He wasn't being disrespectful.

He took it down because there are still a lot of people in Houston who associate McCarthy with the hotel, and think of him as someone who was once nearly as famous in Texas as Sam Houston himself, and the manager knew very well that McCarthy's portrait would wind up being stolen by someone who wanted the ultimate souvenir of an era past.

So they took the portrait down.

But Glenn McCarthy doesn't want to talk about that.

He'd rather point to the pictures he's got on his office wall, pictures of his children and maybe even talk about his grandchildren.

All five of his kids are married – four girls and a boy – and all of them have children and, he says, there are even now some great grandchildren. How many he's asked. He thinks for a moment, then calls into the next room to his secretary, 'How many grandchildren have I got? And how many great grandchildren?' She says, 'Oh, a real lot.' He nods. 'Yeah, a lot. I don't even know. Can't count 'em all. Got some of the great grandchildren staying with us now. They keep talking all the time. I don't know what they're saying, but they keep right on talking.'

When he's in Houston, he comes into the office five days a week. He's there at 9:30 and he leaves at 3:30. What business he has to discuss is done then, and only then. He never sees anyone for business at the weekend. He never talks business after 3:30.

He says he's got some real estate interests. And, of course, he still likes to dabble a little in oil.

'I sold the last of my oil in 1984 or so, just before the bad times. I'm now waiting to get back. You see, once you become an oil man, especially if you were one in the early stages like me, it never leaves you. It becomes part of your life. It thrills you to bring in a new area. And, believe me, it's not just the money. It's what you're doing.'

And then the talk swings back to The Shamrock.

After all the ups and all the downs, after making two fortunes and losing two fortunes, it's only when you talk to him about The Shamrock that you see some businesses truly mattered to him, that he took some of them personally. And when he lost those, it hurt.

'The Shamrock is the reason that Houston is a large city today and not just a small town. And now it's gone.' He doesn't hide his emotion. 'Some folk tried to muster some support. To create a demand to keep it. They even got 50,000 signatures on a petition to keep it. Didn't do any good though. Guess I never thought it would.'

He says that now. You know, in the way that some people will shrug to show you that they don't care when they really do. But it's a good bet he at least hoped it might have helped.

'I spent $23 million on it. Everybody always says $21 million. Don't know how they got that figure. It was $23 million. You see, in 1949 there wasn't a hotel in Houston worth staying in. Not a one. Couldn't even find an engineer in Houston to build the place. We had builders here but no real engineers. I had to bring one in from New York City.'

Of course, the real reason he built The Shamrock is obvious.

He built it as a monument to himself.

But he doesn't come right out and say that.

'I could have simply put that money into some sort of annuity for myself and my family. But the way I looked at it, the insurance company probably would have put the money into a hotel. So I just took a short cut to get a bigger return. The added risk was just a challenge, which I liked. I don't mean that it was the fastest or the best way to make money. There were a hundred or more businesses which I could have entered with the same investment or much less, and gotten a faster and a higher return on my capital. But Houston needed hotels and I thought The Shamrock was a good investment. Besides, the hotel business interested me. A business which interests me is fun for me. If a business doesn't interest me I do not want to be in it, regardless of the financial return.'

When he built The Shamrock, McCarthy showed great insight into the future of Houston. The mountain did come to Muhammad. But it wasn't always that way. He suggested that Houston have a second airport a long way out of town. The locals said Hobby Field would be big enough forever. Today, Houston Intercontinental is enormous, about 25 miles from downtown, and very much a testimonial to what Houston has become. He also at one point proposed building a major sports stadium in Houston that would have a sliding roof so that baseball or football games would never suffer from poor weather conditions. Again, the town folk thought he was crazy. His stadium never got built. But, less than 15 years later, major league baseball came to Houston and so did major league football, and the Astrodome did get built.

Now, The Shamrock is gone.

In its place they've put up something else.

It's probably important. It has something to do with a medical centre.

But it won't have green lights shining on it all night long. And there won't be green ink in the pens when you sign something there. And it won't have six corner rooms on every floor because lots of people like corner rooms.

And no one will ever drive past it and think to themselves, Glenn McCarthy, the King of the Wildcatters, did that.

8
Boom to Bust

In a recent list of the wealthiest people in the United States, *Forbes* magazine noted that 158 of the top 400 held interests in oil, gas and/or real estate.

Of those 158, an even 50 were from Texas.

The estimated total wealth of those 50 Texans came to $16.622 billion!

In the same issue of *Time* magazine that featured Glenn McCarthy on the cover, there was a small boxed story called 'Seven Big Texans'.

It was half a page of thumb-nail photos and short biographical paragraphs. The introduction read, 'Only their bankers know who the richest Texans are. But these would be on anyone's list.'

The seven, with abbreviated comments, were:

Haroldson Lafayette Hunt, Dallas: 'Probably the richest in oil income, reputedly worth $263 million.'

W.L. Moody, Jr, Galveston: 'He controls banks, newspapers, a large insurance company, vast ranching interests and oil holdings.'

Jesse Jones, Houston: 'Not as rich as some of the others, though he has millions. Wields vast power . . .'

Hugh Roy Cullen, Houston: 'In one day he gave away oil properties potentially worth $160 million.'

Sid Richardson, Forth Worth: 'Probably the richest man in oil reserves . . . drilled many a dry hole, for years lived on credit in a cheap hotel and ate on credit at a drugstore before he hit it rich in 1935.'

Clint Murchison Sr, Dallas: 'An oil rich man . . . last

week he was entertaining the Duke and Duchess of Windsor at his 120,000 acre ranch in Mexico.'

Amon Carter, Fort Worth: 'Oil, ranching and real estate ... whenever he buys a (Frederick) Remington (painting or sculpture), he sends another to Richardson with the bill.'

All seven were, in many ways, caricatures of themselves ... bigger than life, hard-drinking, fist-fighting cowboys who struck it rich in oil. But all seven were also, in every instance, streetwise, canny, shrewd and natural-born businessmen.

Of the seven, only the Hunt, Moody and Cullen names appear on the *Forbes* 400 list. Sid Richardson's fortune is represented in the guise of his nephew Perry Richardson Bass, whose mother lent Sid $40 to get started in the oil business. Bass, in turn, built up a huge oil empire, which he has since handed over to his four sons. And they've proved themselves equally skilful by diversifying out of oil and into more passive investments like stocks and bonds. It's been said of the Bass brothers that if their holdings don't make $1 million a day they start to get very nervous.

As for the Moody and the Cullen fortunes, they were both objects of lengthy law suits with variously entitled family members fighting bitterly to divide up the spoils.

Not that H.L. Hunt's heirs have always fared that well either.

He was a tall, well-built, stern-faced poker player from Arkansas who throughout his life was publicity shy, almost to the point of paranoia. So much so that in 1950 there was only one known picture of him in existence and he often walked the streets of Dallas totally unrecognized.

His fortune can be directly traced to 1930, and a

very ballsy deal he swung with a fellow wildcatter named Charlie Joiner who owned some oil leases on a couple of cotton farms in northern Texas. With less than 20 bucks to his name, H.L. offered Joiner $1.5 million for those leases.

Joiner sold.

H.L. hit oil. And hit it big.

Joiner then spent his money digging one dry hole after another.

H.L. formed his dynasty.

And Joiner died penniless

H.L.'s first three sons – Bunker, Herbert and Lamar – have since proved themselves considerably less publicity shy than their old man but nearly as good at losing millions as Papa was at making them. The youngest and most frugal of the three, Lamar, calls himself an 'economy class millionaire'. He flies at the back of the plane and is said to often wear the same clothes several days in a row. A co-founder of the American Football League (AFL) and the owner of the Kansas City Chiefs baseball team, he was perhaps the smartest of the three because he lost only a small fortune when Bunker and Herbert managed to lose a colossal one on their ill-fated silver bubble.

However, because blood sometimes runs thicker than good sense, the three of them share certain interests.

One of them is an acquired taste for frugality.

As the story is told, Bunker and Herbert got it into their heads at one point in their quest for a silver bubble that the US government might, if pushed too far, bring its wrath to bear and seize whatever silver the brothers were actually holding. So they decided it might be prudent to move their hoard out of the country. They loaded something like $100 million

worth of silver onto a commercial flight bound for
London. And just to be on the safe side – after all, they
had a colossal fortune crated in the hold of the plane –
they got onto the flight with a pair of round-trip tickets
– economy class!

Cramped into the narrow seats in the rear of the
plane, Bunker was on the aisle and Herbert was in the
middle. Just after take-off, the hostess came around
asking if any passengers wanted a head-set for the in-
flight movie.

Again, as the story goes, Bunker refused to pay for
one. But Herbert wanted to see the film so he rented a
head-set.

The movie began.

Bunker stared at the silent screen for the opening
credits.

Then he looked at Herbert, leaned towards his
brother, pulled one plug of the head-set out of
Herbert's ear, stuck it in his own, and just like that
saved himself $2.

Another common interest is the Penrod Drilling
Company, among the world's largest oil rig contractors
and owned by trusts that benefit the three brothers. In
1984 Penrod reportedly lost $100 million.

In 1985 three subsidiaries of the Hunt International
Resources Corp. filed for Chapter 11 protection when
HIR defaulted on a $295 million loan.

In 1980, a respectable New York merchant bank
estimated that the three Hunt Brothers' share of the
Placid Oil Company was worth about $1.9 billion.
Shortly thereafter they were forced to liquidate some
Placid assets in order to secure their $1.1 billion silver
bailout. Then in 1983, H.L.'s first two daughters Caro-
line Schoellkopf and Margaret Hill decided they'd be

better off managing their own affairs, so they took a slice of Placid. They got out just in time.

In 1985 it was estimated that Placid could produce 30 million barrels a year, then at the average price of $26, giving the Hunts a cash flow from operations of over $300 million. But, *Forbes* pointed out, assuming an interest rate of 10 per cent and six years of evenly distributed repayments on the principal, half that $300 million would have to go towards the Hunts' $500 million silver debt. One year later, with oil on the floor at $10 a barrel, even Placid's entire cash flow wouldn't be enough to cover their lingering silver worries.

Once again, the brothers were in trouble.

The banks moved in. To fight back and avoid foreclosures, the Hunt boys tossed Placid into Chapter 11 bankruptcy.

Of course, they're still in the chips. There's really no need to shed crocodile tears for any of the Hunts. At least, not yet. A lot more money will have to go down the drain before anyone worries where their next meal will come from. But Bunker and Herbert, with occasional help from Lamar, are definitely living proof that simply being born to money is no assurance of keeping it.

Especially in Texas.

Clint Murchison Jr was the son of Clint Murchison Sr, who was on that list in *Time* Magazine.

Thirty-five years later Junior died a bankrupt.

Except it didn't take him 35 years to lose all of his money. In 1984 his fortune had been estimated at $250 million. Included among his assets, besides oil and land, was ownership of the $80 million Dallas Cowboys football club. Then came the bad times. His brother's death and the legal battles that haunted the settlement of that estate, his own seriously failing health

and the general downturn in oil stacked the cards
against him. But his massive debts from real estate
ventures delivered the coup de grâce.

In spite of warnings that the market was soft, he
built houses in New Orleans, apartment complexes in
Washington DC and San Francisco, and invested heavily in commercial property in Dallas. Highly geared,
with personal guarantees to back up the borrowings, it
took one failed interest payment to sound the alarm.
His bankers moved in, quickly and efficiently, like
sharks smelling blood, and a series of foreclosures
followed. Bankruptcy was his only salvation, wiping
away both debts and assets.

A lone attempt to come to Murchison's aid was
launched by the Bass family. Sid Richardson and Clint
Murchison Sr had supposedly often bankrolled each
other in their wildcat days. So the four Bass brothers
had some tradition to live up to. But whatever they
offered, it was too little and too late. Murchison never
recovered, from either his financial ruin or his illness.

Less than one week after Murchison went down, the
Metropolitan Life Insurance Company foreclosed on
John W. Mecom Jr, the Houston oilman who owned
the money-draining, game-losing, New Orleans Saints
football club.

John W. Sr was a legendary wildcatter, out of the
McCarthy mould, who started digging for oil with $700
of his mother's money. A millionaire by the mid-1930s,
he was bankrupt in 1970 when he got caught in a
cashflow bind with overly ambitious drilling commitments and a run of dry holes. When the oil crisis hit
three years later, he skilfully managed to buy back a
lot of his old properties and wound up making another
fortune in oil. At the time of his death in 1981, his
empire – oil in Texas, Louisiana, Colombia and the

Middle East, plus hotels, ranches and related ventures – was bringing in something like $300 million a year.

Unfortunately, 'Little John' never had his father's business acumen. Everything simply dissolved around him. He was forced to sell the Saints. Metropolitan foreclosed on $40 million worth of hotels. And it was all downhill from there.

Another football club owner who's had a rough time – maybe someone should do a dissertation on the NFL curse of Texan oilmen – was Kenneth Stanley Adams.

Known as Bud, his old man was Boots Adams, the fellow who built Phillips Petroleum. A co-founder of the AFL with Lamar Hunt, Bud is also known for his leanings towards frugality. Probably just as well. Although he owns over 10,000 acres of Texas ranch-land and over 15,000 acres of California farmland, he has seen less than overwhelming success with his Houston Oiler football franchise and his Adams Resources company. The Oilers lose football games and money. Adams Resources just loses money. Adams nearly sank in 1981 and 1982, but managed . . . only just . . . to restructure his debts and keep the wolf away from his door.

That's more than can be said for Kenneth William Davis, Jr and his kid brother Thomas Cullen Davis, both of Fort Worth. In spite of the fact that they do not own a football or baseball team, they do own Kendavis Industries International and they have seen better days. The two of them used to be worth $250 million, with interests in the oil services industry and the manufacturing of oil field goods. But when oil slowed down in 1985, a group of eight banks – out of 30 with whom Kendavis Industries had financed deals – filed involuntary bankruptcy proceedings against them and shoved a whole slew of subsidiary companies into

Chapter 11. According to the banks, the Davis boys had failed to come up with sufficient collateral for their loans or provide satisfactory cashflow projections. The banks had the courts appoint a trustee to protect their $346 million unsecured position. Shocked that such an incredible thing could have happened, the brothers put the blame on creditors' over-reactions. Responding to that claim, *Forbes* coolly wrote, 'Unlikely'.

By the end of 1987, even though oil prices had come off their $9 floor to about twice that, Texas was still looking like a no-man's land. One-fifth of the state's housing stock was up for sale, the vacancy rate for commercial office space was topping 30 per cent, and more than three dozen banks had shut their doors.

But the bust news of the year was that 'Big John' Connally had joined the club.

A former three-term governor of Texas – he was the fellow riding in the car in Dallas with John Kennedy on that fateful day in November 1963 – a former secretary of the Navy, a former US treasury secretary, and once seriously considered vice-presidential contender, Connally was at the age of 65 reportedly worth $6 million to $10 million.

At the age of 70 he was in the hole for $37 million.

He and his partner, former Lieutenant Governor Ben Barnes, were in the midst of developing $200 million worth of shopping centres, offices and apartment buildings in Texas and New Mexico when the crunch came. They were heavily leveraged, using their bank accounts and personal reputations as collateral. In August, with their assets under siege from their creditors, they filed for bankruptcy.

Said 'Big John' to the press, 'In this environment I certainly don't feel there's any personal stigma attached.'

Added a well-meaning political ally, 'It's almost like a bullfighter's scar. You have to be in Chapter 11 to be one of the gang.'

By the way, it's not only the very rich folk who have got poorer in recent years. Some ordinary rich folk have suffered just as much.

In March 1986, with oil hovering around $14 a barrel, the *New York Times* reported, 'Dozens of incomplete wells have been abandoned, hundreds of slow producing wells have been capped permanently and thousands of others temporarily shut.' Men like Perkin D. Sams – a West Texas oilman who once owned luxury cars, a penthouse office and an expensive art collection – had seen his revenues slip from $400,000 a month to nothing. While some drilling companies in Midland, Texas, which were once paid $200,000 to open a 10,000 foot well when oil prices were riding high, were suddenly struggling to get $90,000 for the same work and were losing money at that. Rigs that once cost $3 million to build were going at auction for $150,000.

Halfway across the state in Tyler, Texas, a lanky, retired drilling supervisor named Nig Spraggins was feeling the pain as well.

He had worked 30 years for the Delta Drilling Company ... once one of the largest independent drilling contractors in the country ... and almost retired as a millionaire.

Except his millions cost him everything.

On 17 March 1981, Delta went public and paid dividends to 87 long-time employees worth $53 million. They received 30 per cent in cash and the rest in Delta shares at $17.50 per. That afternoon, 65-year-old Nig Spraggins was worth $1,638,000. The only condition in the give-away was that none of the lucky employees could sell their shares for 120 days. By then, however, the shares were trading at around $13.60.

Spraggins held on.

By the end of the year those same shares were under $9, and still heading down.

Delta had, as required by law, withheld 20 per cent of everyone's windfall for the tax collector. Spraggins used his remaining $1.5 million in shares as collateral – calculated at $11 a share – for a $287,000 bank loan to pay the rest of his tax bill. As those same shares kept falling, he was forced to use the cash he had as extra collateral just to keep the bankers happy.

In September 1985 *Fortune* magazine reported that Spraggins had since been asked for $221,000 by the bank – his shares were floating at under $1 per – and, believe it or not, an additional $187,000 by the Inland Revenue Service, who were also demanding $93,000 in interest on that overdue tax bill.

Sometimes it's cheaper to stay poor.

Of course, oil is not the only thing you can pull out of the ground. And Texas isn't the only place where the land yields riches. But it probably helps to be a Texan if you're ever going to find it.

Charlie Steen was born in a small town some 75 miles west of Fort Worth. The year was 1919. And his father, according to the legend that Steen helped to create, was once worth $100,000 thanks to Texas oil.

But the Steen fortune was short lived.

The old man blew it all in the fast lane.

Anyway, by the time that happened, Charlie's parents were divorced and he was living with his mother who, he's often bragged, had nine husbands and 500 lovers.

A geology major at college in El Paso, he took a job in 1943 with a mining company in Bolivia, moved on

to one in Peru, came back to Texas and in 1948 got
fired for insubordination.

It seems Charlie Steen has a pretty quick temper.

When no one else would hire him he heard that
there was a fortune to be made in uranium. So, with
his wife and three young sons in tow, he set out to be a
prospector. The region he chose was the Colorado
Plateau, a huge stretch of Rocky Mountain country
covering the 'Four Corners', where New Mexico, Ari-
zona, Colorado and Utah meet.

The five of them lived in a caravan in Cisco, Utah, a
booming metropolis of 45 people – counting the Steens
– about 175 miles south east of Salt Lake City. In the
beginning he staked a few claims but couldn't find a
backer anywhere to mine them. So he sold the caravan
and moved his family into a tar-paper shanty – no
running water, no electricity – for $15 a month and
went right on prospecting.

In 1951 he somehow got enough dough together to
stake a dozen claims 45 miles due south of Cisco, in
the flatlands of the Big Indian Wash.

The following year he convinced an old friend to lend
him some money and a diamond core drilling rig to
start digging.

And, on 27 July 1952, he struck pitchblende, the
richest form of uranium ore.

Hollywood couldn't have written the script any
better.

By the end of that year Steen was mining 500 tons a
day at $52 a ton.

Ten years later he had grossed over $70 million.

During that decade, Steen moved his family out of
the shack and into a custom-built ten-room house on a
hill overlooking the village of Moab. There were plenty
of big cars for himself, lots of jewellery and furs for his

wife, private planes to get him around the country and a 69 foot WWII British Navy runabout that he converted into a yacht at a cost of $150,000. He docked it in San Francisco because a yacht there was, as far as he was concerned, the height of luxury. Occasionally he'd also use the yacht for business. 'Once,' he told a reporter, 'after my miners went for two years without an accident, I took a bunch of them for a cruise on the yacht. We went everywhere, visited all the whorehouses, everything, and I picked up the tab.'

Besides picking up the tab two or three times a week for parties at home, every July 27th he'd invite literally thousands of folk to help celebrate the anniversary of his find. He was so popular that in 1958 he got himself elected to the Utah State Senate. But he backed a few unpopular bills . . . in favour of cigarettes and booze, which didn't go down too well with his largely Mormon constituents . . . and in 1961 he found it prudent to move to Nevada.

In Washoe Valley, near Reno, he blew $2 million building himself a 27-room mansion. Ironically it was just down the block from the house that Sandy Bowers built. Ironic because Bowers struck it rich in the nineteenth century prospecting for silver, blew his fortune on fancy living, and died broke.

A year after he left Utah, the US suffered a uranium glut. Figuring it was time to do other things, Steen sold his company, Utex, and walked away with $11 million. He let out the word that he had money to invest and waited for anyone with a better mousetrap to beat a path to his door.

They descended on him like a plague of locusts.

One after another, anybody with even the most harebrained scheme was shown into Steen's office and given an audience. Most of them got turned away with one of those 'We'll call you' responses. Sadly, a lot of the ones who didn't get turned away should have. He lost $1 million on a cattle ranch thanks to bad management and when the price of beef plunged. He lost another bundle on a California orange grove thanks to bad management and when the weather ruined the crops. He dropped $100,000 on a plan to manufacture homemade Yugoslavian pickles. He lost $3 million on a company refurbishing propeller-driven executive planes just at the time that the Learjet came onto the market.

He also tangled with the IRS.

They claimed he still owed them $2.4 million. He balked, holding them off as long as he could. But the tax collectors are not known for their sense of humour or their patience and in February 1968 the IRS raided his offices. That panicked his creditors who seemed to come out of the woodwork carrying IOUs for $3.1 million.

Steen emptied his pockets but could only put less than $1 million in cash on the table. However, he insisted, his assets were worth upwards of $18 million. His creditors didn't believe it. He had a tough time proving it. A Nevada judge ruled Steen bankrupt. Steen appealed and had the decision overthrown. The creditors tried a second time. Five years of hearings later, a California judge ruled him bankrupt again. And this time the appeals court agreed. Although he established a trust for his children when he was in the chips, by 1975 he was broke, back on the land, looking for another strike.

In Moab these days they tell you he's somewhere in the Colorado Springs, Colorado, area. Yes, they say, he's still prospecting. No, we're certain he's never had another big hit. Yes, he's alive and prospecting out of

Colorado Springs. Yes, that's where he went after he left Washoe Valley.

Except he's not listed in the Colorado Springs phone book.

And there's nothing on him in the library at the *Colorado Springs Gazette Telegraph*.

'The next time it will be different,' he promised when he left Washoe Valley without a cent in his pocket.

But, then, what else would anyone have expected him to say?

'Put your money in land', goes the old adage, 'cause ain't nobody making any more of it.'

And so what if there is another old adage that goes, 'Never invest in anything that eats or needs repainting,' because land – and even repaintable real estate – has always been the traditional hedge against inflation. Land is especially flexible because, besides digging under it, you can build on top of it or just buy a parcel of it and do nothing more than move it along to the next fellow.

On paper, then, land and property are an almost sure way of coming out ahead.

And many of the world's greatest fortunes revolve around those two.

The British Royal Family, for example, are massive land owners with farms spread throughout the country and real estate in the heart of London. In particular, the Prince of Wales, who is also the Duke of Cornwall, has enormous property holdings in the Duchy, almost certainly making him one of the wealthiest land owners in Europe. At the same time, the Duke of Westminster has got to be one of the wealthiest men in the world thanks to his Grosvenor Estates. He owns and controls several square miles of absolutely prime residential and commercial property in the very centre of London.

So impressive are such titled holdings that, in the United States, the legendary robber-baron John Jacob Astor actually tried to model himself on Britain's landed gentry.

An immigrant from Waldorf, Germany ... hence, eventually, the name Waldorf Astoria ... Astor first went to London in 1781 where his brother was selling musical instruments. Two years later, at the age of 20, he sailed to New York with, by his own account, 'One good suit of Sunday clothes, seven flutes and five pounds sterling'. He found a job in the fur trade, saved his money and before too long opened his own business, having learned to defraud the Indians out of their furs in exchange for trinkets and liquor. His huge profits there were then invested in shipping and by 1800 he was already a man of considerable wealth.

By all accounts he was also a thoroughly unscrupulous fellow, even though his fortune is now thought of, in American terms, as old respectable money. There is no doubt that Astor openly flouted the law. There is even less doubt that those same methods would today see him sent to jail. It's just that in those days officials were much easier to buy. Too, there were no taxes, which meant serious wealth was a more easily attainable goal than it is today.

While visiting London, sometime early in the nineteenth century, Astor became aware of the admiration British society held for the landed classes. He liked the way land owners were elevated to an exalted position so closely associated with nobility. After all, he knew, the feudal concept of royalty was based almost entirely on land holdings. He appreciated the power and stability of English fortunes founded on property. Especially appealing to him was the term 'landlord' – lord of the soil – and all of the authority under law that came with the title. So on his return to New York he deliberately set out to establish himself as the richest and most important land owner in the United States. By the beginning of the twentieth century, the Astor family might very well have been just that. Their land interests in New York City alone were guestimated at over $300 million.

Following in that tradition, Marshall Field bought up downtown Chicago while the Rockefeller family used their Standard Oil money to buy up as much of New York's Fifth Avenue as they could muster. The Vanderbilts and the Goulds headed west, buying and leasing land for their railways. The Guggenheims and some Rothschilds headed west, buying land for mining. Add to them the Fricks and the Mellons, the Morgans and the Carnegies, the Dukes, the Kennedys, and the Woolworths. They all had land.

So, too, lesser known dynasties.

Philip Belz came to America from Austria in 1910 with his mother. They settled in Memphis, Tennessee, and spent what little of their own money they had on property. 'Buying vacant land with other people's money is a very dangerous thing,' he was fond of saying. Today the Belz family are the largest landlords in the state.

James Campbell ran away from home in Ireland in 1839, as a stowaway. He was shipwrecked, captured by cannibals and somehow made his way to Hawaii where he bought land. Today his heirs own over 80,000 acres in paradise, including 10 per cent of Oahu Island.

Panayes Dikeou came to America from Greece in 1921, started his business career by selling popcorn, put his popcorn profits into vending machines and then put his vending machine profits into real estate. His idea was to buy small parcels of land, located in downtown areas, and wait for someone to come along with a land-assemblage deal. When that happened, he made it his business to be the final holdout. Today the family controls 15 acres in downtown Denver, Colorado, plus land surrounding airports in Denver and Houston, and shopping centres in Florida.

John Galbreath was an Ohio real estate broker who was wiped out by the Depression. He bounced back by coming up with package deals, where he'd find a tenant, then a builder and finally arrange for a bank to finance the marriage. Today the family has massive interests in midwestern farmland, commercial property, game reserves and Hong Kong commercial property.

Ray Hugh Garvey was a Topeka, Kansas, newspaper boy who saved $500 in 1917 and bought a half interest in a land company. Today his heirs control an estate comprising oil and gas holdings, farmland, office buildings, shopping centres and grain trading.

Richard King was a steamboat captain on the Rio Grande. He invested his money in the 1850s in Spanish land grants along the Texas side of the river. Today his heirs own the land, farm on, graze on and lease oil rights under 823,000 acres – that's larger than the state of Rhode Island or about the same size as the English county of Kent or the French *département* of the Alpes Maritimes – known as the King Ranch.

William Scully left Ireland in the mid-1800s to wind his way through the Midwest, sampling the soil, buying whatever land anyone would sell him: Before the turn of the century he owned hundreds of thousands of acres of farmland in Illinois, Kansas, Nebraska and Missouri, plus swampland in Louisiana.

Today his grandchildren lease that land to tenant farmers and have long since found oil in the Louisiana swamp.

Frederick Weyerhaeuser left Germany in 1852 to work in a Minnesota saw mill. When it went out of business, he took it over, made it profitable, then started buying forestry land, heading west from St Paul all the way to Seattle, Washington. Much of the land was bought at $6 an acre from railway tycoon James J. Hill. 'The only times I ever lost money', Weyerhaeuser liked to say, 'was when I didn't buy.' Today his heirs own a part of the company that still bears his name, in addition to interests in forestry, mining and banking.

Leslie Townes Hope left England in 1907, was raised in Cleveland, Ohio, and won a Charlie Chaplin imitation contest in 1913. That launched a career in show business. From 1941 to 1953 he was one of Hollywood's top money-making stars. A lot of what he earned went into real estate. The same was true of his late pal, Harry Lillis Crosby. Today Hope and Crosby head a list of the wealthiest stars ever to come out of show business. They are also considered to be the largest land owners in the state of California. In fact, Bob Hope once said that the only reason he kept working well into his 80s was not because he needed the money to live, but so he'd have enough cash to help pay the taxes on his land.

In 1980 I met a man in Kansas City who told me that the secret of life was nickels.

'If you got yourself a nickel coming in from here,' he explained, 'and a nickel coming in from there, and another nickel coming in from somewhere else, well, then, those nickels will add up fast and you'll never have to worry about money.'

Songwriters have long ago discovered the joys of being paid every time a disc jockey plays their music. This fellow simply applied the same game to real estate. He had, once upon a time, been an accountant who woke up one day suffering from that desperate treadmill feeling. Having saved some money, he decided to give up his job and take a chance at saving his own life. With a firm belief in his '5-cent philosophy', he invested in an old house on a small tract of land. He and his wife lived there while they fixed it up. When it was ready they didn't sell it, they rented it. With that money coming in every month, he mortgaged a second property and did the same thing. Thirty years later, with lots of nickels arriving all the time, he was one of the most important residential landlords in the Midwest.

Yet, for as many ways as there are to make money with land in theory, there are just as many ways to lose money with land in practice.

William Zeckendorf owned, and ran with an iron fist, a New York based company called Webb & Knapp. For more than three decades he was to world-class real estate what Pele was to world-class soccer.

Simply put, Bill Zeckendorf ruled the game.

Born in 1905, and after a less than spectacular school career, Zeckendorf went to work for his uncle, a real estate agent in lower Manhattan. Beginning with a clerk's job handling rentals, he learned the business literally from the basement up. Before long he branched out to sales. And at the age of 25 he finessed a $3 million property deal that not only netted him $21,000 in commission but also firmly established him as one of the young lions in New York real estate.

Eight years later he was offered a partnership in the highly respected firm of Webb & Knapp. Ten years after that he paid his partners $6 million to become the firm's sole owner.

Under his influence, Webb & Knapp went into office buildings, supermarkets, railways, oil wells, factories, warehouses, night clubs and airports, expanding the empire from Manhattan to 35 states, Canada, Mexico and the UK. He retained architects like Le Corbusier, and hired I.M. Pei. He handled deals for Macy's, Gimbel's, Montgomery Ward, *Time*, Woolworth's, the State of Israel, the New York Philharmonic, the Rockefellers and the Astors. In fact for a number of years he single-handedly managed the entire Astor family real estate portfolio.

After the Second World War, Zeckendorf spent $6 million purchasing an 8 acre tract of warehouses, run-down flats and a slaughterhouse in mid-town Manhattan, along the East River. He planned to construct a $150 million office, hotel and recreation complex that might, perhaps, one day bear his name. But 'Zeckendorf City' was not to be. A better offer came along. John D. Rockefeller wanted that land, so Zeckendorf sold it to him for $8.5 million. Rockefeller in turn donated it to be used as the headquarters for the United Nations.

'What I like to do', Zeckendorf once said, 'is to recognize a great piece of land and conceive a suitable edifice for it.'

Over the years, either as an active real estate magnate or towards the end as a consultant, his insights and skills went into such projects as the Roosevelt Field shopping centre on Long Island (the first of America's modern shopping malls), Century City in Los Angeles, the Place Ville Marie in Montreal, the Mile High Center in Denver and L'Enfant Plaza in Washington, DC.

For a time his trading partners were the likes of General Motors, Alcoa and, in London, the Philip Hill Investment Group.

Lord Keith, chairman of Philip Hill, remembers Zeckendorf fondly. 'He had immense charm, and was a great visionary. He was also a remarkable salesman. He assembled prime sites and put spectacular buildings on them. Everything he did came to fruition and became, at the end of the day, extremely successful. But those spectacular projects took longer than he anticipated and a good deal more money than he anticipated. If he'd have just slowed down and done one at a time. I think he got carried away. The trouble was, I think, he had too many visions all at once.'

By the late 1950s the same imaginative Zeckendorf spirit that had taken Webb & Knapp out of the ranks of conservative real estate holdings and turned it into the world's largest land development empire, had also brought it close to the brink of extinction. Instead of following his well-proven formula for success . . . using a minimum of cash and a maximum of ingenious borrowing techniques to finance cash-generating projects . . . he went beyond his scope of expertise and put the company into hotel management, construction, urban renewal and an ill-fated New York amusement park called Freedomland. That was supposed to be a Bronx version of Disneyland but it was a very poor imitation, and lost money right from the start. The property was finally sold for a housing project. And Freedomland has since become synonymous in New York lingo for a lemon real estate deal.

In 1959 Webb & Knapp reported assets of $300 million.

In 1960 Webb & Knapp reported construction projects under way worth $500 million.

Yet as he piled one vision onto another, costs skyrocketed and interest payments mounted. Debts quickly passed the $100 million mark. And he was forced into mortgaging assets, borrowing money at near-usury rates. It was obvious to lots of people what was happening. But he told his critics, 'I'd rather be alive at 18 per cent than dead at the prime rate.'

A framed inscription on the wall near his desk reiterated the point. 'If I tried to read, much less answer all of the criticisms made of me and all of the attacks levied against me, this office would have to be closed for all other business. I do the best I know how, the very best I can; I mean to keep on doing this, down to the very end.'

But by now the end was in sight.

Webb & Knapp reported $20 million losses in 1962 and $32 million losses in 1963. Assets were sold to try to stop the slide. That left less and less with which to do new deals.

The list of creditors grew. US Steel. Lazard Frères. Chemical Bank. Royal Bank of Canada. In one particular instance sometime around 1960 or 1961, as recalled by a New York lawyer who was there that day, Zeckendorf began negotiations for a property sale at 9 A.M. The meeting, in his office, dragged on non-stop until just before midnight, when Zeckendorf finally had to give in because he needed the money from that sale to meet his interest payments the next morning.

It was the Marine Midland Trust Company that finally cried, enough.

In the spring of 1965, holding $4.2 million of Zeckendorf's IOUs, they put Webb & Knapp into bankruptcy.

And Zeckendorf's innings was over. 'You could say that I feel resigned now that all the harassment is over,' he explained to *Newsweek*. 'We had as much advance warning as the United States Government did at Pearl Harbor . . . We have always managed to avert bankruptcy and we could have come up with something this time too. But what can you do when you're hit on the head?'

He went down, so short of cash that Webb & Knapp couldn't even hire an auditor to go through its books or issue a final annual report.

Slightly less grandiose was the sinking ten years later of Walter Judd Kassuba, a Palm Beach, Florida, based real estate magnate whose empire was once valued at $800 million.

Specializing in the building and managing of apartment complexes, shopping centres, mobile home parks and motels, Kassuba, like Zeckendorf, operated from a highly geared position. However there were a few very important differences between Kassuba's bankruptcy and Zeckendorf's. Where Zeckendorf's liabilities totalled only some $60 million, Kassuba's ran closer to $500 million. And, where Zeckendorf lost everything, Kassuba managed to sidestep total disaster. He filed for Chapter 11 protection, getting his creditors to agree to settle for extended payment terms, reduced interest rates and, in a few cases, debt moratoriums of up to two years.

Under Chapter 11, the party seeking protection is not supposed to be able to rewrite the terms of the loans. However, Kassuba turned out to be such a salesman that he convinced his creditors their only other alternative was to foreclose and manage the properties themselves.

Right from the start, this was one of the few liquidations where everyone realized the debtor was going to come out a lot better off than his hapless creditors.

Of course, that's got to be the aim – whether stated or not – of every financier who gets into trouble.

It certainly must have been what London solicitor Friedrich Grunwald – a.k.a. Fred Greenwood – had in mind. Except his attempted take-overs of several property companies in 1960 wound up being England's most spectacular financial swindle since the Second World War.

A refugee from Hitler who came to the UK in 1938 at the age of 14, Grunwald borrowed £200 from his father to establish a small legal practice in 1948. As his client list grew, he was able to move into London's fashionable Mayfair district. And it was there that his association took hold with the State Building Society, a publicly owned savings and loan institution. State, through their managing director Herbert Murray, handed cheques over to Grunwald, entrusting him to secure certain mortgages. Instead, Grunwald used the money to take over property companies, giving himself and Murray the controlling shares. Those companies were then used as security for loans with State to replace the original 'borrowings'.

It was such a neat system that it worked very well the first four times Grunwald and Murray tried it. The fifth time – going after the Ely Brewery in Cardiff and a company called Lintang Investments that owned, among other properties, Dolphin Square in London, the largest block of flats in Europe – it all went wrong.

The brewery and Lintang were joined together through the holdings of the Jasper Group, controlled by merchant banker Harry Jasper, a sometime associate of Grunwald and Murray.

Even though Jasper was cleared of all subsequent

charges linking him to any fraud, had Grunwald, Murray and Jasper been able to pull off this fifth deal they would have had property holdings valued at around £20 million. But bringing the brewery and Lintang into their stable meant coming up with more than just the State Building Society's money before the terms of the deal expired. Murray and Jasper put up their share. Grunwald mistakenly believed that he could get the rest.

As he later wrote, 'On paper at least we had more than enough. It may sound odd to those who don't know the City, but I assure you that no thought of a crash ever crossed my mind. Why should it? Everything I had touched so far had turned to money. I was the man with the golden fingers, the chap who couldn't go wrong.'

Except he did.

When the deal fell through, the entire pyramid collapsed. The Board of Trade got curious. It aroused the Fraud Squad's interest as well. Apparently there was money missing from the State Building Society's books. Like £3.25 million! Grunwald, Murray and Jasper wound up side by side in the dock at the Old Bailey, where only Jasper walked free. Grunwald and Murray were sentenced to five years and both served three and a half.

Happily for the public who stood to lose in a building society crash, their funds were returned, with a token shilling per pound on top as compensation for lost interest. Grunwald fared less well. He walked out of prison penniless.

'Nothing would have been wrong', he told Fleet Street when he was released from jail in 1963, 'if I had got the money I was promised. But I was let down.'

That's not quite the way the jury saw it.

'I am not a rogue,' he went on. 'But there is a saying in Britain that if you succeed in the City, you get a knighthood. If you fail, you wind up in Wormwood Scrubs.'

At least he proved half of that.

9

William Stern – Record-Breaking Bankrupt

William Stern is not the easiest of men to pin down.

It takes a lot of chasing, suggesting perhaps to anyone who can take a hint that he doesn't particularly want to be pinned down.

Born in Hungary in 1935, he was interned briefly as a child with his entire family by the Nazis at the Bergen-Belsen camp, raised in Switzerland until the age of 17, then educated in New York and Boston where he got his bachelor's degree, became a US citizen and also got a law degree from Harvard.

When you first meet him he is chilly and stand-offish, perhaps suspicious of anyone with a tape recorder who has come to invade his privacy.

But, once he agrees to tell his story, there are frequent glimpses of the reputed Stern charm. He is easy to chat with, obviously extremely bright and remarkably open.

'I met and married my wife in 1957. After being admitted to the New York Bar, in July 1960, pursuant to a so-called premarital agreement with my late father-in-law, Osias Freshwater, who required a member of the family alongside him in business, I came back to England with my wife to join the then rather small Freshwater Group. I started in the lower ranks of management, writing out cash books, banking the rents, inspecting boilers, dealing with tenants' repairs. In 1964 I got into the financial side of the business and became joint managing director. I was basically in charge of financing, until 1970 when due to the fact that two younger children in the family had grown to manhood, I felt it was better for each of us to row our own boat. So we parted company. We divided the assets, and I established what became known as Stern Holdings in late 1972.'

Less than three years later the mainstay of his property empire, Wilstar Securities Ltd, crashed with the rest of the London property market and he was straddled with debts totalling £142,978,413.

Between 1979 and 1985, he had the rather dubious honour of being listed in the Guinness Book of Records as the largest personal bankrupt in history.

These days, finally released from his bankruptcy, he talks about his spectacular rise and even more spectacular fall like a man who has had plenty of time to put it all into some sort of perspective.

'From 1961 until 1971, English property lending was subject almost incessantly to arbitrary limitations of one type or another made by the Bank of England. They were trying to limit inflation by limiting the amount of credit to the economy. Therefore, anyone who was able to expand during the 1960s had an uphill task however good his balance sheet might be. You had to face the challenge of a bank manager who'd say, "I'd love to help you but our credit is limited to within 5 per cent of our lending of last year. With inflation at 5 per cent that effectively means we are limited to an unchanged ceiling which has been taken up by other customers and therefore I cannot let you have the money." The only way you could get any money was to shop around between ten or twelve banks to find the one which had some room within those artificially imposed limits. Believe me, I could tell stories unending of the most wonderful deals that couldn't be financed.'

At the same time, during the mid-1960s, the big four joint stock banks wanted to expand, so they created subsidiaries. They capitalized those smaller banks at £50 million or £100 million, whatever, and sent them out into the world. But before too long the managing directors were complaining that they couldn't lend because they weren't allowed to take deposits above the artificially imposed limits.

Then came 1971.

The Bank of England decided to throw open the shutters and let the sun come shining in. They did an about-face, wiping away years of artificial restrictions on lending. The new policy was to let market forces dictate, to let credit seek its own natural levels and to allow anyone with money to lend to anyone who wanted some.

'It was a new era. Now the philosophy was, let any institution go out and compete for deposits. Let the little merchant bank offer half or one point more than Barclays. Let them attract deposits and let them lend to anyone for any purpose as long as there is a market. This had the effect of pouring into the property sector a few billion pounds which previously were not in property. Of course, when you have a lot of money chasing a finite amount of property, prices will rise. Coupled with the fact that when you have a free credit policy it generally creates a feeling of affluence. Credit was generous. People who could spend did spend. And the value of property, the value of rent, the value of houses, it all went up dramatically between, I would say, December 1971 and the summer of 1973. It was an upward-only spiral.'

In his own case, Stern was new on the scene as an independent but well known in property circles and around the City.

'My own business was barely six months or a year old. Yet I had banks literally knocking on my door, saying, can we come to see you, can we invite you for lunch, would you like two, three, five million pounds for your expansion, we would like to be in with you on the ground floor, etc., etc., etc. They couldn't have done that, even if they wanted to, four years earlier because of the credit restrictions.'

Throughout 1972 and well into 1973 large amounts of money continued to pour into property. Prices rose in 1971, but now they soared. Valuers appraised accordingly. And the banks continued to lend against these higher appraised values.

But in the autumn of 1973 a series of seemingly unrelated events began that, Stern now believes, triggered off the crash.

'First and foremost was the Yom Kippur War with the subsequent unprecedented rise in the price of fuel oil. That unsettled the finances of the western world and had a ripple effect in virtually all western economies. Then, there was a conference of the Institute of Directors held at the Albert Hall around the autumn of 1973, when Ted Heath, who was prime minister, proudly and stupidly said that Britain had no problems other than the problems associated with success.'

Within five months, England had a miners' strike, it was unlawful to leave office lights on for more than a few hours a day, offices were unheated and industry had to shut down because it didn't have enough power to operate. The miners' union successfully challenged the Conservative government of the day and forced the calling of an election. And Heath was defeated.

'A minority socialist government was elected. What I mean by that is even though they had a majority in the number of seats they had a minority of the popular vote, which hence led to the mistaken belief that the government would be short lived. That helped to continue the uncertainty. In the middle of all this, on December 4, 1973, came the collapse of London and County Securities, a fringe bank which grew on the back of this huge expansion and which found itself short of liquidity. England being England where secrets are well kept, the Bank of England extended to that first bank the beginning of what became known as the lifeboat.'

At least in the beginning, he says, those lifeboats were such well-kept secrets that even some bankers who were directly affected didn't know where the money was coming from.

Stern's group was at the time 75 per cent partners with the First National Bank of Maryland in a small merchant bank called First Maryland Ltd. On holiday with his family in December 1973, Stern had just arrived in Miami when he got a call from the general manager of First Maryland.

'I was on the board of directors and majority owner but I did not run the bank, preferring to leave the bankers to run it. He said, we have a problem. He said we could not renew our market deposits. He said it may be useful if I returned to England. So I came back right away and got on to our main bankers, Barclays. And they gave me an unusual response. Normally large banks were not particularly keen to help the expansion of the small ones, understandably. Get your deposits from the public, not from us. But instead this time they said, oh fine, Mr Stern, what liquidity do you need? Two million? Three million? Unbeknown to us, Barclays was doing that at the bidding of the Bank of England, which had organized the lifeboat and which eventually took £1.25 billion needed to keep the banking system afloat.'

But the lifeboat policy was, in an ironic way, the infamous double-edged sword. The Bank of England pumped money into the system so that the world would believe everything was hunky-dory. Except they couldn't keep it secret long enough and all the rumours that came hand in hand with the lifeboat helped to create even more uncertainty.

'There is nothing more corrosive than uncertainty or fear. From the miners' strike and the beginning of the bank collapse in December 1973, within a 12-month period, to the beginning of January 1975, there was a total collapse of confidence in Britain. You could not give property away. It is not that prices collapsed. That would simply mean property had found a new level of prices. No. They were not trading at all. The bargain sales were in 1975 and 1976. In the year 1974 you literally could not give property away. People pretended to continue to keep talking. Institutions pretended to keep buying. The talk in the profession continued but no contracts were signed. I challenge anyone to point to any deal done in the year 1974.'

When the crash came, the Stern group – by then a conglomeration of nearly 50 companies dealing in property, banking and insurance – was in the midst of building on 40 different sites in England.

'It's like a manufacturing activity. Except, instead of building widgets in a factory, you build buildings in the fresh air. We had banking lines and very adequate banking lines. But there was an unspoken assumption. It was that the finished building would either rent within a reasonable period of time, say six to 12 months after its completion, or if vacant it would sell.

The one assumption that was not programmed into the computer was that business life could come to a halt.'

He never dreamed he would not be able to meet his interest payments. But his loans were, depending on the period you select, running at over £150 million. His own reserves could only take them one more quarter. The collapse in the market became evident in January 1974. He made good on his 25 March interest payments. But now the coffers were empty.

'That's when I decided to test the market. I took a lovely building which we owned in the centre of Dublin, thinking that the Irish might be a little insulated from what was happening. To make a long story short, agents were telling me that it should fetch about a million. I put it out to tender. One then had the usual activity of people going to the solicitors, inspecting the deeds, inspecting the planning, and I was waiting anxiously for the opening date of the tender. You know how many offers we had? None. There was not a single tender. Not for a million. Not for £800,000. Not for £500,000. Not for £100,000. Nothing. The market had disappeared. Within days of that I went to our main bankers and explained that come June we could not meet our quarterly interest payments. In mid-May they brought in liquidators Cork Gully.'

It was little compensation, but Stern was not alone.

Bricks and mortar had turned to mud.

Property speculation is a high-leveraged game. You use as much of the bank's money as you can. As inflation is part of the formula, in the time it takes you to develop the property and resell it, the property should appreciate enough in value to cover a good part of the interest rates you've been paying. As land is the traditional hedge against inflation anyway, once the property is developed you stand to make a handsome profit. That's the way it works. That's the way it's always worked.

Except after December 1973 it stopped working that way.

Property speculators were suddenly faced with what is now sexily called 'negative revenue outflow'. In the old days it was known as having your back against the wall. The banks wanted their interest payments but no one was buying property. If you owned some flats and people were paying rents . . . in other words if you were using property as an investment . . . you either had money coming in or could always lower your rents to get some money coming in. People will always need places to live so you had a fighting chance. But if you were building property, if you were on the development side, all you had were bills to pay. You can't sell a house without a roof. So until the roof is finished your cash flow is a one-way street.

These days when you speak to any of the property people who went through those years – survivors or victims, it doesn't matter – the first thing they all say is that no one ever expected the crisis to last as long as it did. One, two, three years perhaps. But not five or six.

A well-known City figure who successfully came out of the crisis put it this way: 'One of the lessons of that era is where you have real assets that can earn, if you have the time and patience, those assets will come through for you. A lot of people grew up in those days. But anyone with a large development programme was in trouble.'

For instance, Guardian Properties admitted they were having serious problems in March and went into receivership three months later. The Lyon Group asked for a debt moratorium in May but soon crashed with a £50 million debt. Town and Commercial Properties eventually sank, as did the David Lewis Group, as did Northern Developments. They were all fairly big names in those days. And even some of the very big names in property these days had their troubles then too. MEPC, British Land, Town and City Properties. There was just no escaping it. This was a horror movie, just as scary as *The Bugbear That Ate Cleveland*, except it was called the crash that nearly busted Great Britain.

For instance, there was Pat Matthews and the First National Finance Corporation.

Founded in 1960 as a shell company called Birmingham Carriage and Wagon, Matthews built FNFC up in just a decade to one of the largest operators in London's secondary banking and property market. Said to be worth £550 million, when the crash came the Bank of England stepped in. Their lifeboat team decided FNFC was worth saving, and subsequently sunk £360 million into the company. In October 1975 FNFC reported an £83 million loss, claiming a world record for the banking industry. Matthews resigned and was given a £57,000 golden handshake.

For instance, Amalgamated Investment and Property.

For the most part, Amalgamated's money was tied up in a few very large development properties. Therefore, when the crunch came there was an outflow of cash and nothing to sell to cover the rising costs of staying in business. The buck was passed to the few institutional investors that were willing to keep the company afloat. But then Amalgamated had been one of the go-go, wealthy, beautiful, well-selected property companies, so why shouldn't the institutions continue to back it? All the more so because it was headed by Gabriel Harrison, everybody's blue-eyed boy and the darling figure of the property world. Sadly, in the middle of all this, in 1976, Harrison died while undergoing surgery. Within two months of his death, the company went into insolvency.

Stern insists that the insolvency was not created by Harrison's death. He says it was simply that the institutions were no longer prepared to go on fooling themselves. They understood there was no longer any point in supporting the company, they divided the spoils, sold out, and said good day.

So no, Stern was not alone. Not by any stretch of the imagination. 'As long as you had faith in the recovery of the country, values did come back. Imagine that some tooth fairy had told the Stern Group, whatever your cash requirements are, don't worry, finish the buildings and as soon as the economy picks up, we'll wait until you rent it and let interest accumulate throughout the period. If that had happened, we would today be a very very wealthy company.'

But, to have pulled it off, you absolutely had to have that tooth fairy to stand by you.

'In the property world, Town and City is the only one I can think of. In the banking world, while no depositor suffered, 30 merchant banks folded. The shareholders of 30 institutions lost the value of their investment. The exception was FNFC. They lent heavily to the property sector. When that first bank got into trouble in December 1973, FNFC held out a helping hand. Apparently, a promise was made that they would have the goodwill of the Bank of England for that helping hand. So they were not allowed to collapse.'

Thanks to the Bank of England as tooth fairy, Stern points out, FNFC's balance sheets make an interesting read.

'That's a unique study. Normally if you saw a printed balance sheet with a £70 million excess of liabilities over assets, you'd think the company was bust. But they weren't. Yet when my balance sheet showed a £30 million excess of assets over liabilities, I was broke. It has to do with the definition of solvency, or your ability to meet your debts as they fall due. Despite properties notionally worth £30 million, I did not have that ability. FNFC, despite £70 million excess of debt over liability, had a tooth fairy in the person of the Bank of England saying we'll pump in money for as long as the liquidity crisis lasts. The liquidity crisis, as far as they're concerned, finished in 1984 or so. And today FNFC is happily trading with a value on the exchange approaching £100 million. But they were technically insolvent for a period of years.'

Those companies not supported by institutions, like his, ran as fast as they could just to stand still.

Now, you don't have to be a major league risk taker to know that if someone refuses to lend you money, while you may not make any, by the same token it's very difficult to lose any.

So a healthy part of the blame for the massive losses that took place in those days has to rest squarely on the shoulders of the banks. They were the ones lending the money. As Stern says, banks were banging on his door with plenty of loot for the taking. But property developers were looking to support long-term projects, while the banks wanted their money back in three to five years. And it doesn't necessarily take the benefit of hindsight to see that's obviously not the right combination. You can hardly blame the developers for taking the banks' money. But even if bankers today won't admit it in public, they know damn well their lending policies in the early 1970s were wrong. The proof is in the pudding. These days you can't find a single banker who remembers lending property money in 1972–74. It seems they just don't exist.

With the economies of western nations so tightly tied to each other, the British property crisis was not an isolated incident. The effects of it were felt in other countries.

It was especially dramatic in France, where British capital had been heavily invested in property development. In fact there was an almost copycat occurrence of the English events. The market disappeared in 1974. Subsequently values dropped to a level from which they only recovered two or three years after property bounced back in England.

In America, and in particular in New York City, residential property was foreclosed by the thousands of buildings. Savings and loans associations had their hands full for the same reason that the bottom fell out of the property market – the energy crisis. And those two problems were compounded when New York itself came so very close to going bust.

Besides Great Britain, Stern had holdings in France, Belgium, Denmark ... 'They were small and quite frankly a boom in Denmark would not have saved my British group' ... and in Israel. But it was in England where the devastation was the most unbearable because it came without any warning.

'Other industries in Britain, normal manufacturing industries, continued their slow decline for reasons unique to themselves. But they didn't collapse. The collapse was limited to two sectors of the British economy which are intertwined, property and finance. The financial sector was supported artificially by the Bank of England. But the property sector was not, with the exception of one or two of those companies I mentioned. The collapse was total.'

He likens it to a shutter coming down suddenly.

'No one saw it coming. No one had any advance warning. I've said this many times before, but I defy anyone to find one single quote from a banker, investment manager, insurance company chairman, or any financial commentator, published up to December 1, 1973, which would warn of an overheated market, likely to come down, watch your prices, watch an over-expanding X-Y-Z, can't last, etc. No one. And the proof, I repeat to you, is Heath saying, we've only got the problems of success. England was thought, wrongly and mistakenly, to be on the wings of an unending expansion, financially, materially, even in terms of the manufacturing industry. It was an illusion which collapsed within a short three to four months. Without any forewarning whatsoever. There is no pundit you can quote who forewarned it.'

Cork Gully were called in as liquidators in May 1974.

'As soon as I realized that because of the collapse of the market we couldn't meet our interest payments in June 1974, I went to see the group's main bankers who were National Westminster. They sent in their accountants. And they submitted a voluminous report which basically found two things. One was that, on reduced value, the group had an excess of assets over liabilities of £30 million. But as we were building on so many locations, in order to stay alive in the corporate sense of the word, over the next 12 months we would need a vast amount of money, which I seem to

remember was in the order of £30 million. The bank
considered it and on one famous Thursday afternoon,
May 9, 1974, they came to me and said, we are afraid
we can no longer support you and we suggest you see
your solicitors. Which I did that same evening. My
solicitor's advice was to call in Kenneth Cork of Cork
Gully to look at the affairs of the group. I saw a partner
of Cork's the next day and his advice was to call
a meeting of the group's main bankers for Monday,
May 13.'

On that day, a dozen bankers met in Stern's boardroom, representing between them two-thirds or more
of the group's debt. He told them, basically, 'We are
illiquid.'

Kenneth Cork was then asked by those bankers to
supervise the affairs of the group. To all intents and
purposes Stern could now do nothing without Cork's
approval.

'It was immensely upsetting, bearing in mind that
every step we were taking, due to our size, was subject
to newspaper comment. There wasn't a day that my
wife or members of my family couldn't pick up a
national daily without seeing some aspect of the
group's affairs being reported on.'

Cork's first job was to keep Stern's group afloat for
as long as he could. He studied the books and met with
the bankers and worked with Stern and decided, there
is a temporary crisis in liquidity. He told the banks,
instead of the £30 million net asset value that Stern
had, as verified by his accountants on normal balance
sheets six months earlier, he'd downgraded it to £18
million. But that meant Stern's group was, with £18
million of assets over liabilities, still alive, merely in a
temporary crisis of liquidity owing to a depressed state
of the market. Cork reiterated that his role was to stay

in and supervise sales until such time as liquidity was re-established.

'A year later when the depressed market did not pick up, when the expected salvation did not material-ize, when the country remained at bargain basement level, with all that accruing interest, it became silly to continue pretending. We were working with an appraisal evaluation which by that time was 15 months old. No one would buy that or even 30 per cent less. Then came the sudden slashing where values simply disappeared.'

The example he gives is a development site he had off Oxford Street, in London's fashionable West End.

'We had planning permission. There were no doubts. There was no delay. All we needed was a builder to put up 14,000 sq. ft. And I say 14,000 sq. ft. because if I said 140,000 you'd say it was oversized, there would be traffic problems, not enough parking. But this was a 14,000 sq. ft. little nothing in the heart of the West End. We bought the site in 1973 for £1.25 million. Lest you think I was a fool for paying that much, the bank's valuers appraised the property at £1.3 million. They lent against it the usual 75 per cent, I forget what it was, £900,000 or £950,000. They sold it in 1976 for either £150,000 or £175,000 but definitely below £200,000. A sixth of its value or less within a period of 18 months. And today it's a beautiful office building. The fellow who bought it then made a fortune. It was a total collapse of confidence. The banks couldn't believe that an office building there would have a taker.'

Those were not only difficult days for the property market, they were also personally difficult times for Stern.

'It was only small consolation that one saw trouble

everywhere else. One knew that one wasn't alone. But they were very upsetting times, mostly because of the publicity. We live in a fairly small circle of friends who obviously were every morning looking at me, meeting me, knowing everything about what was happening to me.'

During the worst part of the crisis, a good part of 1974, he says he was on tranquillizers because the pressure was so great.

'They helped me keep some sort of even keel. But I was fortunate, in a way, that many other people in similar situations effectively closed the door behind them and somebody else sorts out their affairs. I had to stay on for 18 months to work for Kenneth Cork in helping him sort out the affairs of the group, providing information about the properties. In a way that was helpful because I had to apply myself to duties instead of wandering the streets and commiserating about what had happened.'

His main concern was to try to keep his troubles as far away from his family as possible.

'I found myself at one point with, I think, not £5000 to my name anywhere. When the curtain came down, all I wanted to do was to be able to lead a normal life at home with my wife and children, for them, on a day-to-day basis. That was, I think, the single greatest challenge. After all, you can't stop children from hearing things at school about their father when their friends repeat what they've heard at home. So it was very important to me to maintain a normal home life. It's one's faith and one's family which enables one to get through.'

Throughout this period, Cork tried to avoid Stern's personal bankruptcy, saying that it would accomplish nothing. Anyway, the creditors needed Stern to help

sort through the very complex group of companies.
Everybody wanted to avoid a free-for-all sale of assets,
so Stern was named a director of the group under Cork,
which couldn't have happened had he been put into
bankruptcy. Stern was kept on a salary ... 'I don't
know if I could live from it but I was certainly kept on
a salary ...' which started at £15,000 per year – a lot
of money in those days – but diminished as the liquidation proceeded. In the last few months he was on
£1000 per annum consultancy basis. That finished
when Stern stopped working for Cork in December
1975.

Early in 1977, Cork called Stern to say that he could
no longer delay the personal bankruptcy issue.

'That came to me as a shock. Because in a way it
meant that as long as I could be useful to the whole
body of creditors I would be kept out of bankruptcy.
The moment I fulfilled my functions the inevitable
would have to happen.'

The creditor chosen to do the deed was the Keyser
Ullman Bank. They started the bankruptcy proceedings against Stern, claiming debts of £20 million.

'That was an interesting choice because Keyser
Ullman itself was a merchant bank which had suffered
from the crash and wouldn't have then been in existence if not for a Bank of England lifeboat.'

Advised that they intended to take judgement on his
personal guarantees, Stern offered up all his worldly
goods and also agreed to submit himself to any form of
cross-examination by counsel, but in private, if there
was any way of avoiding a formal bankruptcy proceed-
ing. The answer was, no. It was felt that, since a
number of banks were owed such large sums and as
there had been such public interest in the matter,
everything should all be seen to be above board and

public. The creditors felt that anyone wishing to cross-examine Stern should be able to do so.

At that point someone suggested to Stern that he file for his own bankruptcy. That would have cut short the Keyser Ullman procedure and perhaps saved Stern some of the prolonged discomfort of a contested battle. With that looking like the least painful option, Stern sought counsel's advice. But he was told not to do that if there was any glimmer of hope that he might avoid bankruptcy.

'So I defended the action.'

He put up technical defences, which were overruled.

'I thought, if I lose, so be it. Which I did.'

The judgement was entered for the sum total of the Keyser Ullman involvement, £20.5 million.

The other creditors piled onto the bandwagon.

And William Stern was on his way to the record books.

One very curious fact that he points out, substantiated during the bankruptcy hearings, was that the banks accepted his personal guarantee without ever having asked the most basic questions or even wanting to see his personal financial statement.

'There are two elementary questions they should have asked. What are you worth? And to whom else have you given guarantees? Had they asked those questions, they would have been told that I was worth personally, other than my shareholding in the group, perhaps a quarter of a million pounds—being my house and personal effects. And that I had freely given guarantees to all the lenders because, being a private group, it was the accepted custom that banks or public companies did not require guarantees but any agreement with private companies did.'

But then he feels that if someone were to ask any of the bankers involved in the lending of 1971–73 if they were indeed relying on the personal assets of William Stern outside the group, the answer would be no.

'Because they never contemplated that. Had they had any doubts about the assets against which they were lending, they wouldn't have lent. But the legal facts of life are that a personal guarantee means just that. Against all expectations, if that which forms the reason and the basis of the lending collapses, they can look to the person down to his last penny. That's what they did. So I couldn't really feel that they were dogs. I had effectively made nonsense of the group's limited liability by freely giving my guarantees.'

Looking back on the Stern affair, Kenneth Cork agrees.

'The market was agin him. He only went bankrupt personally when he borrowed £200 million, which would be £1 billion today. Now you know bankers are renowned for their stupidity. So when they said what security are you putting up, Stern said, I'll give you the whole of the shares in my company and I'll also guarantee the debt personally. So the idiot bankers take that, not realizing that if the company couldn't pay its overdraft or pay its borrowings the shares are valueless. So Willie pledged his shares and gave his personal guarantee. He didn't hide behind his company.'

Stern continues. 'I'll tell you something about how banks work. You have the people who lend and then you have the receivers. When a loan goes bad or a group collapses, you may have known and worked together with people in the bank for however many years, but those who take the liquidation decisions are totally different from those who are on the lending side. Every bank of any size has a recovery department where people deal with nothing but loans which have gone wrong. To those people you are nothing but a debtor who, on a personal guarantee after the assets have been realized, owes an amount which represents a deficiency and they will go for that regardless.'

While any number of bankers admit to having been charmed by him, Stern's aloofness seemed to keep them at arm's length. He wasn't one to encourage business relationships that overflowed into social relationships. Maybe that's the reason, he says, why he could never turn around after the crash and say, so and so was a good friend but he let me down.

'It wasn't in the power of the people I knew to really do anything for me. I wouldn't have expected the general manager of a large bank to not proceed because I was a nice guy. I did not spend my time being wined and dined with the establishment. I attended to my business. I never expected any outlandish favours from anyone in a position to influence matters.'

In that respect his situation was, he feels, very different from so many other businessmen who ran into financial difficulties around the same time. Jim Slater, for instance.

'He was a much more visible chairman of a group which was in the papers almost weekly with a new deal. He had a bank. He was wining and dining with the Bank of England and when things went wrong I'm sure he was let down by people whom he may have felt had the ability perhaps to take a different course of action. Specifically the Bank of England. I was always much less visible, more inward looking. So in a way I think, not only with hindsight but also at the time, I felt what was happening to me was perhaps inevitable.'

It all comes back to those personal guarantees.

'Had I not given my personal guarantee, I could have built up the group and then, when it looked as if everything was turning sour, I could have sold the shares, walked out and gone to the Bahamas. I signed personal guarantees because the banks wanted to ensure that the person they saw across the table remained the party running the show. I never negotiated limitations and I never tried to get out of them.'

Business is business, he says, so even during those darkest days he never took it personally.

'Not really. I was trained as a lawyer and I think in a way it's affected my temperament. I ask myself, is it fair and reasonable. Only when I think somebody is trying to put a knife in my back would I get upset and feel vengeful. One cannot say that I could objectively feel that way if banks who had accepted personal guarantees then took the logical step of suing on them.'

He also insists he's never felt any bitterness about the way the bankers treated him.

No bitterness at all? No resentment? Not even a little?

He says, no.

Then he thinks about that for a moment.

'If there is any bitterness at all it's towards the press. They publicized my affairs in such a totally provocative manner. I'll give you an example. When there was something to do with the sale of my house to my late father, I remember the *Express* published a photograph of my garden taken from a balcony overlooking my house. Now the garden is under 1 acre. But the picture of the garden in the paper that day looked like some feudal manor with about 60 acres, out of the reach of any ordinary person who happened to look at it. I have quite a nice house with a decent garden, but certainly nothing like it was made to look. They were trying to underline what to them seemed not only unusual but morally wrong: that I could be legally bankrupt yet proceed with a lifestyle which to them seemed undistinguishable from that of a wealthy person.'

Perhaps to the press photographer who took that picture it was undistinguishable. But, as far as Stern was concerned, his lifestyle had altered from what it was. From where he stood, the differences certainly were distinguishable.

'I was living with my family's assistance, which barely enabled me to maintain a house and a standard of living above that of the average salaried executive in the UK. It was literally a fraction of what I spent when I was spending my own money rather than money being made available as loans from my family.'

Often described in the press during that period as living lavishly, he claims that's just not true.

'I don't live flamboyantly. But comfortable living, depending on which year you choose, cost me somewhere between £30,000 and £50,000 a year, which is, yes, more in spendable money than most executives make. But if you go on living in the house where you used to live, it's implicit that you require that amount of money because it's a large house and there are continual expenses. You must understand that I never made a secret of it and declared it on all occasions when asked. I never denied that funds were made available to me through my family. And for this I was punished, if I may use that word, by the press, with the net result that today it has created an inhibition in me when I deal with anyone who hasn't known me

pre-crash. I know that anyone who has known me
before the crash knows that Willie Stern has always
kept his word and that his word is his bond. But when
I deal today, say with a lending institution, although I
am facing the manager face to face, I know deep down
there is a credit committee or the board of anonymous
gentlemen who never met me and who only know of
Willie Stern depicted by the press, and who is not the
sort of fellow I would want to do business with.'

Looking closely at the stories that were generated
about him over those years, three points in particular
stand out.

Bones of contention, if you will.

First, there are Stern's 'lavish' Christmas gifts to
various bankers. There were lots of stories about that.
But when you read them closely you found out that (a)
the gifts were not all that lavish ... you can hardly
consider £23 fountain pens, £4 desk lighters, £6 leather
blotter books or even a £400 tea set to be lavish, (b)
Christmas gifts from businessmen to their bankers,
clients and suppliers were not invented by Willie Stern
nor are they exclusive to the property business, and (c)
for personal reasons he did no other business entertaining throughout the year ... no 'weekend meetings'
on a yacht off Antibes, no £100 a head 'evening
meetings' over candlelit French cuisine with wives and
girlfriends present, there weren't even £10 liquid
lunches at Fleet Street wine bars on the company's
account ... so he's always claimed those Christmas
gifts were simply his chosen way of showing some
usually accepted courtesies.

Secondly, when the group was his, pre-crash, and
had a net asset value of £30–80 million, depending on
which year you were looking at, his wife borrowed half
a million pounds from the group. Some of the news-

paper stories made hay with that fact as if it was a truly shocking revelation. However, he says the loan was announced from day one and it clearly made up part of his auditor's report. All the banks he was doing business with could see his reports, so they all knew about it.

Thirdly, that he managed to sell the house to his father, who in turn allowed Stern, his wife and their six children to continue living in it in a manner that effectively precluded the creditors from seeing them evicted.

Realizing the roof over his family's head might eventually be at risk, Stern wanted to sell the house to his father who would then put it in trust for Stern's children. He approached Cork Gully and explained the situation. Stern was not bankrupt at the time nor was he for the two years that followed the sale of the house, which is a stipulation of the bankruptcy laws. Cork Gully said ideally he should put the house up for auction. But Stern told them he wasn't keen on doing that and asked if there was any other way. He was instructed to get two valuations and sell the house for the higher. He did as he was told to, but one of the valuations had a severe qualification attached to it. The house was valued at £125,000 but the appraiser added that he couldn't sell the house at this price, nor could he say when he could sell the house because there was absolutely no market for it. When Stern's father said that his lawyers could not act on such a valuation, Stern commissioned a third valuation, this time with a firm of appraisers used by Cork Gully.

'I now had two unqualified valuations. One was, I think, £85,000 and the other was £110,000. So we sold at £110,000. But there was in the background this £125,000 with the qualification. And later it was thrown in my face. I was asked why I didn't disclose I had a valuation of £125,000. I answered that it wasn't an evaluation because it went on to say we cannot market it at that price because there is no market. But a great deal of political capital was made about this because it was the only contradiction. So, when you ask me, do I have any hard feelings, the answer is no. But I am quite certain that a great many ordinary people with whom I have never had any dealings were made to feel by the press that there was something quite wrong with a system which allowed me to continue to live in what was seen to be a wealthy man's lifestyle.'

Much of the press attention he received and still receives – after all, he is included here – stems from the previously unheard of size of his personal bankruptcy. A company goes down for a couple of hundred million and that's that. One person goes down for a huge sum and that's news. 'The Man with Debts of £100 Million,' barked one front-page banner headline. But in the next breath a rival national daily made light of a quote from the Official Receiver who said, 'This is just an ordinary bankruptcy with noughts on the end.'

Even after the affair quietened down, after the newspapers went on to other matters and the history of Stern's bankruptcy was left to book writers, there is still that slight edge that creeps into the texts. It's not nastiness. It's more like a slight twinge of jealousy. Stephen Aris, a former *Sunday Times* journalist, wrote, 'What offends in the Stern case is that there appears to be one law for the rich and the well-advised and quite another for the poor and the confused. And what makes Stern's behaviour so open to criticism is that he deliberately and cynically took advantage of what, to other, more scrupulous, folk might have seemed to be a crushing liability.'

That there is one law for the rich and another for the poor is almost certainly true. That's the way life works. No one ever said the rules were fair. No, that doesn't make it right. Yes, changes may be sorely needed. But that Stern was able to defend himself within the workings of the system should not expose Stern to criticism. That he had a wealthy father who was willing to help him is the luck of the draw, an accident of birth. But, again, it doesn't seem fair to use that as grounds for criticism either. Stern contends that everything he did to maintain his lifestyle was done with the knowledge and the blessing of the liquidators. If he hadn't been open and above board at every step along the way, they would never have allowed him to continue. To say that he deliberately and cynically took advantage of the situation sounds more like sour grapes than a serious comment. What he did, he did within the law. Lawyers were involved and banks were involved and the courts were involved and so was the reputation of someone as upstanding and respected as Sir Kenneth Cork.

This is not meant to sound like a defence for Stern, or anyone else.

Let everyone involved plead his own case if in fact there is a case to plead.

The point is that Stern did whatever he was legally permitted to do.

What too many people seem to forget is that, in at least one respect, he did something none of the other bankrupts from the era did. He took his medicine.

Notes Cork, 'I found Willie very honest to deal with. But he was treated the biggest bloody crook of the lot. Now all the other fringe bank crisis and property dealers had limited liability companies which they hadn't guaranteed. Therefore they were never made personal bankrupts and nobody abused them. They all had limited liability. Now, how do people get away with limited liability when all the creditors whistle for the money. Well, Willie didn't. Willie guaranteed all his debts. So Willie was made bankrupt because he was the only man who didn't have limited liability. But he had people going for him as though he were a man who escaped it.'

The pill Stern had to swallow, in addition to the obvious humiliation that takes place when someone hangs your dirty washing up in public, was nearly seven years of commercial punishment, almost like a business prison sentence.

'At certain times I felt that a short shock custodial sentence would almost be more pleasant than this sort of notionally free but effectively restrictive freedom. It is, in the business sense, a prison sentence.'

During that time he sold his services as a consultant.

'But that is not the most pleasant way of earning your living because people who use you feel they are doing you a great service. Very often your brain is picked and you're told, thank you very much we'll contact you, and you don't get to hear from them again. Even when you are in employment the feeling remains, because of your status, I am doing you a favour. It was not something which was very helpful for one's self-respect.'

At the end of 1982 he applied to the courts to be discharged from his bankruptcy. But one of his former creditors felt too strongly about him and objected. What could have been a routine hearing wound up being a long and expensive legal wrangle.

'They referred to me as this proud man who only

needs the discharge for his pride. The fact that one
likes to earn the money one lives on rather than
receive it by way of gifts or loans from one's family did
not seem to matter very much.'

It took the better part of a year's worth of court
hearings and appeals before his discharge was finally
granted. When it was, the decree carried with it a
30-month postponement. As the judge put it, he
wanted to make certain that Stern had learned his
lesson.

In September 1985 Stern regained his commercial
freedom. He went back into business, for himself,
quietly minding his own business.

But this time it's not quite like it used to be.

The world of finance has changed. The property
business has changed. And so has William Stern.

Older and wiser, to be sure. Maybe even more
philosophical. What happened is behind him. No bitterness towards anyone, except maybe the press. Yet
deep down, when he looks back on what happened,
now having had all those years to reflect on it, he says
he does have to admit that there is one small twinge of
disappointment.

It seems, he says, in 1974 he was led to believe by
Kenneth Cork, and through him by the Bank of England, that because his group was totally clean he might
have been able to avoid the trauma of the personal
bankruptcy.

'You realize that I was never interviewed by the
Fraud Squad or anyone else like that. There was
never anything which anyone got concerned with
about the group, let alone found anything. And I
would have felt that, having been kept out of bankruptcy during the period when I was of use to the

creditors, I shouldn't have been put into it after my usefulness then ceased.'

He shrugs.

'Let me put it to you differently. If I was going to be made bankrupt, it should have happened in 1975.'

10
The Eccentrics

The maturity of a society can be judged by its eccentrics. Some people believe that eccentrics in America are the norm rather than the exception. Consider the Yank who found national fame by burying a slew of cars, nose down in the Texas desert. In England, the eccentric is a respected stratum of a class-conscious society . . . especially upper-crust eccentrics. Take for example John Mytton as reported in the *Telegraph*, who during his short career drank several hundred dozen bottles of port, became Sheriff of Shropshire and piddled away his personal fortune to the point of total penury. He also set his shirt on fire for no other reason than to demonstrate a cure for hiccups. Then there's the French. The late sculptor Alexander Calder once said that the reason he lived in France was because the French appreciate eccentrics more than any other group. And while he may not have been as eccentric as many sculptors, the French after all do eat frogs' legs and snails. Imagine the very first Frenchman who decided to find out if such things taste good.

However, at least where minus millionaires are concerned, there are eccentrics and there are eccentrics.

The world of eccentric minus millionaires is hereby divided into two groups. Good ones. And bad ones. A purely arbitrary categorization. The good ones do what they do for love, or just to have a fun time. The bad ones do what they do for greed and can be dangerous.

The good ones are amusing. The bad ones sometimes wind up in jail.

First, a few good ones.

And who 'gooder' than Doris Day.

The freckle-faced movie star, whose real name is Doris von Kappelhoff, not only managed to maintain her virginity through more than 40 films . . . including *Teacher's Pet, That Touch of Mink, Pillow Talk, Lover Come Back* and *Move Over, Darling* . . . but she also made more than $20 million doing it.

In 1951 she married her agent, Marty Melcher, who immediately began handling her finances. He entrusted her money to a Beverly Hills lawyer named Jerome Rosenthal because 'Rosenthal is a genius'. The Melchers found themselves invested in land bank bonds, venture capital projects, hotels, plus oil and gas deals. Everything seemed to be going great for Day. At least it looked that way on the surface. Years later, an *Esquire* magazine profile of her noted that during the final five years of her 17-year marriage to Melcher the couple didn't have sex.

Too bad. Because in 1968, when Melcher died, Day reached into the piggy bank and discovered to her horror that she didn't have any money either. Melcher had either mismanaged, along with Rosenthal, or embezzled her entire life's savings.

'I was the big fish as well as the bank,' she was quoted as saying at the time. 'I was working away, knowing nothing and trusting.'

Minus her millions, she filed suit against Rosenthal.

It took five years to come to trial, and the trial lasted 99 days, but in the end she proved that Rosenthal had commingled her funds with his, took kickbacks on deals he arranged, got clients into bogus transactions and then charged them exorbitant fees for trying to rescue their funds. The trial judge held that Rosenthal was liable for $22.8 million, concluding that he had been running 'A private Community Chest for drunken and dishonest operators'.

One of the reporters covering her case concluded differently. He saw a moral in the story. 'Hard as it is to make a fortune, it seems almost easier these days to make it than to keep it.'

Rock star Mick Fleetwood discovered that was true, the hard way.

In 1984 the lead singer of the extremely successful pop group Fleetwood Mac filed for bankruptcy in California. His personal debts had reached $3.7 million. His assets covered only about $2.4 million. He was forced to sell his houses – including his $2.2 million 'Blue Whale' in Malibu – his cars, £20,000 worth of guitars and an extensive collection of Dinky Toys.

Fleetwood's lawyer, Mickey Shapiro, told *Rolling Stone* magazine, 'Mick loves great drums, cars, beautiful women and magnificent pieces of real estate. But he is not in the classic sense a heavy roller. He's not on the Beverly Hills Diet, champagne and cocaine.'

Fleetwood's problems began in 1980 when he bought some property in Australia. Because Australian law requires foreigners buying land to pay for most of it in cash, Fleetwood had to borrow half a million dollars from a Californian bank. The loan was guaranteed by Warner Communications who in turn took certain collateral from him. That included a deed of trust on Fleetwood's Beverly Hills home, plus shares in various companies. Fleetwood had supposedly intended to move 'Down Under'. After three weeks of living there he decided it was just too far away. He sold the house, but came out on the short end of the stick, mainly due to exchange rates. In December 1981 he bought the

'Blue Whale', having secured a mortgage with another Californian bank while Warner Communications took a second mortgage on the Beverly Hills property. But by this time interest rates were unreal and Fleetwood was looking at monthly payments in the neighbourhood of $20,000. Then certain investments started going bad, like the oil and gas drilling scheme that cost him over $600,000. At the same time, his annual earnings began to drop. Where he had once been making over $1 million a year, by this time he was down to under a third of that.

The burden got to be too much.

'There was literally no money,' he told *Rolling Stone*. 'I'm not being flippant about what has happened. It was put off as long as it was physically possible to be put off. But you start getting into a situation that doesn't do anyone any good. It's lovely to have money and certainly more preferable not to have this sort of thing happen. But the perspective in which you approach having money is much, much more important than the money.'

And to that he hastily added, 'I'm doing just fine now. I'm not a raving lunatic. If you let the whole thing collapse and don't have any sense of humour, I think you're in big trouble.'

His bankers may not be so quick to agree that a sense of humour will win in the end, but even bankers are likely to admit that not everybody in show business is eccentric. That not everybody in show business collects houses, beautiful women, cars, guitars and Dinky Toys. Buster Keaton didn't and he went broke. So did singer Eddie Fisher. Chico Marx was a gambler who managed to lose his fortune. When he found he didn't have enough to live on in the 1950s, Groucho and Harpo agreed to a somewhat melancholy comeback – they were long past their prime – in a made-for-television film. Judy Garland died broke and it took the generosity of Frank Sinatra to pay for her funeral. Sinatra also supported former heavyweight boxing champ Joe Louis in the final years of his life. Josephine Baker went broke, although she probably never earned really big money and anyway what she earned was spent on all those adopted children, so you might say her money went to a good cause. Betty Hutton, the 'Blonde Bombshell' who starred in such films as *Annie Get Your Gun* and *The Greatest Show on Earth*, reportedly earned over $10 million during her Hollywood career. But spent it too. In 1967 she filed for bankruptcy and promptly disappeared from the public eye. Seven years later she was found, broke, working as a cook and housekeeper in a Rhode Island Catholic rectory. Much the same happened to Veronica Lake. The blonde with the 'peek-a-boo' hair style was once a big earner, and romantically linked to both Aristotle Onassis and Howard Hughes. But by the early 1950s, while married to director André De Toth, she filed for bankruptcy and eventually disappeared. Ten years later a newspaper reporter discovered her working as a barmaid in a New York hotel. Bud Abbott also had money problems. He and Lou Costello earned huge money on the music-hall circuit, in films and later in television. Then they split up. Costello wanted top billing and another partner. The team that gave the world 'Who's on First' just couldn't come up with a punchline for real life. Costello drowned in his swimming pool, while Bud Abbott died penniless in an old actors' home. What happened to all of his money is anyone's guess.

Where Peter Bogdanovich's money went is less of a mystery.

The director of such award-winning films as *The Last Picture Show*, *Paper Moon* and *Mask* filed for bankruptcy at the end of 1985 saying that, apart from his house, all he had left of a $6 million fortune was the $21.37 in his bank account and the $25.79 in his pocket.

The money was spent trying to immortalize the woman he loved.

Her name was Dorothy Stratten. She was *Playboy* magazine's Playmate of the Year in 1979. And she was the star of a film he was directing called *They All Laughed*. The two fell in love on the set and he later said they planned to marry. But in 1980, just after the movie was completed, Stratten was murdered by her estranged husband who then committed suicide.

Devastated by her death, Bogdanovich spent $5 million to buy the rights from Time Incorporated and distribute the film as a memorial to her. Unfortunately it wasn't a very good picture and the public didn't take to it. Ticket sales generated less than $1 million, only about half of which came back to him.

With $6.6 million in debts, the 130 creditors who lined up at his front door quickly wiped him out.

Love also got to a London casino owner named Alf Barnett.

A modern-day, albeit poor man's, version of the infamous Tommy Manville . . . who squandered tens of millions of dollars on women and gambling . . . Barnett's club was a money-making proposition, especially during the 1970s when Middle Eastern gentlemen came to town, their pockets bulging, creating the boom time for petrodollars. But in 1979 Barnett and his wife split up. He sold out for £1.3 million, gave her their house in North London plus £120,000, and found himself with money to burn.

Over the next four years he bought a Rolls-Royce, hired a chauffeur, rented a Mayfair penthouse, and discovered that certain young ladies can smell money from miles away. To keep them happy, he blew £20,000 on a chartered yacht in the Caribbean, £140,000 on jewellery and furs, £60,000 on air fares, and something like £50,000 just thrown around in cash. At his bankruptcy hearing he admitted to having gone through £150,000 in restaurants and £60,000 on polo. An additional £380,000 was lost on business ventures, while £120,000 was spent on a country house.

'I lost my senses,' he told the court. 'It was the first time in my life I had such a large amount of cash in my hands. I was crazy, mad. Put it down to that time of life.'

In all he managed to swing his way through £1.8 million before the Inland Revenue asked for their share of the casino sale. They demanded nearly £660,000 plus interest.

By then most of the ladies had found greener pastures.

By then all he had left was £394.

Someone defaced a library book.

On the title page of *Norah – The Autobiography of Lady Docker*, an anonymous borrower felt compelled to write in ink just below her name, '. . . Who knows the price of everything and the value of nothing. Wilde must have had her type in mind!'

Needless to say, long after her disappearance from London's social scene, Lady Docker still has her fans.

'I am a most peculiar woman,' is the first line of *Norah*. 'I can't even boil an egg. But I have cooked the world. And I washed it down with pink champagne.'

If you think she's being modest, that's only the start

of her ego trip. She goes on to brag that she has grilled wags and waiters, roasted playboys and princes, and planted her feet delicately but boldly on red carpets in the palaces and castles of the most sacred dynasties across the world. 'I have sinned and brought others to learn of their own sins.'

She writes, 'For many years, people have endeavoured to analyse the reasons for my success. Was the secret in my hazel eyes?' Or, she hints, 'that I had to be good in bed. Oh dear. Take it from me that sex doesn't bring any achievement, except for an organic one. So, never be fooled into submission on false promises, because I never was ... I have never been promiscuous. Indeed, by all modern standards I have been prudish. I have never undressed in front of any of my husbands. Not because I was ever ashamed of my body, but I hold the opinion that lovemaking does not need to be a visually sordid experience.'

Eventually she comes forth with the secret of her success. 'I applied a simple rule, to make myself expensive ... Through life, I set both my sights and my price high.'

Three millionaire husbands and three squandered fortunes later, she died alone, in a tired hotel room in a less than chic London neighbourhood next to a less than chic railway station, to be buried in a small country churchyard next to her third husband, after a funeral where just about nobody bothered to show up.

Champagne Lady Docker was one of four children, born Norah Turner in the provinces in 1906.

Arriving in London at the age of 18, she had it in her head to become an actress. In the end she settled on a job as a taxi dancer at the then fashionable Café Royal, off Piccadilly Circus.

Like the song says, 10-cents a dance.

But right from the start she believed 'there's only one way of getting on, and that is to make oneself expensive.' So she lived by the rule, often stating, 'If men are rich enough to have money to burn, why not let them burn it on me.'

And they did.

She danced for eight years, earning handsome money in the ugly days of the Depression. When she decided it was time for a change of air she went to Southport and got herself a job selling hats in a department store. Except that didn't last very long. Not a lot of chances to meet millionaires. So she went to Birmingham and worked in a local dance hall. As that proved too depressing, she hied herself to London, this time to the Savoy, where taxi dancers were known as hostesses. But that didn't work out too well for her either, and before long she was dancing again at the Café Royal. And now it seems the wealthy roués of the era were lining up to be with her. One of them, an Old Bailey judge, decided she couldn't spend her life dancing so he bought her a country hotel to run. Left to her own devices and business sense, within 18 months she was broke. The bailiffs came in. Faced with bankruptcy, the judge helped bail her out.

Norah returned for a third tour of duty at the Café Royal.

Over the next year or so she agreed to several engagements to be married. Each young man being wealthier than the next.

'I believe that pre-marital relations are generally a good and useful experience,' she liked to tell people. 'The only danger is that promiscuity might follow.'

But it wasn't until she met Clement Callingham that she actually tied the knot.

Callingham was chairman of Henekeys, the wine

and spirit merchants, and a frequent visitor to the Café Royal. Claiming to be someone who loathed girls with freckles ... 'I regarded that as a personal affront for I am covered in freckles from head to foot' ... he was 13 years her senior but more than wealthy enough to keep Norah in the style to which she fully intended to become accustomed.

Although Callingham was married at the time, that didn't stop her. They took a house together and right off the bat the servants called her Mrs Callingham. They married as soon as his divorce was finalized. She was just 32.

He had a Rolls-Royce. She had a Daimler. Together they had a weekend barge in Holland, holidays on the Riviera, and one son named Lance.

The marriage ended in 1945 when Clement Callingham passed away.

For the next year Norah played the grieving widow. Callingham left her £175,000 ... generally speaking enough to get by ... but a good part of it was eaten up by duties and taxes. Then she met Sir William Collins, chairman of Cerebos Salt. She was 40 and he was 69. As she herself put it, 'I married him for his money.'

Now she had a 16-bedroomed country mansion, a staff of 16, and no less than 15 cars. At one point in her book, well into her marriage with Collins, she explains, 'Since Clement's death, I had not slept with anyone, and had never felt any desire to.' That may or may not suggest poor Collins was among those left out. Of course it doesn't really matter. More important is that she almost got left out when he changed his will.

It seems that sometime before his demise he drafted a new will and, for whatever reason, it did not include Norah. She found out about it, obviously panicked, and made damn sure he changed it back just in time.

He passed away in 1948.

As his sole heir, now there was more than enough after duties and taxes that she could be a grieving but extremely wealthy widow.

That's when she met Sir Bernard Docker, KBE, chairman of the Birmingham Small Arms Company (BSA). In her own words, she 'shamelessly pursued him'.

They married in 1949. She was 43. He was 53. And now there was a 2400 acre country estate, an apartment next to Claridges, the *Shemara* – which was said to be the largest and most luxurious yacht in the world – a gilded coach, lots of cars, a family flag flying from the top of the house whenever the Dockers were in residence, and the title 'Lady'.

'How the hell does she do it?' Norah writes, convinced that *tout Londres* had such questions on the tip of its tongue, good manners being the only barrier to actually voicing the thought. 'I wanted to tell them that it was relatively easy. All a lady needs to know is where she is going, and what she demands of life. I can safely say that, on those two counts, I was never in any doubt.'

Hardly.

This is, after all, the same woman who once admitted, 'I do not think I could have ever married someone poor. Not even for love. That may be regarded in some respects as a heartless and uncompromising attitude to life, but I have applied it only in a matrimonial sense . . . I am not saying that the rich should marry the rich, or the poor the poor, although that has its recommendation.'

Her future secure, now Lady Docker really started to live.

There were thousands of couturier dresses to keep

her in the limelight at thousands of charity balls. There were hairdressers scattered around the world to keep her feeling elegant no matter where she was.

And there was the famous gold-plated Daimler.

In 1951, the Daimler motor car company was a subsidiary of Birmingham Small Arms. As Norah professed an interest in cars, Bernard gave her a job to help promote Daimler. Her idea was to design a smaller, family version of the limousine. At the time, chrome was in great shortage. But gold wasn't. So gold leaf was sprayed on all the fittings . . . from the exhaust pipe and the hubcaps to the petrol tank cap and, of course, the shakers in the cocktail cabinet. To finish the effect, gold stars covered the bodywork. Almost instantly, she and the car became virtually inseparable. They toured together, promoting Daimler, and even wound up in Paris in a scene of the Jane Russell film, *Gentlemen Prefer Brunettes*.

She followed that with a powder-blue Daimler, which boasted a blue lizard interior.

Then there was a blue-grey metallic Daimler with scarlet crocodile interior.

But in 1955 she came up with the Docker-Daimler Mark V . . . a cream and gold sports car, with ivory fixtures and zebra-skin upholstery. And when asked why zebra, she told the world – as if it was obvious – 'because mink is too hot to sit on'.

Besides cars, there was also a penchant for jewellery. By the mid-1950s her count was £150,000 worth. Today that figure would be multiplied several dozen times. 'If you marry three millionaires and they plaster you with jewellery, there is little you can do about it, is there? You can't really object, even if you want to.' It was later stolen, found by thieves in the false-bottomed bidet in her bathroom where she was certain thieves would never even imagine to look.

Finally there was the *Shemara* . . . 836 tons and 214 feet from stem to stern. Launched in 1939 just in time to serve in the Royal Navy during the Second World War as an anti-submarine ship, she maintained a crew of 31 and cost the Dockers in excess of £30,000 per year to maintain . . . something they did for 19 years.

Their cruising took them through the Mediterranean, not only because the weather is good and the coast is beautiful . . . and there are plenty of casinos, although she always swore they were not heavy gamblers . . . but because Monte Carlo is there.

And Monte Carlo was the place where Norah Docker had her much publicized fight with Prince Rainier.

Very much a storm in a tea cup, Norah made a lot more out of it than it was worth. But then, for a woman who loved the limelight, this was the best limelight in town. What happened was that over several visits to Monaco in the early 1950s she voiced her opinion about the way she and Bernard were being welcomed. One afternoon in a state of anger, she plucked a miniature Monégasque flag off a restaurant table and ripped it up. She and Bernard then left for Cannes to stay there. The next morning they were officially banned from the principality. At the time she published her autobiography in 1969 she had not been back. However, she did return some years before her death, supposedly planning to buy a hotel there. Prince Rainier, who is much too big a man to worry about the likes of a silly grudge with Norah Docker, obviously couldn't have cared less if she returned or not. But it's a good bet that when she did she was treated with a great deal more respect than she showed to anyone in Monaco way back when.

Then, too, getting herself thrown out of a fashionable place was not an isolated incident. She also got herself tossed out of the Royal Enclosure at Ascot.

She and Bernard had spent several racing seasons there. But in 1953 a letter came from the Duke of Norfolk as Chamberlain-Controller of Royal Ascot, saying that it had come to his attention that Norah had been named as a guilty party – i.e. co-respondent – in Clement Callingham's divorce suit. Therefore, as a woman with a wicked past, she would no longer be welcome in the Royal Enclosure. She and Bernard stayed away three years until that ban was also relaxed.

In the mid-1950s Bernard Docker ran up against the law. With the constant publicity that surrounded them, especially her, questions were being asked in high places about their lifestyle. Although they were limited to an exchange control quota of £25 each, as she put it, 'My liking for pink champagne, minks, diamonds, the *Shemara* and the golden Daimler did seem to cause rather a lot of headlines, and banks are very sober and sensitive.'

Currency violations were levied against Bernard, who spent £25,000 in legal fees to fight the case, which ended in a £50 fine. Although it also subsequently led to Bernard's resignation from the board of the Midland Bank.

However more trouble was soon on the way.

The BSA board had been gathering its forces to get Docker out of the chairman's seat. Too many things were sticking in their collective gullet. One was a £7910 bill on the company's books for Norah's wardrobe while attending the Paris motor show. Another was that the Daimler division – which was posting heavy losses – was being run by Norah's brother-in-law.

So in May 1956 Bernard was voted out.

Feistily, Norah appealed directly to the 17,000 shareholders, sending them each an autographed photo of herself, while Bernard appealed directly to them on television. But in an extraordinary general meeting, the shareholders supported the board. The Dockers were out. Fifteen years later, BSA went into bankruptcy.

Like most royalty in exile, the Dockers left home for pastures new. They chose the Channel Island of Jersey. They said it was for tax reasons. But before long Norah was banned from her local pub for causing a rumpus.

Banned from Monte Carlo. Banned from the Royal Enclosure at Ascot. Finally banned from a pub. 'The world, as I know it today', she said at the close of her book, 'is no longer big enough for me to live in, because I have exhausted all there is to do. There is no longer anything that sparks my ambition. There are no more challenges left to meet. The party is over. On to the next one!'

From Jersey the Dockers went to Spain, to Palma de Mallorca. But by then the days of wine and roses were long gone. There were no more apartments at Claridges. There was no more dancing at the Savoy. On their visits to London they stayed at the Great Western Hotel in Paddington. And there is some kind of irony in that. Once the largest hotel in Europe, it too had long since been passed by as the ultra in chic.

When Bernard became ill, he was brought back to England, confined to a hospital in Bournemouth. Norah stayed on alone in a small flat in Palma. Just before his death in 1978 she told a women's magazine, 'I thought the halcyon days would go on forever.'

She followed him five years later.

One morning in 1983, a maid came into the single room at the Great Western Hotel where Norah was propped up against her pillows. She had gone in her sleep.

The head porter, Fred Wright, still remembers her with great affection. 'She was a small, frail woman. But her hair, champagne colour, was always perfect and she always tried to dress well. She wasn't flamboyant towards the end. There was no handfuls of pound notes. She was a very truthful person, which means if she had something to say to you she'd say it. And she liked to talk to people. She'd go into our bar and someone would ask her if she'd have a drink and she'd always reply, I'll have a bottle of pink champagne.'

She was, he says, terribly fond of Bernard. Although a story that goes around the shooting set has it that once, while hunting birds, someone accidentally plastered her bottom with buckshot. Bernard is said to have shrugged, 'No bother. She's just a runner.'

The *Guardian* wrote after her death that 'silliness and spending' were 'Naughty Norah's' fortes. But, then, they felt that she carried them off with an undeniable charm.

Perhaps.

But she was also outrageous. 'There is no such thing as an impotent man,' she was often quoted as saying, 'just an unskilled woman.' A little known fact is that she happened to have been a two-times British Women's Marble Champion, in 1954 and again in 1955.

As long as the pink champagne flowed she had a thousand friends.

At her final public appearance, only 29 of them showed up.

She left a provision that she wanted a red onyx

headstone on her grave. Alive and rich, she almost always got what she wanted. Departed and nearly broke, she didn't. The vicar at the small church in Maidenhead where she is buried decided her final wish wasn't in keeping with the quiet of a country churchyard.

As Jon Akass wrote about her in the *Daily Express*, 'For a lady who lived in so grand a manner, filling the gossip columns of a decade, her last occasion was sadly small.'

Some people marry money and then blow it.

George Huntington Hartford II was born to it and blew it.

A grandson of the man after whom he is named ... GHH the First founded the huge A&P grocery store empire that once stretched across the USA ... Huntington Hartford II grew up as the $90 million heir to the throne in the lap of utter luxury. Born in 1911, he reached adulthood having dropped the George and the II, preferring to add after his name such titles – at various times in his life – as magazine publisher, museum benefactor, art collector, author and property developer.

Had there been any room left on his calling card, he might have also put down something along the lines of, general all around but otherwise likable loser.

Speed-Park, an automated parking garage that never got built, cost him $2 million. New York's The Gallery of Modern Art/The Huntington Hartford Collection cost him $7.4 million before the paintings were sold in 1974 to raise money and the building was turned into offices for the Department of Cultural Affairs. A now defunct afternoon newspaper in New York called *P.M.* hired him as a crime reporter and in

return he became an investor, and that cost him
$100,000. Then he sank $600,000 into the Huntington
Hartford Foundation, an artists' retreat in California,
which he eventually sold because he publicly opposed
the so-called Modernist Movement and artists who
came to retreats in those days were all modernists.

With the Huntington Hartford Theater in Hollywood
he hoped to ram culture down the throats of the laid
back southern California folk. But the theatre flatly
refused to make a profit while he owned it. In 1964 he
gave up and sold the place. More than 20 years later
the management decided to rub his name off the
marquee.

As long as he felt he had a flair for the theatre, he
penned an adaptation of Charlotte Brontë's *Jane Eyre*
and produced it himself with Errol Flynn in the lead.
But by that time Flynn was a drunk, couldn't remember his lines, demanded a teleprompter to help him
and walked out before opening night. *Jane Eyre* cost
Hartford $500,000.

In the early 1960s he gave magazine publishing a
whirl with a glossy named *Show*. It failed and with it
went $8 million.

His crowning glory however came in the Bahamas.
He 'discovered' a 700 acre island called Hog Island and
bought it that very same day. He saw it, wanted it and
signed the contract immediately. It never seemed to
dawn on him that he ought to have his lawyers come
down to read through the small print on an $11 million
purchase.

The idea in the back of his head was to develop Hog
Island into one of the world's great resorts. The first
thing he did was rename the place Paradise Island.
Then he dropped another $19 million trying to make it
look like paradise.

Running into cashflow troubles, he sold part of his interest in the island for $750,000. Then, inexplicably for someone with cashflow worries, he turned right around and lent the man who bought those shares $2 million. Strangely, he accepted repayment in unregistered stock, which he quickly discovered he couldn't sell to anyone. Still strapped for cash, his partner arranged to help him with a $1 million loan, which was supposed to have been guaranteed by anyone but Hartford. Except it somehow wound up being secured with another hefty chunk of Hartford's Paradise Island shares. Then – suddenly and maybe even suspiciously – the original guarantees were pulled and the loan was called in. Hartford's shares were sold. And the net result was that his $30 million investment in Paradise Island managed to produce a $28 million tax loss.

Besides possessing a thorough lack of good business sense ... or possibly any business sense at all ... he constantly broke what's got to be known as 'The Inheritor's Golden Rule'.

That reads: 'Never invade principal.'

Instead of putting his inheritance into shares and living on, or playing with, the interest, Hartford fooled around with his own capital and in the course of half a century managed to lose more than $80 million.

Easy come, easy go.

That's one way of looking at it.

Or, oh well, it wasn't mine anyway.

Whatever the excuse, man's ability to rationalize definitely helps soothe the bankrupt's conscience.

Apart from someone of Hartford's ilk – and he's a fairly unique case – it's likely that no one has ever seen money appear and/or disappear quicker than a gambler.

Rosario Leonardi, from Milan, played the Italian football pools every week until he won nearly £2 million. He took his winnings, sank it into various businesses and managed to lose it all. Sadly, in January 1986, at the age of 37, he was killed while trying to jump onto a moving train.

Just as tragic is the story of an English woman named Vivian Nicholson.

In 1961 her second husband Keith won the pools and Littlewoods handed him a cheque for £152,319. It was then a gigantic sum. It is now probably worth eight to ten times as much.

And Vivian went wild.

She blew Keith's winnings on clothes, parties, race horses, a bungalow called The Ponderosa and, especially, booze. As her story was once described in the *Financial Times*, sudden wealth transformed her from 'a sluttish mother of four who stole mashed potatoes to feed her family into a sluttish mother of four who drenched herself in champagne and Chevrolets.'

When Keith was killed in a drunken car accident, what little money was still left quickly disappeared. Three more husbands followed, as did health problems, the discovery of Jesus, a book called *Spend, Spend, Spend,* a television play adapted from the book, and a low-budget stage musical adapted from the television play.

'The set makes the point,' wrote Antony Thorncroft in his FT review of the play, 'covered with cheap rubbish in the first half, with expensive rubbish after the interval.'

But playing the pools, or Lotto, or any of those state lotteries where the first prize is $20 million, is really nothing more than an innocent pastime, like parish hall bingo, when compared to those serious, heavy gamblers you sometimes see in places like Monte Carlo . . . perhaps the most famous emporium of its kind in the world.

Opened in 1865 by François Blanc, the idea was to provide an arena where punters with a perfect scheme could live out their fantasies in exchange for a small cut of the action. Blanc came to Monte Carlo with very clear-cut ideas in his head about how to separate punters from their money, having learned his business the hard way, running other casinos – some not so successfully – across Europe. In one of them, he was literally wiped out by Prince Charles Bonaparte. It seems the Prince had more money to play with than Blanc had to defend himself with. So at Monte Carlo he put into practice a pair of rules. One, the house must always have more money than any of the gamblers. And two, the house must establish a betting ceiling, so that infinite sums of money cannot be bet against it. Those two rules, first used by Blanc, make up the backbone of every casino operation in the world today.

These days the casino at Monte Carlo has been restored to its earlier ornate splendour. There are carpets and paintings and sculptures and ceilings in gold leaf. There are roulette wheels and crap tables and chemin de fer tables surrounded, on any given night, by enough people to earn the casino profits well in excess of $100 million a year.

Hanging around those tables – especially in the private rooms where the nickel-dime bermuda-short tourists are never permitted because they'd only get in the way of the dinner-jacketed Italians and Givenchyed Middle Easterners who play for important lolly and where 50,000 FF chips get tossed around like cream eggs at Easter – you often hear the expression 'professional gambler'.

And yes, they'll tell you at the casino, professional gamblers do exist. But anyone in the casino business will also tell you that professional winners don't. True, some people win more than others. But that's because they defend their money better. Anytime you win and you think you're playing with the casino's money, you're wrong. Any money in front of you is yours. You own it. You can quit and walk away and it goes with you. And that's one of the big differences between winners and losers. Winners know when to quit. Losers don't quit until they've lost.

It may sound surprising, but there's nothing a casino likes better than a big winner. Just look at how much publicity the Las Vegas casinos thrust on someone when the one-armed bandit pays out a million dollar prize. The reason is simple. One big winner is guaranteed to lure in masses of losers. And losers keep the place open.

While no one has ever broken the bank at Monte Carlo . . . and no one is ever likely to either . . . there are probably more big money and 'if only' stories about this place than anywhere else on earth, with the possible exception of the NYSE.

At the turn of the century a British engineer named Jaggers came to Monte Carlo with six assistants to test his theory that it is impossible to maintain a perfectly balanced roulette wheel and that imperfections in the wheel will cause some numbers to hit more frequently than others. After months of compilations, Jaggers spent four days at the tables and won the then princely sum of $180,000. The casino's directors immediately adopted the rule that all the wheels in the house would be checked and rebalanced every day. That rule still stands.

By the way, that's another difference between winners and losers. Casinos learn from their losses. Punters risk more by trying to win it back.

One of the most often told smart-loser stories ever to come out of Monte Carlo is the one about the gambler who dropped his entire fortune at the tables, but who also understood the monetary value a casino would put on bad publicity. Just as a big winner will bring the punters in, a sore loser will drive the crowds away. So, when his pockets were empty, this particular fellow faked his own suicide. Using a smoking pistol and chicken blood, he panicked the management so much with his corpse that they stuffed £2000 into his pockets before the ambulance arrived. It was, they believed, cheaper than a nasty scandal in the newspapers. But he had other plans. As soon as he had this fresh stake he stood up, brushed himself off and went straight back to the tables.

The game must go on.

Luck will out.

And of course luck is a singularly important factor.

But timing is just as important. It's not much good being lucky when there isn't money around to win. You have to be lucky when the money is there. The answer, as explained by one of the directors of the casino at Monte Carlo, is courage. The courage to bet small when you're losing and to bet big when you're winning. It's Jim Slater's 'pressjack' all over again. If you lose ten straight hands at £100 and win one at £1001, then you're a winner. Where most people make their big mistake, he claimed, is in thinking that a pile of winnings in front of them is grounds for courage. They figure, I can afford to lose so I'll bet big. They believe that because they're ahead they can take chances. What happens is that they win a little bit and ten minutes later give it all back to the casino, plus some more. The smart gambler takes his winnings and defends them. He limits his losses by saying, I've lost enough for today. I won't run after that money. It's gone. Too bad. Tomorrow is another day.

It's only common sense that the longer a gambler stays at the table the more chance he's giving for the house edge to catch up to him. But that's how casinos pay their bills.

A few summers ago in Monaco, the biggest player of the season spent 12 hours a day at the tables, winning some, losing more. As August wore on towards September, someone asked him how much longer he would be in town. He answered that he was leaving the following day. Except the following day, there he was, still at the tables. In fact he kept returning to the casino until the summer had long gone. Then, sure enough, he finally announced to the manager of the Hotel de Paris that he would be checking out the next morning at 10 A.M. The staff and management helped put his luggage into a waiting Rolls, gave orchids to his wife and bade them a hearty farewell. But just as his wife was getting into the car, he glanced across the Place du Casino and mumbled, 'I'll be right back.' Nine hours later he came out of the casino, ordered his bags to be unpacked and stayed another week.

The most spectacular story of all in Monte Carlo's history took place in the summer of 1979.

With oil prices going through the roof and vast fortunes being made in the petroleum business, a group of Arab sheikhs invaded Monte Carlo. Their camels' saddle bags were literally oozing with petro-dollars. They hit the tables at the Sporting d'Été around midnight, installing themselves in front of a roulette wheel, and betting as heavily as the table limits would allow. By 5 A.M. they were $2.4 million ahead. But that's when Lady Luck took a powder. In less than two hours they were $1.4 million in the hole. In under 120 minutes the roulette wheel had turned around some $3.8 million. And that works out at a losing speed of $527.70 per second!

Pretty sickening when you imagine that the money could have been put to better use.

But then, compulsive gambling is often considered an illness, much like compulsive drinking and compulsive eating. In this case Grandma would have been right. Any damn fool can piss it away.

Gamblers Anonymous happens to be an absolutely wonderful organization, helping tens of thousands of people to reshape their lives. Nevertheless, the tales that get told at their nightly meetings are pretty sad.

Such as, 'I gambled because I really liked the action. I loved it. It wasn't boring. It wasn't mundane. I loved the idea of making a decision. Sometimes I would be right and get paid for being right. I loved the feeling in the pit of my stomach waiting to find out if I was right. I eventually became immune to losing. Losing meant nothing. I was there for the action.'

And, 'I remember putting a fiver on a horse that didn't have a prayer, and it won. Listen, if God decides you're going to be a compulsive gambler, you can back a 6000-1 shot and it will win. I started with a fiver a week. Before long I was losing £200–£300 a week.'

And, 'I didn't mean to hurt anybody, but the company had so much money and I needed it to pay for my losses and I never thought they would have found out.'

Some people say winners are contagious. They may be. But losers definitely are.

* * *

And now for a few bad ones.

In February 1983, the Imperial Wizard of the Invisible Empire, Knights of the Ku-Klux-Klan, filed for protection from the Klan's debtors under Chapter 11 of the federal bankruptcy code.

More and more, in recent years, the intent of the Chapter 11 law has been twisted. Some companies in the States have found they could avoid all sorts of interesting problems by filing for Chapter 11 protection. When its Dalkon Shield contraceptive didn't work, the A.H. Robins Company – a financially sound operation – sought Chapter 11's shield from pregnant customers. When Continental Airlines found itself in difficulty with the labour unions, it used Chapter 11 to break contracts. So, naturally, when the Baton Rouge, Louisiana, Ku-Klux-Klan was handed a bill for $8650 from the Internal Revenue Service for unpaid taxes, penalties and interest, Chapter 11 was its first choice.

'This will not hamper our operations,' noted the Imperial Wizard. 'It preserves our cash flow and freezes our obligation. But you won't find that bookkeeper around here any more.'

Next, Murph the Surf.

Although he was never technically a minus millionaire, $410,000 in 1964 would be a respectable fortune today so he sort of qualifies.

Born John Roland Murphy in 1937, and for nearly 20 years known as Inmate Number 024627 at Florida State Prison, he gave up a minor career as a prodigy violinist, a fairly decent tennis player and a Florida surf bum for jewel thievery. Starting small, he worked his way up to the theft of $50,000 worth of jewels from actress Eva Gabor in Miami in 1964. He was identified by her but never convicted. And from there he graduated to the major leagues with one of the most daring gem heists of the century.

In the late autumn of 1964, Murphy and two pals headed north to New York where they rented a three-bedroomed suite in a fancy residential hotel on West 86th Street, just three blocks from the Museum of Natural History. Over the next several days, they visited various museums, including the Guggenheim and the Metropolitan, photographing rooms and access points wherever they could. But the first hit on their list was the J.P. Morgan Hall of Gems at the Museum of Natural History.

One dark October night, Murphy scaled the outside of the building . . . a dangerous enough task . . . then risked life and limb to make his way along the narrow fifth-floor ledge towards an unlocked window. That's when – the way it always happens in bad movies – he tripped over a bunch of sleeping pigeons, sending them fluttering in all directions. He later admitted it scared the life out of him.

After catching his breath he had to wait while a museum guard shone his torch around the room before he could slip in through the window. Hiding behind show cases, Murphy waited patiently in the darkened hall until a plane flew overhead. The noise of the engines covered the sound of breaking glass as he smashed into the display case housing the stones he was after.

Then, with the 563-carat Star of India – at the time it was the largest sapphire in the world – plus the Midnight Star, the DeLong ruby and 20 other precious gems literally bulging from his pockets, Murph the Surf hurried out of the window and across the narrow ledge to meet up with his pals at a Times Square bar for a couple of drinks.

For the next 48 hours they were fabulously rich, even if they didn't yet have the cash to spend.

Then the cops descended on them. Murphy's fortune was gone.

Years later Robert Conrad starred in a film about him called *Love a Little, Steal a Lot*. But by then he was doing time for a double murder and the sleaziness of his new image quickly tarnished his romantic jewel thief reputation.

Where Murph the Surf wound up spending most of his life in jail for stupidly turning to crime, and where someone like John De Lorean risked a jail sentence for something as stupid as a cocaine deal, some minus millionaires wind up doing time for being stupid about the greedy way they handled their business affairs.

Emil Savundranayagan was born in Ceylon in 1923. After being educated at a fashionable school and serving in the Army during the war as an officer, he shortened his last name to Savundra, and started buying surplus goods from the military which he'd sell to anybody who wanted them. In one of those deals he picked up some cameras, which he quickly moved along to the Chinese. Except not really. Yes, the Chinese saw the samples, and, yes, the Chinese paid for the cameras upfront and, yes, they took delivery of a shipload of heavy crates. But when they opened the crates there were no cameras . . . only bricks.

He repeated the performance in 1950 with a petroleum deal. One of his companies, Trans World Enterprises Ltd, claimed to have been acting as an intermediary between a bank in Ceylon and another in Belgium. He was paid over $230,000 for the deal, which turned out to have involved forged documents. Then he tried it yet again, this time with the Portuguese government and a shipment of rice. It netted him about $240,000.

By July 1953 he had left Ceylon and was living in London.

That's when he was arrested and an extradition fight ensued. The Belgian government was demanding justice. That's also when he suffered his first heart attack. The British judge finally ruled that he could be extradited. A Belgian court sentenced him to five years and added a heavy fine, although the fine was later reduced and he only served a few months before being released on the grounds of ill health.

In 1958 he turned up in Ghana trying to buy exclusive mineral rights from the government of the day. He registered a company there called Ghana Minerals Corporation, claiming to have £5 million capital. But there was a bribery scandal and at least one government minister resigned and Savundra found himself deported.

Next stop was Costa Rica where he tried to corner the country's coffee crop. Local banks put up credits in excess of £560,000 and that money disappeared, along with Savundra.

Eventually he decided on a gentleman's career in insurance.

On 14 February 1963 – Valentine's Day – the Fire Auto and Marine Insurance Company was born. Savundra's gimmick was to insure the otherwise uninsurable. He programmed his computers for all the permutations. A quote for anyone in 63 seconds. Even one-eyed, one-armed drunks. Except that a clause in their auto policy ruled out any liability on a car 'being driven in any unsafe or unroadworthy condition or manner'. In effect, the clause excluded just about every possibility except an act of God.

But the one-eyed, one-armed drunks didn't know that ... and nobody else would insure them even if Savundra's premiums were very steep ... so for the next three years money poured into the company.

Savundra awarded himself an invented doctorate, used bogus CD plates on his car to keep the traffic wardens away, and bought some social status by becoming a powerboat enthusiast. He lavishly furnished his homes, and just as lavishly furnished his offices. 'I've got two televisions at home,' he once told some IBM salesmen, 'I've got twin engines on my boat, I want two computers in my office.' Those computers wound up costing nearly £400 a day to rent. But Savundra never batted an eyelash.

While riding high, he hired a legal adviser to look into a knighthood. He wanted to find out what it would cost and who had to be paid. Around the same time he tried to start a correspondence with Prime Minister Harold Wilson by writing him letters explaining how wonderful they both were. Later, when his business collapsed, he wrote to Wilson suggesting the PM nationalize all car insurance firms, especially Fire Auto and Marine.

Known as a roué, legend has it that as a young army officer he rode around chasing ladies in a Cadillac with a specially built extension ladder that came out of the truck so he could get over the walls of the Wrens' quarters. His name was also, for a time, linked with Mandy Rice-Davies and the Profumo scandal. More mysteriously, there has even been talk of his having been involved with the 'Great Train Robbers'. One theory has him as the mastermind behind the plot. Another names him as the launderer of the funds. But no one has ever been able to prove either, or in any way link him to the robbery.

A man with heart problems, some of them serious, some of them convenient, his ill health often got him out of town and into a rest home, far away from problems, just in time. At other times he proudly and outrightly faked a seizure, scaring away prying journalists, then coming back to life and announcing to startled friends that his performance was worthy of an Academy Award.

Known as a devout Catholic, he set up and supported a convent in Ceylon. But he also kept some of his business records there. What could be safer? When problems developed, he is known to have cabled the Mother Superior, telling her to burn them. She is known to have cabled back, 'All documents destroyed. Praying.'

In 1966, more than a quarter of a million British motorists found themselves uninsured as the accountants were sent in to look at Fire Auto and Marine's books. They discovered £1 million missing. As they unravelled the web of companies that threaded through England and Liechtenstein, Fire Auto and Marine collapsed with £2.25 million worth of liabilities. Within a year Savundra and his partner, Stuart De Quincy Walker, were both up on fraud charges. Found guilty, Walker got five years plus a £30,000 fine, while Savundra – still claiming to be innocent – was sentenced to eight years plus a £50,000 fine.

Calling himself 'The original black Englishman' and 'God's own lounge lizard', he stood in the dock at his trial and cried poverty. 'I have never been anything more than a poor church mouse.'

Unable to meet that fine, or pay any of his other bills, the man who had lived on Millionaires Row in Hampstead and who came to court every morning in a

Rolls-Royce was adjudged bankrupt. All of his assets were sold.

In 1974, after 6½ years inside, Savundra was released from Wormwood Scrubs, still insisting that he was never guilty of any wrong-doings. 'When you English see a loophole in the law,' he said 'you drive a Mini through it. I, Savundra, drive a Rolls-Royce.'

Two years later he was dead.

Ever true to form, just before he died he offered to sell $200 million worth of property in Sri Lanka to the US Army so that they could have a missile base there. His only stipulation was that they had to name his wife Queen of North Ceylon.

If Murph the Surf's take was adjusted for inflation, and that was added to the money Savundra made and lost, it still wouldn't even come close to the all-time winner of the world bankruptcy stakes.

In 1985, Rajendra Sethia, then just 37, earned his place in the Guinness Book of Records by going broke, personally, for £170 million.

His story begins in the City of London with the 1984 collapse of a company called ESAL Commodities. It had been a money spinner for Sethia, selling sugar and rice to Nigeria and the Sudan. But in 1983 sugar prices fell through the floor and the world's sugar market dissolved. Then came a coup d'état in Nigeria, toppling the government of President Shagari, with whom Sethia had a working friendship. That was followed by allegations of illegal currency dealings, which firmly put the damper on Sethia's business in Lagos.

Caught in the squeeze, ESAL Commodities had run up massive loans with banks that the company couldn't pay. Having established lines of credit with several banks, Sethia borrowed from one to pay the other. The downward spiral continued until he had dug himself into a hole so deep that he had in fact buried himself. Many of those loans were personally guaranteed by Sethia. Among them was a £70 million loan from the Punjab National Bank, India's second largest. Also included in the list of creditors was the Central Bank of India, the Union Bank of India, the Allied Arab Bank, the London and Overseas Sugar Company, the Inland Revenue, and the ill-fated Johnson Matthey Bank, which was subsequently the object of a Bank of England lifeboat rescue. ESAL owed JMB £6–10 million, depending on who's counting.

Before the crash, ESAL Commodities boasted a £300 million annual turnover on a capital base of £5 million. Afterwards, ESAL's total corporate debt was £280 million. In addition to that, Sethia found himself personally committed for £170 million.

The fifth son of businessman Sohanlal Sethia and younger brother to two highly respected London businessmen, Rajendra's family name and his London School of Economics credentials made him a natural bet for a successful City career. After graduation from the LSE he took his place in the family jute business. In 1969 he borrowed £10,000 from his father and started playing the metal markets. He reportedly lost over £50,000. By 1973 he decided to leave the family business and go out on his own. He took with him a company called Rusel Fibre Dealers, diversified that company out of jute and put them into sugar and rice. He made millions until the world sugar markets crashed and he was declared bankrupt. For the next 18 months he tried to eke out a living playing the horses until his brothers came to the rescue and gave him a job in Nigeria. There he made the right contacts to deal again in sugar, set up ESAL and came back to the City. With a great deal of money pouring in again, he paid off his debts and started living higher and faster than ever before.

Within a matter of months he had three Rolls-Royces, two Mercedes, 40–50 race horses, and his own Boeing 707. ESAL paid $3.6 million for the plane and another $600,000 outfitting it with a boardroom, bedrooms, gold-tapped baths, a sauna and a jacuzzi. He also purchased a £3 million house in Hampstead, although he never bothered to move in. At a banquet he once hosted at the Dorchester Hotel, he substituted krugerrands for after-dinner mints. Especially fond of gambling, there were evenings at some of London's more glamorous private clubs where Sethia would invite his guests to the gaming tables, allow them to keep their winnings but personally pick up their losses. Among the legends that have grown up around his gambling exploits is one particular night when he posted a £100,000 loss.

Almost as soon as his empire crashed in January 1984, Rajendra decided that the weather on the south coast of Spain might be better for his health. So with several ESAL directors in tow, he went into exile.

Scotland Yard issued a warrant for his arrest.

Nine charges in all were lodged against him, covering fraud, forgery and theft.

In an exclusive interview in November 1984 with The *Sunday Times*, Sethia – living in a rented villa between Malaga and Marbella – announced that he was busy putting together some new deals. He said that he intended to pay off all his creditors. And added, 'I know I am on the road to greatness. I may not get there for 15 years and I may have to crawl on hands and knees through a long tunnel first. But I'll get through it.'

Before achieving his promised greatness, he returned to India. The British government immediately requested extradition. But the Indian government had ideas of their own. They charged him with fraud and threw him into jail to await trial.

A journalist interviewing him in his Delhi cell was told, 'I will soon be the richest man in the world.' Claiming to spend several hours each day in prayer and meditation, Rajendra Sethia seems to take a philosophical view of his fate. 'My present problems are sent to me by God. But I will be back and next time I shall build a business so big that it cannot go bust.'

Famous last words.

Tune in next week.

11

Vintage Bugattis and the Brothers Schlumpf

First there was a phone call from London to Basle, Switzerland.

He said, 'What do you want to know? When would you want to come to visit?'

Both questions were answered.

'Yes. I think that should be all right,' he said. 'But send me a letter and tell me again.'

The letter was written and sent to Basle.

His answer, in a curt handwritten note, was, 'I'm sorry but I will be out of town. I cannot see you.'

That was followed by another phone call from London.

'No, I'm sorry. I won't be here. I'm going away on a trip. I'm sorry.'

Then there was a third phone call, this time from Basle on the eve of the originally agreed to but since broken rendezvous.

A woman answered. She asked, who's calling? When she heard who it was she said, 'Just a moment.' Forgetting to cover the mouthpiece, she whispered to her husband that the man from London was ringing and now he was in Basle. He whispered back, 'No, no. Say to him I'm not here. Say I've gone away on a trip.' She whispered to him, 'Take the phone. He's here in Basle.' Again he said, no. And again she tried to pass the phone to him.

Only after a lot more whispering would he come on the line.

An appointment was made ... reluctantly on his part ... for the following morning.

The Gellerstrasse is one of the most fashionable residential streets in Basle. The block of flats where they live is modern. The lift rose to the penthouse and opened directly into the hallway of their very large flat. The man who stood there, courteous but unsmiling, wore a blue blazer with a white shirt and bright yellow tie. A yellow handkerchief was fluffed in his blazer's breast pocket.

Although he is almost totally bald, shockingly huge white mutton chops cover his cheeks.

At the age of 80, his blue eyes are very bright.

But if you look closely into those eyes, you can see the reason for the broken meetings and all that whispering.

Fritz Schlumpf is a man who harbours an enormous amount of suspicion.

Mulhouse has never been confused with one of the more scenic, one of the more beautiful or even one of the more touristy corners of France.

And for good reason.

This is not one of those French towns with a fantastic local cheese or a little known local wine or even a whole cluster of restaurants where the Michelin man can lose his cool in handing out stars. It's a factory town, half an hour from the Swiss and German borders ... one of those European cities that has kept very little of the fine old in favour of a lot of the bad new. It's a factory town, like so many factory towns late in the twentieth century where old people grow old and young people aim only to escape.

'Mulhouse, a City Full of Surprises.'

That's what the local tourist office promises in its brochure.

They offer a zoo and some outdoor sculpture ... maybe in the bright sun of August it all looks surprising but the rest of the year it definitely doesn't ... plus a history museum, a railway museum, a fire engine museum, a fine arts museum, an annual Bach festival and local theatre. But deep down Mulhouse is still a factory town where the local crop used to be textiles. Maybe that's why there's also a wallpaper museum and a museum dedicated solely to the craft of textile printing.

However, Mulhouse is these days very much on the map because it is also the home of France's National Motor Car Museum ... which is truly surprising, even though it more properly should be called the Schlumpf Collection ... except it isn't actually a national museum because it now belongs to the city of Mulhouse and some regional authorities, although it is without any doubt whatsoever a world-class attraction.

It is exquisite.

There are nearly 600 antique automobiles and other types of vehicles on display. There are 98 different makes of cars and the world's most complete representation of the output of 40 different French auto manufacturers spanning the era 1878–1950.

If you will accept the premise that motor cars are a marvellous reflection of social history, then the social history – at least the European social history – of the past 90-odd years unfolds here with great ease. There are all the grand touring cars of the 30s and most of the modernist cars of the 50s. There are Grand Prix racers from the 20s and rally racers from the 60s. There are Gordinis from the 50s and Maseratis from the 30s. Mercedes range from the 1907 model 39/75 to the 1956 model 300SC. Benz's span the entire decade of the 1890s. There are Panhard & Levassors from 1893 onwards, and no less than 26 De Dions to cover the years 1901–14.

There is a 1906 Sage, a 1904 Hermes Simplex, a 1920 Sunbeam, a 1933 Talbot Londres, a 1924 Mathis, a 1908 Sizaire Naudin racer, a 1906 Piccolo, an 1896 Bollée Tricar, a 1927 Ravel, a 1912 Barre, a 1914 Maf, a 1906 Corre-Licorne, a 1911 Le Gui, a 1907 Gladiator, a 1907 Delaunay-Belleville, a 1934 Mayback-Zeppelin, a 1906 Fouillaron, a 1927 Peugeot 174, a 1903 Decauville, a 1904 Dufaux, and a 1921 Ballot that ran in the Indianapolis 500 that same year.

There are Rolls-Royces – including every Rolls model up to the mid-1930s – and Bentleys and Daimlers – one belonged to the British Royal Family – and Hispano Suizas and Lorraine Dietriches and Maybachs and Le Zèbres and Delages and Darracqs and Gardner Serpollet steam cars.

But most of all there are 123 Bugattis.

It's the largest and most important accumulation of Bugattis in the world ... including the absolutely unique Coupé Napoléon, which was the private car of Ettore Bugatti himself.

Spread across 5 acres and all under one roof, as far as you can see there are red tile walkways and 845 lamp posts copied exactly from the street lights along the Alexander III Bridge in Paris, and all those cars polished to perfection.

The effect is absolutely breathtaking.

It is such a truly astonishing sight that when French President François Mitterrand came to visit the museum his initial reaction was, 'What a folly. It's worthy of Mad King Ludwig of Bavaria.'

To that Fritz Schlumpf says proudly, 'Why not? My

museum is a superb folly. What a beautiful compliment to be compared to Ludwig. Everything you do in life you should do with passion. Otherwise it's not worth doing.'

And there can be no denying that this collection was a passion.

'In 1963, the Bugatti factory was in difficulty. They owned 23 classic Bugattis including the Coupé Napoléon, the two 7-cylinders and the racer which ran in the 1930 24 Hours at Le Mans. So I bought them all.' He is said to have paid 120,000 francs (then about £10,000 or $24,000) for the cars, some extra motors and the factory full of spare parts. Among those spare parts were 23 Bugatti compressors, factory fresh and in working order, which he turned into a wall sculpture to form the letters EB. 'It's beautiful,' Schlumpf insists, although to be perfectly frank it is not nearly as beautiful as it is silly. *Aficionados* jealously weep, 'It's ridiculous,' because serious Bugatti collectors would give their eye-teeth for just one spare Bugatti compressor. It seems that they are easily rated among the rarest items on earth.

'Then I bought another 30 Bugattis from someone in Chicago. That collection included the second Royale.' A private American collector named John Shakespeare had been asking $105,000 for his Bugattis. Schlumpf offered $70,000. The final price is said to have split the difference.

The buying spree continued.

Throughout the 1960s train-loads of antique automobiles were brought into the Schlumpf factories in France. Some of the cars were unloaded only under the darkness of night. All of the cars were always covered with heavy tarpaulins. All of the shipments were always surrounded by intrigue. It was all straight out

of a paperback spy thriller. There were barbed wire
fences, guard dogs and floodlights. Some 40 workers
from Schlumpf companies were sworn to secrecy,
employed full-time to restore the cars of this collection.
As the legend has it, Fritz Schlumpf relentlessly
patrolled the area on a bicycle, forever checking the
security. Once when he caught a worker trying to peek
at a newly arrived car, he fined the man a heavy sum.
Another version of the same story says he fired the
worker on the spot.

'It took me 30 years to put that museum together. I
dedicated it to the memory of my mother who was from
Mulhouse.' But only 33 VIP visitors were ever allowed
into the museum in the ten years between 1966 and
1976. 'I wasn't interested in letting anyone see it.'

That's when he lost the collection.

It was taken away from him.

Except he says it was stolen.

The two brothers are as different as night and day.

Fritz is stern. Hans can be outgoing. Fritz can be
arrogant. Hans is prepared to allow his brother the
limelight. Fritz passionately loves automobiles. Hans
is more at ease with nature.

As the story is still told in Mulhouse, Hans used to
keep pigeons in the back yard of their family home. He
adored his pigeons and loved to watch them fly around
the property. But Fritz was more concerned with what
the pigeons were doing to the statues scattered around
the property. So he made Hans sell his birds.

Another story is told about their beds. Fritz's bed in
France was king-sized, and propped up on a stage-like
base. Hans's bed in France was in a smaller room, and
single-sized.

Yet another story is told about the way they conducted their business. Fritz was the president-director general – the dreaded P-DG in French lingo – who ruled with an iron fist, who signed every letter that left their factory, no matter how banal, who often threw temper tantrums but who always spoke his mind. Hans was director of personnel who used to visit the factory floor and ask the employees if everything was all right.

Hans was born Giovanni Carlo Viterio Schlumpf in Italy in February 1904. Fritz was born Federico Filippo Augustino Schlumpf in Italy in February 1906. Their father was Swiss. Their mother was French. Immediately following Fritz's birth the family moved to Mulhouse. After finishing school, Hans worked as a banker and Fritz learned the textile trade. By 1935 the two brothers joined forces to start a woollens business. Then came the war and the German occupation of the area.

There is no doubt at all that during the war years the Schlumpfs cooperated with the occupying army to supply textiles. There is no doubt that the Nazi flag flew in their factories, interestingly enough alongside the Swiss flag. Nor is there any doubt that photos of Goering and Goebbels adorned the walls of some offices. They also supposedly sent a telegram to Hitler, congratulating him for having survived the assassination attempt of 1944.

When the war ended they were accused of being collaborators. In April 1946 their assets were temporarily seized and an investigation was launched. Fritz Schlumpf claimed all along that it was a charade. He said that when you find yourself in a pack of wolves there's nothing else to do but howl like a wolf. One report said that the Schlumpfs took too literally the expression, 'The end justifies the means,' and would have cooperated with anyone as long as they were allowed to continue doing business. But their employees stood by them. A motion passed by 97 per cent of their workers in 1946 affirmed, 'We never had such good bosses, so understanding, so caring.'

A textile merchant named Bernard Thierry-Mieg was appointed by the Free French to look into the Schlumpfs' war years and he concluded that, while they had indeed cooperated with the Germans, they were certainly not the only ones. His recommendation was not to prosecute the brothers. But the basis of his recommendation was that as Swiss citizens they might in this case actually be beyond French law.

Their assets were returned and the Schlumpfs tried to put that episode behind them.

They made the headlines again a few years later when Fritz's first wife Paule – the mother of their mentally retarded daughter who died in childhood – was put on trial for the murder of her lover. Fritz testified on her behalf. She was sentenced to eight years, and while she served her sentence the two were divorced.

Between the years 1946 and 1957, the Schlumpf brothers expanded their empire by taking over four regional textile concerns. At the same time they steadfastly refused to make excuses for their conduct during the war years. They just as steadfastly refused to join other industrialists in the area to create a single front against foreign competition. The only thing that apparently interested them was moulding their businesses into a major French texile group.

Then, in 1957, the matriarch of the family passed away.

Although Fritz had always collected cars in a small way, and loved to drive some of them himself in local rallies, when Jeanne Schlumpf died something must have snapped in Fritz's brain. That's really the only rational explanation for the compulsive collecting that followed ... that somewhere a fuse blew or a wire short-circuited. Both brothers were bowled over by their mother's death. But Fritz, who was always the more outwardly emotional of the two, manifested a hidden passion by suddenly buying every antique automobile that came his way. His idea was to put together the most magnificent car collection in the world, which he could dedicate to his mother's memory.

A fortune was spent on the cars, on restoring them and then on transforming one of their factories in Mulhouse into the museum. 'I spent every afternoon with my cars. At least two hours a day for 30 years. It was my life.'

That collection became such an eccentric obsession that it eventually got in the way of his businesses.

The first signs of problems came in the early 1970s when the labour unions manifested their discontent with violent demonstrations. They even burned Fritz in effigy.

Then the market turned sour.

'In 1974 there was a worldwide crisis in the textile business. It happened to many others. I wasn't alone. It was a very difficult period. There was a sudden fall in demand while at the same time costs and wages shot up to crazy heights. The unions were also giving me big problems. Everything got out of hand. I finally decided, that's enough. It's finished.'

He announced his intention to close the factories, to shut down the businesses and to devote himself solely to the museum.

Faced with massive unemployment in an area where unemployment figures were already high, the unions began accusing the Schlumpfs of running their businesses into the ground, of misusing company funds to support the car collection. Fritz and Hans offered all four factories to anyone for the symbolic sum of 1 franc on condition that the new owner assume their debts, said to be in the region of 60 million francs (then about £5 million or $12 million).

There wasn't a single taker.

'When we ceased doing business, all of our accounts were in profit. Then the unions took me to court and they demanded audits and even then the auditors appointed by the courts decided our accounts were in the black. It wasn't until the liquidators came in to sell everything and they sold all our assets at the lowest prices.'

The Schlumpf Group was put into receivership and a well-known French company director, Albert Sallan, was appointed to try to save the group. He saw the possibility of a solution by tying the museum into the group's debt repayment. He went to see Hans Schlumpf and explained that, if the car collection was made into a foundation, they could raise funds on that to relaunch their textile business. It seemed to Sallan a viable solution. He even told Hans about an art collector who had just saved his business with his paintings and had a wonderful art museum in his name to show for his troubles.

But, Sallan recalled, he couldn't make the Schlumpfs understand. 'They were convinced that they simply had to close their factories. They imagined that would then save their car collection. They never doubted that if they went bankrupt they would be allowed to keep their personal assets. I don't believe they are great thinkers.'

Seething with frustration and faced with massive

layoffs, in October 1976 the workers occupied the factories. The Schlumpf brothers, together with Fritz's companion – whom he refers to as his wife – and their daughter were forced to retreat to their villa in Malmerspach.

The unions then organized the siege of the villa, surrounding the house and virtually keeping the Schlumpfs prisoner there for 72 hours.

Says Fritz, 'I finally decided enough was enough and called for the police.' The CRS, the special French riot police, arrived the following morning at dawn, armed, to free the Schlumpfs and escort them to Mulhouse where they took a taxi to Basle.

By this time the world's press had focused on the affair. And now stories circulated that the Schlumpfs had miraculously escaped in the dead of night, like fugitives, fleeing to freedom in Switzerland.

'It's not true. We left October 2, 1976. We were free to leave.'

For some time before any of these problems began, rumours were already spreading through the town hall in Mulhouse about the collection and just how splendid it was. Every so often, someone from the mayor's office would approach Fritz Schlumpf to suggest that he might bequeath the museum to the city after his death. 'I said, no. That museum is mine. It belongs to me. What happens to it later, well, I'll think about that later. Anyway, I'm going to live to be 100. I'm 80 now so I've got another 20 years. After that it goes to my wife and daughter.'

Eight days after their departure from France, another delegation came to see him. 'They said to me, if you donate your museum to the city of Mulhouse, to the *département* of Haut Rhin and to France, all your problems will disappear in five minutes. I told them,

"Merde", and kicked them out the door. They came back three times. They tried to blackmail me. You know, without me there would be no museum and, without that museum, the city of Mulhouse would be nothing at all. It's because of me that Mulhouse is now known throughout the world.'

That's when the unions filed suit against the brothers, accusing them of having diverted company funds to support the museum.

The French courts then issued a warrant for their arrest.

'They did that to try to keep us from defending ourselves in the French courts. They accused me of taking money out of the companies and putting it into the automobile collection, when they felt I should have reinvested the money to keep our companies afloat. The warrant was issued, so they said, for our supposed mishandling of the companies' assets. They said we mishandled our own fortune, that we mishandled our business and that the collection was bought with the companies' funds. It's totally untrue. We had 25 companies, and not one single car was bought with company funds. I can prove that everything was bought with our own personal money. They also tried to keep my lawyers from pleading my case because, they said, we were fugitives from justice. They said that we fled Mulhouse and escaped to Basle. Do you know that for ten years the courts pretended not to know our address?'

The company was made bankrupt and so were the two brothers. 'The courts took over and they made me bankrupt. They had to do it that way so they could steal everything we owned. It was all part of their plan.'

That's when the workers occupied the museum. They

threw open the doors and called it 'The People's Museum'. They claimed the collection for themselves. They escorted visitors through the huge room, where cars were still covered in layers of dust, told them how communism would one day triumph in France and compared the price of each car with their own monthly salaries.

'Our problems arrived very suddenly,' Fritz explains. 'We didn't see them coming. There was no way we could have seen those particular problems coming. My mother was from Mulhouse and the collection was put together in her memory. There was no way we could have taken the cars and simply left. After all, there were 560 cars. How would you want me to take them away? It would have created a single uninterrupted line of cars five kilometres long. That's three miles. It was unthinkable. And don't forget these are all antique cars. You can't just take them out and put them on the road in the rain or in the snow. And even if you could, where would you then find 20,000 square metres of space to show them. That hall is magnificent. You can't find space like that easily.'

He notes that over the years he had offers from various countries to relocate his museum. The Franco regime made him an offer to take the collection to Madrid. He also had offers from Italy and Argentina, among others. 'If I had built the museum in Switzerland, today I'd be happy. The way it stands now I am very unhappy. But what could I do? My mother was from Mulhouse. You know, if I had taken the money and bought a yacht or bought property on the Riviera, today I wouldn't have any of these problems.'

There is a certain irony in what he says. Even at the town hall in Mulhouse, the General Secretary of the mayor's office, a certain Monsieur Gessler, agrees that

if the Schlumpfs had spent their money on a castle in
Spain, they never would have suffered the way they
have. 'They were very secretive about their museum.
It was difficult to contact them. It was almost as if they
didn't want to know about anything or anyone, except
their museum. As early as 1967 or 1968 the mayor of
the day was prepared to put 1 million francs (£80,000
or $200,000) into the museum and at no time did we
ask on behalf of Mulhouse for the ownership of the
museum. All we wanted was to be given the museum
as a bequest when the two brothers passed away. But
they said, no. Yes, it is slightly paradoxical. They were
charged with misusing funds, with diverting monies
from their enterprises and putting them into their
museum. But without that, obviously, there would
never have been a museum. After all, they could have
easily spent the money in all sorts of other ways and
that would have been the end of that.'

Here Fritz is in total agreement with the authorities.
'There is nothing in the law that would have prevented
us from wasting money on gambling in Monte Carlo or
on women or on anything at all and if we had done
that we would have had nothing. But instead we spent
our money on that museum and now they have that.'

In a philosophical tone, Gessler believes part of their
problem stemmed from the fact that the Schlumpfs
never played the game. 'They were never part of the
industrial society of Mulhouse. They never socialized
with the other industrialists. In some ways they were
considered *arrivistes*, outsiders who were not part of
the same caste as the high industrial society in the
region. I guess that was because they were very special
characters. Very peculiar. But they were always
apart.'

Again Fritz agrees.

'Of course we were never members of the Chamber of Commerce, or for that matter of any association at all. We didn't have the time or the inclination. We were at the factory every morning by 5. And we worked 16 hours a day. Every afternoon I went to the museum. In 40 years I only took three vacations. Work is what keeps one young. Laziness makes you old. Being a part of Alsatian society just didn't interest me. A foreigner, a Swiss, a rich man who said "Merde" to everybody, that's enough to create a lot of jealousy. They're dying of jealousy. We were the fourth largest textile manufacturers in France and the largest in Alsace. We provided work for 50 years. We were employing 2200 people. And the unions simply threw all of that away.'

Another part of the troubles, as Gessler sees it, came from the Schlumpfs' staunch paternalism. 'There was a long-standing problem with their workers. Everyone knows that for many years they were considered to be very good employers who looked after their workers. But their style of paternalism was no longer viable after the war. The unions took over that role. The Schlumpfs were of the old school. It's well known that one or the other brother was always available to drive a worker's pregnant wife to the hospital when her baby was due. But times changed. If they hadn't, the Schlumpfs would be heroes today.'

Now Fritz says that their fatherly approach to employee relations had nothing to do with their problems, that paternalistic attitudes where employees were concerned could never be outdated. There were workers' cottages and company-sponsored family outings. There were company restaurants and company Christmas parties where Père Noël had gifts for everyone. 'We were too good to our workers. We had excellent relations with our personnel until the unions arrived and they destroyed everything. The union chiefs said to our workers, even if the boss is 100 per cent right, we've got to pretend he's wrong. They said, we are against the bosses so they will never be right as far as we're concerned.'

Many employees however remember it differently. They claim that Schlumpf paternalism – especially during the 1970s – was merely a façade. Some are still quick to accuse the brothers of being stingy with wages, inaccessible, and authoritarian. There are also those who claim that Fritz used to spy on his employees through holes in the roof.

Answering that, Fritz sees red. 'The unions infiltrated my workers and united them against me and to them I say, "Merde"! What the city of Mulhouse has done to my brother and me is shameful and a scandal.'

And he's not alone in believing that.

Oddly agreeing with the Schlumpfs was the very same man who investigated their wartime activities, Bernard Thierry-Mieg.

In 1981, at the age of 78 . . . purposely not having spoken to either of the Schlumpfs since judging them collaborators . . . Thierry-Mieg told a reporter that in his opinion the brothers had indeed been treated shabbily. He said he believed they went bankrupt, not because they had misused company funds, but because the European textile industry was no longer competitive. Anyway, he felt, the Schlumpfs were poor managers. 'But nothing the Schlumpfs may have done justifies confiscating their cars. Everything that has happened since they went bankrupt in 1976 was done with the intention of buying the collection as cheaply as possible. The whole thing stinks.'

* * *

Unable to obtain the museum in any other fashion, and by now realizing the vast tourist potential of such a collection, the city of Mulhouse joined with the *département* of the Haut Rhin and other regional authorities to take advantage of the Schlumpf bankruptcy. They purchased the museum from the liquidators after certain 'experts' valued the collection at 44 million francs (£4.4 million or just about $6.6 million). The city of Mulhouse, the *département* of the Haut Rhin and those other regional authorities came up with the money and just like that laid claim to the cars.

But establishing the true value of a collection as important as that is not quite as easy as the French courts made it out to be.

Fritz Schlumpf claims it is today worth more than 600 million francs. That's in excess of £60 million or over $90 million.

But when one says that a certain collection is worth so much, the important question to ask is, to whom?

And here the French were very clever.

The first step they took, before valuing the collection, was to declare it an historic monument. Under very strict French laws, that decreed the cars could never be exported. They would have to stay in France. Instantly the market for them shrank. The courts also ruled that the collection had to be sold as a whole, not individually, and not at public auction. By so completely restricting the possible buyers to just one – the consortium consisting mainly of the city of Mulhouse, the *département* of the Haut Rhin, the Mulhouse Chamber of Commerce and local tourist boards – the courts totally erased the international auction value the collection might have otherwise had.

On an international market, Schlumpf's eight different Type 55 Bugattis alone, covering the years 1932–35, could probably come close to being worth 44 million francs. Not long ago Sotheby's sold a Bugatti Type 55 for £420,000. That was then just over 5 million new francs. Although the value of each would vary in an international auction because of the different versions Bugatti made of the same type, the French experts valued each of Schlumpf's eight Bugatti 55s at only 60,000 francs.

Then there are the Type 41 Bugatti Royales.

Worthy of the Guinness Book of Records, under the category of largest automobile ever built for private road use, the first one was finished in 1927 for King Alphonso XIII of Spain. It measures some 22 feet long (that's 6.7 metres), and the bonnet alone takes up one-third of the body. A six-seater, with the most luxurious interior possible, the Type 41 was powered by an 8-cylinder, 12.7 litre engine. The car was capable of speeds up to 120 mph.

Only six Type 41s were ever built. Four of them are in the United States, while two are in the Schlumpf collection.

Establishing the true market value for a Bugatti Royale is easy. One of the six – part of the famous Harrah Collection – was sold in June 1986 at a public auction in Reno, Nevada. Knowledgeable antique car collectors estimated that the price might reach anywhere from $4 million to $6 million. And nobody would have been surprised to see it sold for more.

The hammer price was a staggering $8 million, which at the time converted to £6.5 million.

In November 1987, a London auction house sold another Royale, this one having belonged to race driver and yachtsman Briggs Cunningham. The hammer price was £5.5 million. When converted to the then current dollar rate, this Royale goes into the record books at $9.6 million.

However, one of Schlumpf's two Royales is the 1930 Coupé Napoléon and there are some people who think that might be the most prestigious motor car in the world.

Putting a price on that is anyone's guess.

It is a unique automobile. A one-off work of art. And Ettore Bugatti built it for himself. The bonnet takes up nearly two-thirds of the entire car, with the world's longest running boards stretching, in a single piece, the entire length of the machine. Everything is in perfect proportion. The lines are sleek. The wheels are magnificent. The interior is phenomenally luxurious. There are two seats uncovered up front . . . the chauffeur and perhaps a footman . . . and two seats covered behind that, for Monsieur Bugatti and friend.

Even unexportable, it is still almost certainly the most valuable automobile in the world. One conservative estimate suggests that, should it ever go onto the international auction block, it could fetch twice the price of any other Type 41.

And that makes the French experts' valuation of 44 million francs for the entire collection decidedly ludicrous.

'Before putting a value on the collection,' Schlumpf recalls, 'they said the cars were ugly, no good, worthless, not authentic, poorly restored. There was nothing but bad mouthing about it to set a low price. They stole it from me. Now it's the most beautiful museum in the world, the best collection in the world. What they once called worthless is now sensational. Let me repeat to you that, without Fritz Schlumpf, there would be no museum. And without that museum, the city of Mulhouse would be absolutely ignored.'

One of the experts named by the courts to catalogue and value the collection was Hervé Poulain, a Parisian auctioneer who usually flogs old master paintings, French furniture, Oriental ceramics and contemporary sculpture.

Poulain spent three months in Mulhouse, after which he proclaimed, 'Many of the cars are not museum worthy and there are some counterfeits.' That's an obvious reference to the Type 41 Bugatti Royale that Schlumpf ordered built as a replica but that was never completed. 'Some Mercedes, for example, make you think of poor imitations. This is a garage, not a museum.'

Schlumpf of course immediately takes great exception to that . . . as any antique motor car enthusiast might. 'He's an auctioneer and knows nothing about antique automobiles. But the real plum of the valuation came when a certain Monsieur Chapelon, an engineer from the Museum of Arts and Crafts in Paris, inspected the Bugatti Royale, Coupé Napoléon. He asked that the bonnet be opened so that he could see the motor which is one metre long. As he had to list in his report the number of cylinders, he counted the number of spark plugs and wrote, *quel horreur*, 16 cylinders! It's scandalous. Bugatti designed the Royales with two spark plugs per cylinder, so there are only eight. Chapelon should have known better. That he didn't is deplorable.'

To prove his point, in 1981 Schlumpf enlisted the aid of Christian Huel in Paris – the only antique automobile expert in France accredited to the French Court of Appeal – and the international auction firm, Christie's. 'Huel did his valuation in a serious, conscientious and honest way and valued my cars at 307 million francs. But I can better that because Christie's valued the collection at 325 million francs. It's shameful to have given away this collection for two times nothing. It was organized theft.'

Part of the Christie's team who helped do the valuation for Schlumpf was Robert Brooks. And he doesn't hesitate a second to say it is an extraordinary collection. 'I don't know of any other collector or collection that has been put together in that way. It is quite remarkable and quite unique. There are all sorts of motor cars in the collection which are very very interesting, more or less across the board. It certainly stands out as one of the most spectacular in the world.'

But what's it worth today? He won't commit himself. 'Let me put it this way. I'm not going to tell you what I think the Coupé Napoléon is worth because it belongs to a collector who we'd been advising and we're not in a position to discuss our valuations. But in my view, and I think you will find in many people's view, the Coupé Napoléon is one of the two most desirable Royales. There are six Royales in existence and this is one of the two most desirable. Many say the most desirable. Certainly it is more desirable than the Berline de Voyage which was sold at the Harrah's sale.'

However, what Brooks will say is that prices for antique cars have accelerated rapidly over the past few years, at least since Huel and Christie's valued the Schlumpf collection. 'The market at the top end has become a lot harder and more spectacular with the figures that are being achieved. The million pound motor car now is not a rare exception that one never sees. It's something that's being proved time and time again. Call it the million dollar car and one's seen it on several occasions recently. But it then hardly goes without saying that when certain Bugattis are worth and have been proved to be worth on the open market prices as high as 1 million pounds sterling, it doesn't take a lot of imagination to draw conclusions about the Schlumpf collection from there.'

In the early 1980s, two 'Schlumpf' books were published in France. One on the bankruptcy. One on the collection.

Not surprisingly, Fritz Schlumpf has objections to both.

L'Affaire Schlumpf was written by two journalists then based in Mulhouse, Francis Laffon and Elisabeth Lambert. It is subtitled, 'The secrets of the most fabulous museum in the world'. Laffon and Lambert do not hide their leftist leanings and are openly partial to the union's cause.

Say Laffon and Lambert, 'The private life of Fritz and Hans has hardly been an average one. It's rather an odd combination of a quasi-mystic adoration for their ever-present "dear mother" and dramatic episodes worthy of "boulevard" theatre. Old men and their old habits, attached to their traditions but motivated by more worldly desires. The Schlumpf brothers are either angry with you or they are smiling at you. But they never win your sympathy.'

Says Fritz, 'He's (Laffon) nothing. He came to see me once and I threw him out. He came without a tie. He wrote the book and made money off my back.'

Collection Schlumpf – Une Folie Superbe is an outsized, overpriced full-colour coffee table book that does more justice to the collection than the Laffon–Lambert book by keeping the text to a minimum and simply showing the pictures of the cars. However, the introduction was written by Jean Panhard ... as in Panhard & Levassor ... who is president of the French

Automobile Club and vice-president of the Museum Association. On that introductory page there is a colour photo of him, surrounded by the text, propped up and grinning in the driver's seat of the museum's 1908 Panhard & Levassor two-place racer.

Says Fritz with great annoyance, 'Those are my cars and he's sitting there as if they're his.'

But, then, just about everything concerning the way the collection has been handled since the workers' occupation of 'The People's Museum' in 1977 and the official opening of 'The National Museum' in 1982 annoys Fritz.

'When they inaugurated the museum, they cut the ribbon just in front of the portrait of my mother. It wasn't someone else's place to cut the ribbon. It's my museum. It's scandalous. The union was there. They sang the Internationale. And no one said anything. No one. They stole from me a collection worth 600 million francs today and they sang the Internationale. I'd like to give them all a kick in the arse.'

From that morning in October 1976 when they left France, Fritz and his wife, with their daughter and Hans in tow, have lived in Basle. For the first six years they occupied penthouse suites at the Three Kings, one of the most renowned hotels in Switzerland. Then Hans took a flat and Fritz did too. Today Fritz and his wife live in that modern penthouse, with a huge terrace, in rooms that are overcrowded with antique furniture, Persian carpets and mementoes of the good times past. They don't give you the impression of being on their uppers, but they are quick to tell you that in order to get their own furniture to Switzerland they actually had to buy it back from the liquidators at a public auction.

Because none of his cars are allowed to be auctioned,

he couldn't possibly get any of them back that way.
Which might well be why the courts decided not to
auction the cars in the first place. But when you ask
him if he still has any antique autos you get a hesitant,
'Hmmm ... yes.' Then he changes the subject,
obviously and understandably, very reluctant to go
into detail, not at all disposed to tell a stranger which
antique cars he still owns or where they are. He'd
rather talk about new cars. 'I have my own cars. My
wife drives a Mercedes 190 and we also have a
Mercedes 500. Then I have a Ferrari Testa Rossa. It's
the most beautiful car in the world. I can drive it at
300 km an hour. We're talking about 400 horse power.
I do 200 km an hour easily. Why not, I'm still a young
man.'

Young enough, he insists, to fight on.

But old enough to realize that the war he is waging
is not an easy one.

When the workers occupied the museum, which is
still housed in a factory that once belonged to a
Schlumpf company called HKC, they found accounting
ledgers and invoices that, they claimed, proved without any doubt the Schlumpfs had used HKC's funds to
support the museum. In particular, there were bills to
show that HKC had paid for a good part of the
restoration on the collection. A lower court ruled in
the workers' favour and the Court of Appeal in Colmar
upheld that decision. It called HKC 'a mere façade',
which was used as a funnel for certain deals out of
which HKC took a 6 per cent commission. It was this
money that, the court said, the Schlumpfs used to
finance the collection. 'A large part of their antique
cars, as well as the street lights, lanterns, candelabras
and other fixtures which went into the museum were
acquired by the Schlumpf brothers through HKC.'

Anyway, the court ruled, the Schlumpfs lived too big. 'The defendants, in spite of their advanced years, exploited their companies and that is incontestable because it brought them more and more personal benefits as seen by the extremely comfortable situation in which they lived but which was out of all proportion to their actual situation.'

Firstly, Fritz answers, 'None of the deals that we did were in any way clandestine. They are all on record either with the intermediaries involved or with the French banks. These deals were known to the shareholders of my different companies. They were discussed at the annual general meeting where the votes were taken. I was in charge of 25 companies and there was absolutely no misuse of funds. That's because these companies belonged to me 100 per cent. No shareholder complained. There were no shareholders who could complain about abuse of funds or the companies themselves.'

Then he points out that the people who complained were members of the employees' committee, but that they were not shareholders. Therefore the way he ran his business had nothing whatsoever to do with them.

'I had two main divisions. The industrial division, which comprised my textile concerns, and my leisure division, which was made up of a hotel we owned, my museum and my collection. I acquired my automobiles before 1973 and I particularly bought most of the cars between 1961 and 1969. My group ran into difficulties in 1974, like so many others did at the time. The one thing had nothing to do with the other.'

Except that the unions and the French courts claim the two are very related. They have repeatedly stated that there are accounting records to show that all of the money sunk into the collection did not come out of the Schlumpfs' personal funds.

Again Fritz objects. 'The experts said the museum cost 26 million francs, of which I merely paid 845,000 francs. That is completely false and I add completely stupid because I can prove I paid 10 million francs out of my own pocket.' But now he qualifies himself by adding, 'The other 16 million francs came from a company called HKC as investments conforming to its statutes and the law.'

Those investments, and in particular a 1.2 million franc auto restoration bill charged to HKC, had been written off in the company's books by Schlumpf as publicity for the group. 'One page in *Paris Match* cost 100,000 francs for one advert for one week. If you buy one page once, it doesn't amount to anything. Advertising must be repeated, to bang people over the head, to get the message into their brain. Therefore, the 1.2 million francs represents adverts in 12 issues of *Match*. The advertising impact is formidable if you take into account the 1 million people who came to see my museum.'

Anyway, he adds, 'We owned 100 per cent of our own companies and there cannot be misuse of your own funds.'

That notwithstanding, he realizes very well that one of the factors that has saved him from a great deal more trouble is his Swiss passport.

'I was lucky to have dual nationality. My father was Swiss so I was Swiss and French. That was very lucky.'

It was lucky because the Swiss would be most reluctant to extradite one of their own citizens to France. But it was especially lucky because, under French laws, his Swiss passport gave him certain rights otherwise denied to French citizens, such as Swiss bank accounts and beneficial but undeclared interests in foreign companies, which he hints that he's managed to keep away from the French authorities.

'Yes, we still have enough to eat and drink every day. And that's one of the things that greatly bothers them in France. We have more than enough money to live on. But they'd like to have seen me ruined.'

Determined to avoid that, a great deal of his time every day is directed at the business of getting his collection back. 'I love my collection with a passion. Naturally I miss it. You don't put together a museum like that for gangsters. And the people who took it away from me are gangsters.'

So he's fighting the French in French courts and also in the European Court on a human rights angle. His lawyers' bills are, to say the least, extravagant.

'Yes, they are expensive. I have 13 lawyers working for me. What I've spent on lawyers could have got me a villa. The most beautiful villa on the Riviera.'

And if one day the courts rule in his favour?

Fritz promises, 'I'll give them all a kick in the arse.' But after that, he says, he'll probably leave the museum in Mulhouse. 'Yes. One doesn't easily move such a collection. I have to leave it there. For my mother.'

12
Eli Pinkas – A Mystery Story

Lausanne, Switzerland.

Tuesday 10 June 1980.

Just after dawn.

The police arrived in a big hurry at La Gentilhomiere.

In the garage they noticed that the bonnet of a Jaguar parked there was hot. Not simply warm but very hot. The car had been driven hard and fast that night.

The villa seemed otherwise quiet.

A maid allowed them inside.

They rushed upstairs.

In the hallway they found the body of the family dog. It was dead. It had been poisoned.

In the master bedroom they found the villa's owner. He was also dead. An apparent suicide by cyanide capsule. Next to the man's body was a note asking his friends to forgive him.

That should have closed the case.

Except . . .

Sometime that very same morning, but definitely before the Lausanne police went to La Gentilhomiere, an anonymous phone call to the police in Cannes, France, summoned them to a woman's penthouse flat at the Grand Hotel.

The front door had a whole series of locks but now none of them were bolted.

In the master bedroom they found the flat's owner.

An apparent suicide by cyanide capsule. Next to her body was a note ripped into small pieces.

'Flo, m'amour, I give you some last advice because I love you. Open these two packages and swallow these four capsules which operate very quickly so that you can join me.'

The letter warned that if she stayed alive she would suffer great difficulties and dishonour. 'I've tried for years to re-establish my financial situation but without success.'

It was signed, 'I love you always and until the last breath of my life. Your Eli.'

At first glance the story has a Romeo and Juliet quality about it.

But first glances can be deceptive.

Eli Pinkas was a cultured man who spoke at least five languages . . . French, English, German, Italian and Bulgarian.

A man who always dressed in a traditional, conservative manner.

A man whose thinning dark hair was just on the verge of turning white.

A man of average build, but with heavy features . . . like extremely large hands and a very large forehead.

Born in 1920, he came to Switzerland at the age of 21, a refugee from Bulgaria. His family settled in Lausanne and he went to school there, finishing with a degree in chemistry. For the next 39 years he lived the life of a successful and respected businessman in Lausanne . . . the sort of serious businessman that other serious businessmen liked to have on their corporate boards. For instance, among his appointments was a seat on the board of the very serious, very conservative, Banque Vaudoise de Crédit. His home

was aptly named 'the gentleman's manor'. Whenever
he could, he spent time there, in his garden, planting
roses. His personal annual income would have been in
the range of 2–3 million Swiss francs a year. Call that
somewhere between $1 million and £1 million. So he
was a wealthy man. But he was quietly wealthy. Never
extravagant. Except perhaps for his love of Jaguars.
He had several.

The only thing that might be considered just a little
odd about him was that – even to people who knew
him very well – he always seemed slightly distant. He
always seemed a bit aloof. Still, he was for the most
part friendly and nobody really thought twice about
his basic aloofness at the time. It's just the way he is,
some people decided. He's a private person. He's shy.
He's discreet.

His business life was a multi-layered series of interests almost all revolving around his background as a
chemist. His company was called Socsil and his factory
in Lausanne – a large, well-guarded, fully mechanized
plant – operated in three distinct fields.

First there was the manufacturing of mechanical
pumps, a process that Pinkas had patented.

Then there was the chemical testing of certain raw
materials being used to make soft drinks. At times
Pinkas even confided that the particular soft drink in
question was Coca-Cola and that he was the only
person outside the United States to possess the secret
Coke formula.

However, the most important and by far the biggest
share of his business had to do with nitrous oxide . . . a
highly explosive gas popularly known as laughing gas.
Primarily, he produced and sold containers of nitrous
oxide to industrial clients all over the world. But,
complementing that, Pinkas had some time ago

invented a chemical process that rendered that gas inert. Having found a way to keep it from blowing up, he quickly realized the potential of a non-explosive nitrous oxide medical kit for battlefield hospital use. Over the years he developed that side of his business and subsequently had financial arrangements with any number of militaries, including NATO armies and especially armies of certain Arab nations. It's important here to note that through these dealings he was privy to selected military intelligence – a force build-up somewhere would be reflected in an increase of orders for the field kit – and that his military contracts allowed him access to various classified information.

Not that classified information was a problem where Pinkas was concerned because he was also a major in the Swiss Army Reserve.

Or maybe he wasn't.

In Switzerland, just about every male citizen has a commitment to the army for most of his life. That's why it was hardly surprising when anyone who knew him saw Eli Pinkas walking through the streets wearing his reserve army officer's uniform with his major's insignia. If he wasn't a reserve army major, Lausanne is just too small a town and everyone would have known very quickly. He told people that he was the Reserve Chief of Gas Warfare for the Swiss Army. That too is not altogether impossible considering that he was a chemist with a thorough knowledge of gases. The Swiss, who are not a nuclear force, happen to depend greatly on gas warfare as a line of defence against hostile attacks. At the first sign of an attack, their battle plan is to retreat into the mountains and fill the valleys with gas. That way, Switzerland becomes just about impregnable. So it was Major Eli

Pinkas, Reserve Chief of Gas Warfare for the Swiss Army.

Except the Swiss military now say that he never had anything to do with their Army Gas Warfare Department, nor was he ever an officer.

In addition to the three main parts of Socsil, Pinkas had his fingers in a few other pies.

In the mid-1960s he bought a 283 acre tract of land outside Lausanne with the intention of developing it into a resort area. He had hoped to enlist the help of an American consortium but Swiss laws do not encourage the foreign ownership of property, and as a result the Americans shied away. Instead he found he was able to use the land as security when he wanted to swing other deals.

Then, quite ingeniously, he also seemed to be in the scrap steel business.

While selling nitrous oxide to the US Army – at least this is what he told friends – he stumbled across the curious fact that where the Americans were concerned there was a big difference between 'full' and 'almost full'. The gas bottles he shipped to them were full. But as the valves on those huge steel cylinders often leaked, not all of them were 100 per cent full when the Army eventually got around to using them. Bottles that were not 100 per cent full, Pinkas explained, were written off by the Americans as unusable and simply discarded as scrap steel. When he discovered this, he immediately started buying the scrapped bottles, repainting them, topping them up with gas ... the missing 10–15–20 per cent ... and right away selling them back to the Americans for the full price. He explained to friends that it was a wonderful business, and even let a few of them in on it. They invested, he showed them their gas cylinders whenever they visited the factory, and, because those friends made some money with his scheme, no one ever bothered looking any deeper into it.

As a contractor to the United States government, Pinkas was in a position to discount US paper. Although one report later claimed Socsil was doing $4.2 million a year in worldwide nitrous oxide sales, he always claimed to do at least $27 million a year just with the Sanitary Division of the United States Army. He even had the paperwork to back up those figures. It goes without saying that Uncle Sam's signature on US Army invoices meant any bank in the world would welcome Pinkas with open arms. But Pinkas did not actually discount the paper. Instead he borrowed against those notes, putting them down as security for his loans. He'd go to a bank and say, look, you know me, I've borrowed here before, I'll even give you my personal guarantee ... he'd say whatever it took to establish a direct relationship between himself and the bank as far as repayment was concerned. He deposited the paper with them but never gave them an opportunity to collect on it. Had he discounted the notes, they would have worked their way into the Federal Reserve system and that's precisely what he did not want. He had to control his repayment channels.

Pinkas's borrowing against that US paper has now been traced as far back as 1948.

One estimate is that he might have been borrowing as much as $50–60 million a year. And that's probably a low estimate, as some of his records were destroyed.

When any of the banks wanted to see balance sheets for either Pinkas or Socsil, he showed them balance sheets. Everyone who asked for paperwork got paperwork. And in every case, the bank wanting to see accounts was listed in those reports as being Pinkas's only creditor. So each bank had US government paper and Pinkas's balance sheets, plus Pinkas's personal guarantee.

Maybe that's why some of the bankers involved forgot the most basic lesson of the lending business. It's on the first page of the bankers' textbook under the heading of basic banking skills: 'Always check with the originator of a collateral note.'

Astonishingly, no one, not even the American banks from which he borrowed against this paper . . . banks such as Citibank and First National Bank of Minneapolis . . . no one ever bothered checking with the United States Army Sanitary Division.

But, then, this was a man who was officially considered by the local office of the Swiss central bank as having a signature 'as sound as the central bank'. That was the way one memo – seen by a highly reliable source – actually worded it. 'As sound as the central bank.' In other words, the central bank was once willing to put its own reputation behind Pinkas.

That memo has since been withdrawn.

The recommendation has since been denied.

Enter now, the former Mrs Pinkas.

Her name was Florence and, sadly, she was a hopeless alcoholic.

Before Eli and Florence were married in 1943, she appeared on the scene as a dark-haired lady from Argentina who spoke beautiful Spanish and French with a heavy accent. After they were divorced in 1964 she faded away from Lausanne. She preferred to live in the apartment in Cannes and only rarely came to Switzerland. She was two years older than Pinkas . . . they never had children . . . and it seems there was often a touch of melancholy about her. Maybe she loved him and didn't want to live apart. Although he'd tell anyone who asked that he was totally devoted to her. And anyway, every Thursday night he always flew to Nice to spend the weekend with her.

It now turns out that she was not from Argentina.

Instead she was born near Lausanne ... her family still lives there ... and he met her when she was working as a barmaid in a local hangout.

Why the masquerade about being from Argentina, no one seems to understand. The important thing is that everyone either believed it or was at least willing to play along with it.

The week of 2 June 1980.

A clerk in the Banque de Paris et des Pays-Bas in Geneva was making a routine check through some paperwork when he noticed that ink was rubbing off his hands. He looked closely at the smudged forms and saw that they were from the United States Army Sanitary Division. How bizarre, he thought to himself, the Americans ought to have better printing facilities than that, and ink on US government forms isn't supposed to rub off, and perhaps I should mention this to someone.

He routinely reported the incident to his superior.

The superior routinely wired the bank's office in Washington DC asking them to seek out some routine information about the Sanitary Division of the United States Army.

The bank in Washington phoned the Pentagon and the US Army answered the query with, 'What Sanitary Division?'

For the price of better paper and better ink, the world was about to cave in on Eli Pinkas.

Instead of ringing him directly, to ask Pinkas what

this was all about, officials at the Banque de Paris et des Pays-Bas immediately called in the public prosecutor.

Being so well connected, Pinkas must have known what was about to happen by, say, Thursday of that week. It's almost certain that he knew, because all of a sudden he started paying back whatever loans were then outstanding and due. A few thousand dollars here. A few thousand francs there. And he paid cash. Looking back, it was almost as if he perhaps desperately wanted to clear at least some of the slate.

That same week, it now comes to light, Pinkas wrote letters to at least six people, excusing himself, asking them to forgive him.

On Friday 6 June, the local prosecutor in Lausanne received a document charging Eli Pinkas with fraud against the Swiss banking laws.

And the local prosecutor was absolutely stunned.

The thought of someone as reputable as Eli Pinkas being involved in a fraud was so worrying to the prosecutor that either on the Friday, or more possibly on the following Monday, he rang Pinkas to say, 'I must see you.' Pinkas allegedly laughed. A rendezvous was set for the week of 9 June.

Sometime following the prosecutor's call, Pinkas rang two friends in the hierarchy of a local bank, saying that he had to meet them.

That meeting took place at the Socsil factory on Monday morning, 9 June.

Pinkas informed them, 'I am being indicted.'

Not surprisingly, they too were stunned.

When they wanted details, he admitted to 'a few wrong-doings'. He assured them, 'It's very little.' He made them understand, 'But it's so embarrassing.'

Knowing Pinkas well, and liking him, they said they

were prepared to help him. However they were also bankers who happened to be lenders, and they had their own patch to protect. While one began checking the bank's files to see the extent of Pinkas's borrowings, the other personally approached the prosecutor to see if his intervention might help Pinkas save face. But by Monday afternoon, everyone concerned was quickly coming to the conclusion that 'very little' was hardly the case.

The next morning, Eli Pinkas was dead at La Gentilhomiere and Florence was dead in Cannes.

The Swiss press announced the Pinkas affair with headlines calling him a 'Fraudster Bulgarian Jew'.

Interestingly enough, he was not a Bulgarian citizen, but Swiss. After his family settled in Lausanne he took Swiss citizenship and carried a Swiss passport.

Nor was he still a Jew. He had publicly converted from Judaism to become a Protestant in the 1950s. Whether he did that for business reasons, or because he particularly believed, no one knows. The point is that he was officially a Swiss Protestant for the last 25 years of his life.

That he was a fraudster, however, is another matter.

When the police went to the Socsil offices after his death, they found that a large number of documents had been destroyed. Pinkas had got to them first. But from what remained they managed to establish that United States Army Sanitary Division invoices, in addition to other paper he had printed from the German Army and a guarantee of $30 million from the Union Swiss Bank, had been used as collateral for loans totalling $300–400 million.

The bogus invoices and whatever paperwork he needed to go along with them turned out to have been printed in Cannes. The printer who did the work for Pinkas claimed that he didn't know what he was printing. All he'd say was that Pinkas always paid for his work on time. The printer was the only person to go to jail in connection with the Pinkas affair. He did two years for accepting cash and not declaring it to the French tax authorities.

Of course, to make everything look absolutely official, Pinkas had to have payments coming into Switzerland from the United States government. After all, if he was supposed to be doing business with the Army, he couldn't simply deposit money and tell the bankers it was from the Army. Somehow he managed to get banks in America to make transfers to Switzerland by order of the US Army Sanitary Division. It's never been explained exactly how he managed that. But one of the banks allegedly making transfers in the Army's name was Citibank in New York.

Over the course of the next two years, the Swiss authorities traced literally hundreds of companies around the world that Pinkas was using to launder funds.

They knew that $300–400 million had come into the system. And they had reason to suspect that figure could be even higher because of undeclared loans. The figures could range as widely as from $300 million up to $800 million.

Yet the grand total of liquid assets attributable to Eli Pinkas once every book was examined, every bank account was opened and every parlour rug was rolled back, came to only $1.5 million.

Even if you take all the lowest limits, to put it mildly, a lot of money has still vanished.

And, for their own strange reasons, it looks as if the Swiss don't want anyone to know exactly how much.

The *Washington Post* reported six weeks after Pinkas's suicide that he had effectively stolen $140 million. Just over $112 million of it came from 18 banks around the world – eight in Switzerland, four in France, one in Britain, one in Israel, and four in the US ... including Citibank and the First National Bank of Minneapolis. Both of those banks admitted to be out $3.5 million. The rest of the money, the *Post* said, came from friends and business associates of Pinkas.

On top of the $140 million total, some newspapers suggested there might be as much as $20 million more automatically written off by creditors who, for legal or personal reasons, cannot publicly admit their losses.

Then, within two months of Pinkas's death, the *Wall Street Journal* was quoting a Swiss banking authority as saying that the $140 million originally estimated was being revised down to $108.7 million.

It's a long way from $300–400 million.

In addition, the Swiss Federal Banking Commission has been content to write off the scandal as a 'folie d'excès d'intérêt'. They say that, because Pinkas was so heavily in debt, he had to keep borrowing just to pay the interest. That created more interest, which in turn created the need for more borrowing.

In other words, they're calling it a 'Swiss Ponzi'.

He was all right, they say, as long as interest rates were low. But when he had to borrow at 19 per cent to pay off loans that had been made at 12 per cent, the interest rates strangled him.

So, you say, fine. A Swiss Ponzi. Folie d'excès d'intérêt. But, where did the money go?

Now they give you two answers.

The first is, 'train de vie'.

Lifestyle.

The other is, 'les jeux'.

Gambling.

The only problem there is that Pinkas apparently managed to live well within his own income, and he was most definitely not a gambler.

As the investigation into the Pinkas affair continued, the public prosecutor's interest focused on three Swiss companies in particular. First there was Socsil. Then there was Vilro, an investment company Pinkas founded in 1970. And finally there was Villas la Roche, the land development company he also founded in 1970 and had obviously hoped to use in connection with that tract of land he owned outside Lausanne.

It was then revealed that Pinkas had long since pledged each of the shares in those companies three or four times to various creditors.

That's not an easy feat to have pulled off, as all of the shares were numbered. To manage it, he had to have copies printed. Then he had to be certain that none of the creditors ever met and – God forbid – somehow started comparing notes.

Suddenly, all of the people who had thought of him as being a little aloof began to understand why.

It turns out he was quite expert at a special technique that can only be called the 'he's got a big mouth' system. It worked like this: Pinkas would strike up a relationship with Mr A. They would be discussing a business possibility when, by chance, Mr B's name came up. Immediately Pinkas would say to Mr A, 'Listen, B is a great guy and I really like him, but this deal has got to be just between us. You see, the problem is that B has a big mouth and, well, he talks too much. If you mention our business to him it will be all over Lausanne in an hour.' Naturally, A would make a point of shying away from B. However, when Pinkas then got involved with B – which he invariably would and perhaps it was even the same business deal he had with A – he'd tell B the same story about A . . . 'He's got a big mouth.'

It was a near-perfect way to keep the people he knew, and who might have known each other, from discussing his affairs. It gave him that aloof aura and more than served his purpose. It wasn't until long after his death that all sorts of people who otherwise knew each other's business – or at least thought they did – came to realize that Pinkas had successfully manoeuvred over many years to keep them apart.

Those same friends had also noted that he was a man with extraordinary control.

Some of them even often remarked that Eli Pinkas never ever got into a fight with anyone . . . that he avoided arguments at any cost . . . that he always managed to keep his temper in check.

Looking now at the glass house where his finances lived, it's no wonder that he never threw stones.

Sometime around 1975 there was a terrible accident at the Socsil factory.

At 6 one morning, while doing some sort of experiment with a product that couldn't explode, the laboratory's chief engineer was killed in an explosion.

There was an official investigation and the report concluded misadventure . . . that the man's death was accidental.

Now there is some doubt.

While this can never be proved because too much water has passed under the bridge, include it in the category of pure conjecture on the part of certain people who are – and perhaps always will be – curious about a man they once thought they knew, called Eli Pinkas.

Those people now wonder if perhaps that chief engineer might have stumbled on something odd going on at the factory, and for whatever reason had to be eliminated.

It is plausible.

Sometime around the end of 1979 or the beginning of 1980, Pinkas showed executives at the First National Bank of Minneapolis a financial statement that listed Socsil's net worth as about $14 million. At the same time Pinkas claimed to be personally worth $25 million. According to his 1978 Swiss income tax returns, he was only worth about $5.4 million.

True, he was by anyone's accounting a wealthy man. The apartment in Cannes was filled with antiques, paintings and carpets. His wife had jewels. She even had 470 pairs of shoes in her closet. Yet she was buried in a commoner's grave. There wasn't enough money to give her a decent funeral.

However, some months before his suicide, Pinkas had added a clause to his will specifically to provide for his own funeral. He wanted a Valkyrie-like affair where his ashes would be sprinkled across Lake Geneva. Could it be just a coincidence that he added that provision when he did?

And what about the woman he loved so much, the woman he asked to die with him. How could he possibly have forgotten to provide for her?

The Swiss banking authorities were greatly embarrassed by the affair. They said Pinkas had been a master swindler. And, as far as the Swiss were concerned, the matter was best forgotten.

Just like that, the case was closed.

These days when you start poking around for answers, that's what they tell you.

Fermé. Closed.

But questions remain.

Questions like, did Florence actually take her own life? Maybe she didn't. Maybe Pinkas drove to Cannes the night before and killed her, trying to make it look like a suicide. Maybe he murdered her, then raced back to Lausanne and took his own life. That might account for the bonnet of his Jaguar being so very hot when the police arrived at Le Gentilhomiere on Tuesday morning.

Or maybe that's not what happened at all. Maybe he drove somewhere else to meet someone else. The note next to Florence's body was said to be in Eli's hand. But it was never officially checked by experts. And anyway, why was it ripped up? And how could he fail to provide for her funeral?

The door of Florence's apartment had a whole series of locks ... it was almost comical and friends who visited there joked that it looked like a fortress. Wouldn't Eli have had the keys? So then why, when the police arrived, were all of those bolts unlocked? Could she have let someone in who didn't have any keys to lock up on the way out?

And, where is the money?

It didn't simply disappear. It had to go somewhere.

Pinkas was a very proud man, someone who was mentally solid. But he was also someone who would never have stood for a jail sentence. He would never have been able to suffer the torture of a public trial. Those who knew Pinkas understood that suicide was a simple way out of the problem for him.

At the same time, some people are convinced that if he still had the money – or any part of it – he would

have returned it. There is nothing a jilted banker
wants more than to have his money back. Bankers,
especially Swiss bankers, would do almost anything to
avoid the sort of adverse publicity that would have
certainly followed the arrest and trial of a man like
Pinkas. And Pinkas would have understood that too.
So if he had the money, or could get to it . . . or even
just had a part of it or could just get to a part of it . . .
he would have been in a position to save a great deal
of face by returning it. The bankers might then have
been in a position to keep the matter quiet.

That he didn't immediately try to return the money
can only mean one thing.

He didn't have it.

Another point . . . here was a wealthy businessman
who absolutely lived within his means. Yet here too
was someone who might have, over the years, had
control of anything from $300 million to possibly as
much as $800 million. But he didn't live like he had
anything even remotely near that. 'Train de vie' and
'les jeux' is ridiculous. There is no proof whatsoever
that he spent any of the money he reportedly stole on
himself.

So, where did it go?

He was certainly not a petty man. He was certainly
not a petty thief. As the money didn't go to any visible
private causes, is it possible then that it went to a
public cause? Could there have been a circuit somewhere in Pinkas's brain labelled, fanatic.

Now a pair of curious facts come to light.

He had, remember, access to certain military information and indeed there were some classified military
documents stored in his factory. It's not unreasonable
to assume that there might be people on one side of the
fence or the other – or just people simply sitting in the

middle of the fence – who would like to know about such things.

Someone who knew Pinkas well believes – for reasons that cannot be disclosed here – that Pinkas was dealing with the Bulgarians. That he was selling them information. Needless to say that would be one source of cash while struggling with financial difficulties.

But that would have brought more money in, not helped him make $300–800 million disappear.

Now the plot thickens.

Every Thursday evening, Eli Pinkas drove to Geneva Airport for the flight to Nice. He returned to Lausanne on Monday morning. When anyone asked, he told them he always spent his weekends with Florence in Cannes. Even the press reported after his death that, although the couple were divorced in 1964, the affair continued on a regular weekend basis.

However, he did not spend those weekends in Cannes.

According to one very close source – who must for obvious reasons remain totally anonymous – it's now known that Pinkas merely changed planes every Thursday night in Nice.

For Tel Aviv.

The person who knew about these trips and was also curious enough to ask him about them was told by Pinkas – in that confidential tone he liked to use when he didn't want anything repeated – that he had an apartment there and had installed a lady friend.

It seemed plausible enough to the person who asked, and that person never bothered to mention it again.

However, after Pinkas's death someone else started looking into the matter and wondered if he could trace Pinkas's activities by locating the flat in Tel Aviv. If he had owned an apartment there, being a foreigner he would have been required by law to register it somewhere and the police would have a file on him. Yet the Israelis categorically denied knowing anything about him, or about his supposed apartment, or about his supposed lady friend.

Now consider this.

The Israelis happen to have, scattered around the world, prominent people who address themselves to selected sources of wealth and help to make these sources available when need arises.

They're known as 'Collectors'.

But Eli Pinkas never talked about Israel.

He wasn't even any longer a Jew.

Anyway, the Israelis insist they know nothing about him. Nor do they care to discuss their 'Collectors'. If Pinkas was one, they're certainly not going to admit that now. After all, $300–800 million later, why should they?

Index

Famous personalities you've always wanted to
read about – now available in Grafton Books

Dirk Bogarde
A Postillion Struck by Lightning (illustrated)	£2.50	☐
Snakes and Ladders (illustrated)	£2.95	☐
An Orderly Man (illustrated)	£2.95	☐

Muhammad Ali with Richard Durham
The Greatest: My Own Story	£1.95	☐

Fred Lawrence Guiles
Norma Jean (illustrated)	£3.95	☐

Becky Yancey
My Life with Elvis	£1.95	☐

Shelley Winters
Shelley	£1.95	☐

Stewart Granger
Sparks Fly Upward	£1.95	☐

Billie Jean King
Billie Jean King (illustrated)	£1.95	☐

Stephen Davies
Bob Marley (illustrated)	£2.95	☐

Pat Jennings
An Autobiography (illustrated)	£1.95	☐

Ann Morrow
The Queen (illustrated)	£2.50	☐
The Queen Mother (illustrated)	£2.95	☐

Pat Phoenix
Love, Curiosity, Freckles & Doubt (illustrated)	£1.95	☐
All My Burning Bridges (illustrated)	£1.95	☐

To order direct from the publisher just tick the titles you want
and fill in the order form. **GM581**

All these books are available at your local bookshop or newsagent, or can be ordered direct from the publisher.

To order direct from the publishers just tick the titles you want and fill in the form below.

Name _____

Address _____

_____

Send to:
Grafton Cash Sales
PO Box 11, Falmouth, Cornwall TR10 9EN.

Please enclose remittance to the value of the cover price plus:

UK 60p for the first book, 25p for the second book plus 15p per copy for each additional book ordered to a maximum charge of £1.90.

BFPO 60p for the first book, 25p for the second book plus 15p per copy for the next 7 books, thereafter 9p per book.

Overseas including Eire £1.25 for the first book, 75p for second book and 28p for each additional book.

Grafton Books reserve the right to show new retail prices on covers, which may differ from those previously advertised in the text or elsewhere.